Medieval film

Manchester University Press

Medieval film

edited by
Anke Bernau and
Bettina Bildhauer

Manchester University Press

Manchester and New York

distributed in the United States exclusively by Palgrave Macmillan

Published by Manchester University Press
Oxford Road, Manchester M13 9NR, UK
and Room 400, 175 Fifth Avenue, New York, NY 10010, USA
www.manchesteruniversitypress.co.uk

Distributed in the United States exclusively by
Palgrave Macmillan, 175 Fifth Avenue,
New York, NY 10010, USA

Distributed in Canada exclusively by
UBC Press, University of British Columbia, 2029 West Mall,
Vancouver, BC, Canada V6T 1Z2

British Library Cataloguing-in-Publication Data is available

Library of Congress Cataloging-in-Publication Data is available

ISBN 978 0 7190 8647 2 paperback

First published by Manchester University Press in hardback 2009

This paperback edition first published 2011

The publisher has no responsibility for the persistence or accuracy of URLs for any external or third-party internet websites referred to in this book, and does not guarantee that any content on such websites is, or will remain, accurate or appropriate.

Printed by Lightning Source

Contents

List of figures

Acknowledgements

'I didn't know they had film in the Middle Ages' was the line that greeted us almost every time we announced our research project, until it dawned on us that play with time was a feature not just of the term but of the films as well. Thank you to all those who made that joke! Some of the chapters in this book were originally given as papers at a conference on The Middle Ages on Film held at the University of St Andrews in July 2005. We thank the participants of this conference for their inspiring papers and discussions, as well as the School of Modern Languages at the University of St Andrews for its financial support.

List of contributors

DR ANKE BERNAU, Lecturer in Medieval Literature and Culture, English and American Studies, University of Manchester

DR BETTINA BILDHAUER, Lecturer in German, University of St Andrews

PROF. RICHARD BURT, Professor, Department of English, University of Florida Gainesville

PROF. JOHN GANIM, Professor, Department of English, University of California Riverside

PROF. ANDREW HIGSON, Professor of Film and Television, University of York

PROF. MARCIA LANDY, Distinguished Service Professor of English/ Film Studies, University of Pittsburgh

DR CAROL O'SULLIVAN, Senior Lecturer in Italian Language and Translation Theory, University of Portsmouth

DR SARAH SALIH, Senior Lecturer in English Literature, King's College London

ALISON TARA WALKER, PhD candidate, University of California, Los Angeles

Introduction

The a-chronology of medieval film

Bettina Bildhauer and Anke Bernau

This volume aims not to collect studies on individual medieval films but to characterise medieval film. 'Medieval film' – the term forces us into a double-take on chronology. Theoretically, it could refer to both films from the Middle Ages and films about the Middle Ages; and it takes a second to work out that the first, intuitive option is (of course) an impossibility. This book argues that such a playful confusion of temporalities is a fundamental characteristic not just of the term but also of medieval films themselves: more so than films set in other periods of the past, the present or the future, medieval films reflect on the fact that they make present a past that was never filmable and offer alternatives to chronological conceptions of time. Both in their plots and in their filmic techniques they frequently show, for instance, anachronisms, time stoppages, time travel and cyclical time. In this introduction we will trace the special relationship to temporality that characterises medieval film to its roots in the overlap of medievalism, film history and film theory. Though frequently not taken seriously by film scholars or medievalists, medieval films are pivotal in challenging both disciplines in their understanding of film and of the European Middle Ages respectively.[1]

According to most recent definitions, 'medieval films' are not just, or even primarily, historical; they need not even be set in the Middle Ages. Martha Driver and Sid Ray, for instance, describe 'medieval film' as a 'genre comprised of films with medieval themes, stories, or characters that can include, besides films set in the Middle Ages, spaghetti westerns, science fiction movies, neogothic films, and even Hong Kong action cinema'.[2] Richard Burt understands medieval film less in terms of genre than in terms of content to mean 'films set in the Middle Ages as well as films with contemporary settings that allude to the Middle Ages or are anchored in them'; while Tison Pugh and Lynn Ramey opt for a cautious combination of genre and content definitions by stating that medieval cinema can be a 'virtually oxymoronic generic classifica- tion', but can also refer to 'modern films depicting the Middle Ages'.[3] In addition they apply what seems to be a quality criterion when claiming that a 'truly medieval' film is one 'successfully depicting the contours of medieval narrative and history'.[4]

Both the generic and the thematic definitions have obvious limita- tions and undermine each other, raising the question of the useful- ness of such a free-floating term as medieval film. Medieval films have not developed coherent genre conventions: unlike western or horror films, they can share the characteristics of these genres and others. Yet defining medieval films solely by their setting, as those whose plot takes place at a time between, say, AD 500 and 1500, would result in the exclusion of a large number of films which are based on medi- eval stories; set in a fantastic Middle Ages; or set at a time before 500 or after 1500, but none the less consistently identified as medieval by film-makers, promoters, critics and audiences. The latter observa- tion might imply the usefulness of classifying medieval films as those which are *perceived* to be medieval films by individual recipients or producers, but this still would leave the question open as to which features of the films lead to such perceptions. We therefore suggest a third, theoretical definition of medieval films: as those characterised precisely by their uncertain temporality. This definition complements generic and thematic definitions, enabling a more nuanced approach to medieval films while also emphasising their relevance for film studies and medievalism in general. In this, it makes possible a move away from the frequent critical dismissal of medieval film, which is justified by its perceived failure to measure up in terms of content to academic standards of historical veracity, or (often in terms of genre) to a suffi- ciently sophisticated or up-to-date standard of entertainment.

Arthur Lindley's work offers a useful starting point when consid- ering medieval film's particular relationship to time. In his now famous essay 'The ahistoricism of medieval film', Lindley argues that films set in the Middle Ages are less concerned with historical accuracy than those set in other periods.[5] He suggests that this is because they try to represent analogies rather than origins of the present, whereas films about the more recent past show evolutionary causes of the present situation:

> Where films about the more recent past habitually construct their
> subjects as existing in linear and causative historical relationship to

the present, films of the medieval period present their *matere* in an analogical relation: as type or anti-type of current circumstances, as allegorical representation of them, or as estranged retelling. The distant past may mirror us – we, not it, are the real subject – but it does not lead to us.[6]

The reasons for this analogical structure, according to Lindley, are that cultural memory does not reach as far back as the Middle Ages, and that modernity relies on a stipulated break between the Middle Ages and the Renaissance in order to found itself: 'After that break, you're dealing with history. Before it, you're in the land of archetypes, *Ladyhawke* country, dreamland.'[7] This medievalist discourse, which posits the Middle Ages as a time before history, affects medieval films in terms of their subject matter, production values and plotlines, but also in terms of their relationship to time.

For Lindley the resulting 'ahistoricism' of medieval film is predominantly negative, 'obscuring' causality and 'sentimentalising' the Middle Ages in a way that denies it 'any real or independent existence'.[8] Other scholars agree with Lindley's judgement both of medieval cinema as ahistorical – more interested in analogies to the present than in historical causality – and in his negative evaluation of this. Susan Aronstein, Roberta Davidson and Kathleen Coyne Kelly, for example, have all recently argued that medieval films are more often than not indicative of a conservative outlook, with medieval analogies confirming traditional political ideals like democracy and monogamy.[9] Like romance or other forms of mainstream popular culture, medieval film is suspected of supporting the upholding of the political, racial and gender status quo. The fact that many medieval films draw on mythical, epic or folklore traditions – for instance, the Arthurian or Robin Hood material – also contributes to its negative critical reception. Dismissed as 'fantasy', the subject matter is condemned as unrealistic, nostalgic and escapist.[10] These aspects have made medieval or medievalised subject matter and themes attractive to writers of children's literature, as the phenomenally popular *Harry Potter* novels and films demonstrate. This, in turn, has reconfirmed the perception of much medieval film as not intellectually, politically or aesthetically 'adult' and modern.

In response to this view we would like to argue that the resistance to chronological history that characterises medieval film can actually be valuable and critical rather than merely or necessarily escapist and conformist. The cause-and-effect chronology of traditional historiographers has in any case come under critical scrutiny in the past three decades and is now widely accepted to be subject to conventions and problems of representation similar to other forms of narrative. This 'narrative turn' in historiography has meant an acknowledgement that generic and disciplinary expectations shape historians' practice, both in the decision of what to study and in the interpretation and evaluation of the selected material. The shared problematics of representation and narration allows a rethinking of the relationship between medieval film and history, moving the discussion away from a preoccupation primarily with questions of authenticity or veracity. In a more recent essay Lindley draws on this recognition when he argues that films are influenced by literary and filmic conventions and precursors as much as by historical data, referring to *Kingdom of Heaven* (2005) as an example of this:

> What we customarily have in medieval film is not just a simulacrum of the medieval past that excludes the actual past and erases historical process – what ever might have happened to connect 1187 with 2005 – ... but one that, as we have seen, is constructed primarily from other historical moments. It is not, in other words, that [Walter Scott's] *The Talisman* and the Western mediate the film's historical subject, it is that they create it.[11]

However, while Lindley now uses the somewhat more positive terms 'multitemporality' (rather than 'anachronism') and 'simulacrum' (valued highly by postmodernists), he still judges the films negatively for failing to provide historical accuracy. None the less, a more positive view is partly implicit in Lindley's earlier argument, in which he suggests that 'all historical film is necessarily mythic: a radical selection and rearrangement of facts plus exemplary fictions into a narrative that embodies an interpretation.'[12] The difference between films representing a later period and medieval ones, however, 'is that the former are much more likely to obscure this fact by particularizing detail' and 'have been and continue to be dominated by narrative codes derived ultimately from nineteenth-century fiction, just as they remain one of the last bastions of Classic Hollywood Cinema technical conventions.'[13] Medieval films, then, lay bare the narrative and cinematic manipulations underlying all historical films. Seen in this way, the ahistoricism of medieval film is not just a deplorable simplification or even falsification, but offers film critics as well as medievalists an opportunity to break out of the stalemate of accuracy versus entertainment and pursue new ways of thinking about history as well as film. Our concern in this volume is not to suggest that one ought to judge films according to the criteria of accuracy expected in academic historiography or literary criticism. It is not even to investigate into the mixture of factors that led to the investment of many scholars and viewers in historical accuracy – including naive expectations of film to be able to record and reproduce reality objectively; snobbism towards a medium that has not been subject to scholarly and cultural interest for centuries; the possessive idea that history and literature are the property of those *writing* about it, preferably in a scholarly fashion. Instead we ask ourselves *why* and *how* the Middle Ages are presented in such an indeterminate, 'inaccurate' manner. Whom and what does this floating signifier serve, either consciously or unconsciously? We suggest that apart from being conservative and ahistorical, as has so often been claimed, medieval film can actually nuance our understanding of history and of film precisely through its strange temporalities. Historical linearity quickly proves an unsatisfactory model when seeking to understand contemporary investments in the medieval past. So does 'memory', the term often posited as a more personal, living counterpart to history (most influentially by Pierre Nora), because the distant past (whether within the narrative of the film or outside it) can hardly be said to be 'remembered'.[14] Medieval film enables new ways of thinking about such questions because of its combination of medievalism and cinematic modes, which makes it less subject to the rigid expectations of historical chronology or genre.

This rehabilitation of medieval film fits in with current attempts to rehabilitate medievalism, that is, the representation and imagination of the Middle Ages in a post-medieval period. Apart from degrees, nothing distinguishes medieval studies from medievalism; there is no entirely objective representation of the Middle Ages nor an entirely invented one, as David Matthews has recently argued:

> To say of a given textual object that it constitutes medievalism rather than medieval studies is essentially to say that it is *bad* medieval studies. Neither Tyrwhitt's *Canterbury Tales* nor Percy's *Reliques* conforms to modern standards of scholarship or editing. Yet the former is automatically sanctioned as good medieval studies, belonging in a tradition which eventually gives us modern academic study of the Middle Ages, while Percy's is bad medieval studies, belonging in a tradition which gives us interesting frauds and fictions.[15]

Academia does not have a monopoly on accurate representation of the Middle Ages, and nor does the written word. Any engagement with the Middle Ages, whether scholarly or not, takes place on a continuum between scientific collection of facts and creative filling in of the blanks. While the conventions of academic historiography have now fossilised into almost universally established criteria of quality, film is as yet less bound by genre expectations and can therefore more easily experiment with new ways to accurately understand the past.

The a-chronology of cinema

Medieval film is uniquely able to demonstrate the conditions of time on which film is based, because medieval time is conventionally seen to function in the same way that filmic time does: as non-chronological in various ways. Films have traditionally been perceived as creating the illusion of a movement in chronological time from what is really a series of still images. This has been linked to the way in which personal memory is created, in particular to the transition from trauma to mourning. The prevalent psychoanalytical understanding of trauma is that it enacts a resistance to historical time and narrative: it cannot be understood and spoken about immediately, and will thus cause a melancholic marching on the spot until it can gradually be conceptualised, spoken about and in this way mourned. Eric Santner and Cathy Carruth have shown the crucial role that films play in the mourning process for the victims of the Holocaust and the Third Reich, analysing the films predominantly as coherent stories that overcome the stoppage of time.[16]

Recent studies have emphasised instead how film also deconstructs the illusion of a flow of time. All films are historical from the point of view of the audience, in so far as there is a necessary time lapse between filming and viewing: the images that the viewer sees on a cinema, television or computer screen were filmed in the past. For the viewer films thus preserve what Philip Rosen, building on the work of C. S. Peirce, has called an indexical trace of the past: 'The indexical trace is a matter of pastness. This already makes it appear that the image is in some way "historical."'[17] Unlike the weathervane, which signals a present wind, a film or photo is a sign of past action or habit, like the 'rolling gait of a sailor' or a fingerprint.[18]

Unlike photographs, however, films extend chronologically as well; they do not simply preserve a past moment, but a whole stretch of past time. Moreover, this is often perceived as 'bringing the past back to life', because each moment in a film has not only a past but also a future. At the beginning of a film the audience does not yet know

what will happen in the next moment in the plot; from the perspective of the first-time viewer each moment thus still has the potential
to go into different directions, as if it were happening in the present.[19]
Rosen, following André Bazin, nevertheless sees this as a process not
so much of bringing the past to life as of embalming time; preserving
that time in the past when what we are seeing was filmed. Films thus
present the illusion of 'mummifying change', of keeping things as they
were.

Laura Mulvey investigates further this tension between change and
stasis, or, in her words, cinema's 'central paradox: the co-presence of
movement and stillness, continuity and discontinuity'.[20] She takes into
account the new ways of viewing made possible by DVDs, where the
viewer is able to stop and slow down a film at will, contemplating image
and sequence at leisure and creating what she calls 'delayed cinema'.
This leads her to explore the delays already inherent in any film, where
early scenes are reinterpreted once the plot has progressed, as an
analogy of how memory works:

> Delayed cinema works on two levels: first of all it refers to the actual act
> of slowing down the flow of the film. Secondly it refers to the delay in
> time during which some detail has lain dormant, as it were, waiting to be
> noticed. There is a loose parallel here with Freud's concept of deferred
> action (*nachtraglichkeit* [*sic*]), the way the unconscious preserves a
> specific experience, while its traumatic effect might only be realized by
> another, later but associated, event.[21]

According to the Freudian concept of *Nachträglichkeit* the subject
belatedly remembers an event that may never have occurred, or at
least not in the way that it is now remembered. This 'memory' is the
result of an accretion of events that cause the subject to remember
something not originally traumatic as traumatic retrospectively. What
is 'remembered' to have taken place at an earlier point in time may
thus be recent thoughts and impressions. Film works in a similar way
in that it forces viewers to interpret the filmic event not just once,
after the time of filming, but also repeatedly at each stage of the plot's
unfolding, as new details emerge in the course of a viewing. For Mulvey
the shared 'storage function' of cinema and memory means that 'both
have the attributes of the indexical sign, the mark of trauma or the
mark of light, and both need to be deciphered retrospectively across
delayed time'.[22]

Important here is the recognition that film does not work chronologically, but that each image or sequence is temporally situated not at

the time of its filming, nor of its screening, nor even at the time of its reinterpretation, but at all of them simultaneously. In short, film works like shifting memory as well as like linear history.

The a-chronology of the Middle Ages

Historical films are particularly suited to exploring the special relationship that filmic images, and indeed sounds, have with the past. In historical films there is an additional time gap, stretching further back into the past, between the time of filming and the time when the action is supposed to have taken place.[23] Although all historical films show this multifold temporality and usually reflect upon it in some way, films set in the Middle Ages do so in a particularly interesting fashion. This is in part because, in historiographic tradition, medieval time has been conceptualised very much like filmic time. In traditional and contemporary historiography, medieval people are portrayed as having perceived their time in the same way that audiences perceive filmic time: as non-linear and memorial.

There is a long tradition of scholarship that argues that medieval people understood history as undifferentiated and atemporal in its providential continuity. According to this argument, time in the Middle Ages was experienced as moving slowly, in a circular rhythm or even not at all, with very little acknowledged to have happened from one generation to the next during the entire period between 500 and 1500. This sense of time, which was allegedly shaped largely by early medieval monastic traditions, was furthermore characterised by an apocalyptic sense of the inevitable and imminent end of time. Ultimately all earthly history was but a prelude to the true life that began after death, and thereby only of interest in the universal moral truths it could help to confirm and reiterate. The past was a natural part of the present. Aron Gurevich, one of the most famous proponents of the idea of stasis as a key trait of medieval mentality, observes not so much a delay (in Mulvey's sense) as an expectation of delay in medieval ideas of time. According to this view, not the reinterpretation of the past but the interpretation of the *present* moment in the light of the Last Judgement occupied medieval thinkers. As Gurevich states:

> Fear of future punishment brought what was to come closer to mind and transformed it into present reality. This way of thinking moulds time spatially by placing past, present and future side by side. This model of the world is devoid of temporal depth and does not bear up the weight

of the centuries which have passed since the moment of Creation. Memory unburdened by knowledge of sacred history only survives for a few generations before it gives way to legend and epos. The representation of a lasting future is absent in so far as the expectation of the end of the world is always present in the subconscious and materializes from time to time in the form of a social or psychological upheaval.[24]

For Gurevich this is a negative, ahistorical model of time as 'devoid of depth'. But this model can also be reread as offering a promising alternative to the limited model of linear chronology; and recent scholarship has attempted such a reinterpretation.

The view of the Middle Ages as 'synonymous with all that is uniform, static, and unprogressive' was criticised as early as 1927 by Charles Homer Haskins.[25] More recently Janet Coleman and Otto Gerhard Oexle have shown that such assumptions ignore the considerable scholarly evidence of a sophisticated historical understanding, at least on the part of medieval elites.[26] To some extent the postulated medieval mentality in which 'nothing changes' appears as an effect of the historical convention of presenting the entire period from antiquity to a stipulated post-medieval period – be it the Renaissance, the Reformation or even the French Revolution – as one long period in which nothing of major significance changed.[27]

More importantly for us, alternative medieval models of time have also begun to receive critical attention. In particular, the notion of *Nachträglichkeit* and of the associated traumatic memory have been shown to be useful for understanding medieval attitudes to time, as well as our relationship to medieval time. Medieval models of memory acknowledged the centrality of pain or trauma and of affect to the workings of memory. As Mary Carruthers points out in relation to the role of violence in medieval memory practices: 'One sees its mnemonic use not only in the cultivation of anxiety-provoking images but in the actual, pervasive brutality of ancient and medieval elementary pedagogy.'[28] Carruthers suggests that the emphasis on a close interrelationship between affect, desire and memory that characterises medieval conceptions of *memoria* is shared by psychoanalytic theory.[29] Critics such as Ruth Evans, who observed similar structures of *Nachträglichkeit* in Chaucer's understanding of memory, have produced valuable new readings of medieval memory practices as a result of such insights.[30]

Evans has also argued that we can use such medieval and psychoanalytic models, in particular the idea that the time of a *nachträgliche* memory is 'displaced ... coinciding precisely with the time neither of its original impression nor of its later symbolic attributions', to understand our own relationship to the Middle Ages.[31] She indicates that is particularly fruitful when rethinking 'the modernist procession of historical periods', because these models resist a linear trajectory, showing the interaction of past, present and future to be more intimately interrelated and interdependent: 'The discipline of medieval studies is not external to the archive of the past that it studies: the "Middle Ages".'[32] As a traumatic memory is remembered and reinterpreted later, the Middle Ages are also mediated by the present of the writer or critic; they cannot be said absolutely either to have taken place then or to have been created in the present. This does not render all attempts at accessing the past futile. Instead, the traumatic rupture that is postulated between then and now, between medievalist scholarship and its object, between the Middle Ages and modernity, can be used productively to develop more sophisticated historiographical methods and a better understanding of medieval perceptions of time.[33] Rather than claiming an abrupt change from the medieval to the modern, we might think of a gradual transition. The very fact that the Middle Ages are so hard to define points in this direction. A tripartite division of history into three great eras – antiquity, the Middle Ages and modernity – has been deeply engrained in academic thought since Christoph Cellarius established this paradigm in 1700. Even when further subdivisions are made, 'modern' cannot be thought without a preceding 'medieval' period. Most films follow the pattern of showing a change from the Middle Ages to modernity to occur some time between 1300 and 1500, while the Middle Ages remain undifferentiated by geography or chronology. But the fact that the Renaissance or Quattrocento can feature both as the beginning of the modern period and still as medieval in different national and discursive contexts hints at the fact that the conventional period divisions should be thought of as crutches rather than miracle cures: they may help to find one's way round history, but they are coarse tools that cannot explain or fully account for historical change, which happens in more hesitant, less teleological steps than normally assumed. If there is any value in seeing the break between the medieval and the modern as a trauma, it is that trauma research emphasises the continuities, delays and gradual merging of points in time rather than abrupt shifts. Given the overlap between conceptualisations of the Middle Ages and of film, medieval film is particularly well placed to develop different models of imagining historical time.[34]

The a-chronology of medieval films

Medieval films do not challenge chronological time just by showing a different view of time in various ways in the plot or in the filmic techniques but also by virtue of claiming to represent a historical period. In this they themselves are both now and then. In a sense, they, too, work like *Nachträglichkeit*, where an event is remembered belatedly, so that this event can be dated neither to the time when it happened (if it happened) nor to the later moment of remembering. They are delayed in three ways: firstly, in Mulvey's sense of all films being delayed; secondly, in the sense that all historical films are delayed in relation to their subject matter; and, thirdly, because the Middle Ages are also themselves perceived to be delayed. So medieval films offer a triple challenge to chronology.

For example, Alexander Kluge's *Der Angriff der Gegenwart auf die übrige Zeit* (The Assault of the Present on the Rest of Time, 1985) shows and makes viewers experience the shock of becoming aware that the past is still present. One of the leitmotifs of the film's series of fictional episodes is that 'the past is not dead, it is not even passed', criticising a presentism that tries to see everything as part of a present in which decision and change are possible, ignoring the control that the past exerts over the present.[35] This is perhaps most poignantly expressed in a sequence on medieval film. We see a beautiful woman's corpse laid out in a medieval crypt; the young monk who is maintaining the vigil begins to look at, touch and finally undress the body. After a cut, the monk is gone, but the dishevelled body begins to move and re-awaken. Even what seems to be dead in this way turns out to be still part of the present. Interfering with it still has consequences in the present and future: the necrophilic rape, as we will discover, has resulted in a pregnancy. The viewers not only share the experience of the surprise that the woman is not dead but now also find out that the entire scene was only part of a film-within-the-film, as another cut reveals its fictional director staring into the projector during a screening of the scene. What we had taken to be the medieval past turns out to be the contemporary set of a film called *The Monk and the Maiden*. The story of the director continues in an interview, during which a journalist asks why the director had chosen a 'medieval story' (the tale of the monk and the girl is indeed based on a medieval fabliau), and repeatedly demands that the film show a 'bridge', an analogy, between the Middle Ages and today. What he does not realise is the allegorical connection, for *The Monk and the Maiden* is about the relationship between the Middle Ages and today (with the monk embodying the present and the girl the seemingly dead past), rather than presenting an analogy between present and past.

Any film-maker doing her homework on a period film by watching other films about the Middle Ages will have come across canonical art house films that reflect on time and chronology, if not Kluge's work, then at least Ingmar Bergman's *The Seventh Seal* (1957) or Carl Theodor Dreyer's *La Passion de Jeanne d'Arc* (1928). The tendency of medieval film to play with linear time goes back to the beginning of film, in part developing out of the early 'cinema of attractions', where sensationalist display was more important than a fluid chronological narrative and which delighted in presenting far away places and time periods. Some of the earliest fiction films represent medieval tales as shaped by Wagner operas. *Richard Wagner* (1913), for instance, is a biography of the composer, during which, in dream sequences, medieval characters from his operas come to life, and attend his funeral in an instance of simultaneity between the Middle Ages and modernity that takes place at the moment of death. Similarly, the earliest version of the *Golem* films (1914), now lost, shows the medieval clay figure come to life in a modern town: a mysterious, even magical, medieval life is thus resurrected in (and for) the present. *Die Nibelungen* (1924) also reflects its medieval source's resistance to linear chronology. It is based on the *Nibelungenlied* and, like the epic, is divided into chapters (or, as the film calls them, cantos), which are self-contained units. While in the medieval epic continuity is disregarded in favour of convincing and spectacular scenes to the extent that continuity errors are left in the tale, the film is superficially coherent, but neglects narrative flow in favour of impressive images at every turn. A tradition of medieval film that engaged with questions of temporality in a range of ways was thus established early on.

It is not just avant-garde or art-house cinema that constitutes the Middle Ages in a deferred action located somewhere between the present and the past: this is a defining feature of most medieval films. Time travel, non-realist elements and anachronism are stock features of medieval film and in part account for its affinity to science fiction and fantasy.[36] Many films are set in a somewhat fantastical Middle Ages that has elements of past, present and future. *A Knight's Tale* (2001) has found much approval from medievalists for such playful use of anachronism as modern music in a medieval setting.[37] Another common way of playing with the preservation of the past ascribed to both film and the Middle Ages is through the popular motif of time travel, where the time elapsed since the Middle Ages is translated into space, so that one can travel back through it. Alternatively, visitors from the medieval past can also emerge into the present, as in *Les Visiteurs* (1993). Although time progresses within each episode, both Middle Ages, the present and often the future exist simultaneously. Time travel has been used in many Hollywood and European box-office successes, from *A Connecticut Yankee at King Arthur's Court* (1949) to *Traumschiff Surprise* (2004). What usually emerges in such stories of time travel is that, beyond the inevitable cultural and technological differences, there is an overarching humanity that allows medieval and contemporary characters to interact in meaningful ways and to learn from one another across the temporal gap.

The Kingdom of Heaven, criticised by Lindley for its ahistoricity, also undermines an ostensibly conventional chronological story through repeatedly engaging with the issue of non-chronological time. It depicts a textbook example of a *nachträgliche* memory as a medieval memory technique. Godfrey, Baron of Ibelin, tells his long-lost son Balian in a few sentences his 'oath' of a chivalric ethos. Telescoping Freud's idea that something is remembered only once it has been connected to a painful experience later, Balian's father slaps him, adding: 'This is so that you will remember.' Here, as in Freud's work on memory and in medieval memory theory, pain is shown to facilitate and even ensure recollection: the slap will make Balian remember the preceding minutes and the words spoken. The remembered event takes place across the moment when the words are heard and the moment when the physical pain of the slap is experienced. For the viewer a similar process takes place: the speech of Balian's father gains additional significance through the slap, reminding the viewer once more of the words that preceded it. This displacement of time is exacerbated by the fact that, as is conventional for simulating violence on film, the actual physical hit is never shown (as it does not take place), just the preceding blurred movement of the arm, followed by the sound of the slap and images of the ensuing reaction of the characters, with Balian bringing his hand to his allegedly stinging cheek. A pause in the dialogue gives both the viewers and Balian time to take in the momentousness of the preceding moments. It takes still another painful experience for Balian to actively recall this motto (or show that he does): during the devastating siege of Jerusalem he fully understands his

1 The moment after the slap in *Kingdom of Heaven* (2005)

father's words as he repeats them to a new generation of men whom he knights, connecting past and future in the present moment. In a doubling of the slapping sequence, we are again led to believe that a young knight has been slapped by being shown the gestures immediately beforehand and immediately afterwards, with the boy bringing his hand to his face again, and his changing expression reflecting an awareness of the significance of the event that suggests that he will remember the previous minutes (Figure 1).

This repetition of the knighting ritual is one of many examples in *Kingdom of Heaven* of events coming full circle, or being repeated in an endless chain of similar events. At first the film seems entirely chronological in the manner of Hollywood father–son narratives and historical epics. Balian, a French blacksmith, has just lost his child. His wife, unable to bear the grief, commits suicide. A crusader knight riding through the village on the lookout for his illegitimate son reveals himself as Balian's father; and Balian joins him on crusade. For him the crusade is a search for redemption that can also be read as an attempt at mourning. Although he does not find redemption, he succeeds his father as Baron of Ibelin, excelling both as knight and as military strategist, and successfully evacuating the besieged Jerusalem before it is lost to Saladin. However, temporal uncertainty intrudes into this narrative of personal and historical progress, through delay, moments of simultaneity and a continuous reinterpretation of the past. The very fact that the passing crusader claims to be Balian's father forces the young man into a reinterpretation of his own history and of the future options open to him; and it is only after a delay during which he burns the bridges to what he had believed to be his past and ancestral home that he follows Godfrey. Balian's rise from the start is not so much an individual narrative of progress as a delayed retracing of his father's footsteps. The characters remark frequently, and the plot emphasises, that he shows the same valour, tolerance and knightly values as his father, as well as inheriting his title, land, looks and characteristics. The film's opening and closing sequences locate the linear story of Balian's life within the wider cycle of continuous crusading and the cycle of seasons. Even the founding of a family turns out to be a repetition rather than a new beginning. What is important happens not in the present or in the past, but in the interaction between the two. The emphasis is thus not primarily on how Balian becomes a knight but on how he becomes his father's son, which is of course also about becoming a true knight.

The same temporal layering applies to the history of Jerusalem. Though the plot is a linear account of the crusaders' loss of the city, this is embedded in the knowledge that Jerusalem has been lost and won many times before, and remains a contested territory. The film's opening title card introduces not only a retrospective approach but also temporal uncertainty when it states: 'It is almost 100 years since Christian armies from Europe seized Jerusalem'. At this stage we do not know from which moment in time this is being spoken; it takes a subsequent superimposition of the words 'France, 1184' to clarify that this is not a film about the century preceding, say, the year the film was released, 2005. Similarly, at the end, it is announced in writing that 'a thousand years later, peace in Jerusalem remains elusive', which introduces the analogical relationship criticised as atemporal by Lindley, as well as suggesting in a way he considers unusual for medieval film a causal link between the failed medieval attempts at achieving peace in the Middle East and our present and future political situation. As Balian points out in his rousing speeches, the historical narrative is accretive rather than linear or analogous:

> None of us took this city from Muslims. No Muslim of the great army now coming against us was born when this city was lost. We fight over an offence we did not give, against those who were not alive to be offended. What is Jerusalem? Your holy places lie over the Jewish temple that the Romans pulled down. The Muslim places of worship lie over yours.

The city here is figured as a palimpsestic memory aid, where time never passes as it does for an individual, but rather accumulates to give present events their significance.

This image of the city as a *lieu de mémoire*, as Nora would call it – as a simultaneous presence of historical events as layers – echoes the imagination of time as space that we have already encountered in the idea of time travel, in Gurevich's concept of medieval time as spatially moulded, in Lindley's reference to the Middle Ages as '*Ladyhawke* country' or in Bazin's idea of mummifying time like a corpse. It is no coincidence that it is Jerusalem that here appears as a memory city, not only because of the analogy between medieval crusading and present wars in the Middle East but also because the 'Orient' is frequently imagined by Western commentators as a contemporary version of the European Middle Ages, out of sync with modernity. That the Middle Ages are perceived as temporally removed in the same way that the 'Orient' is spatially removed is illustrated effectively by Kathleen Davis, who draws on Johannes Fabian's concept of spatialised time to discuss the ways in which an American television documentary on Afghanistan compared travelling across geographical distance to travelling back in time: in this analogy, arriving in Afghanistan becomes synonymous with arriving in the Middle Ages.[38] But again, this can also be seen as the disrupting linearity upon which both discourses of Orientalism and modernity rely. This book hopes to suggest further examples of such new ways in which films that engage with the Middle Ages will be relevant to the present and future. Medieval film is not condemned to perpetuate the status quo, but, through its very position outside the historiographical and generic mainstreams can alter representations of history and cinematic modes.

Notes

1 When we speak of 'the Middle Ages' in this volume, we are referring to the European Middle Ages. When we speak of 'medieval film', we speak of that from Europe and North America, not the considerable and rich tradition of films about the Middle Ages from Russia, Japan or Egypt, for example. Nor are we able to take into account the many differences within the Western tradition, although specific films and groups of films are dealt with by our contributors.

2 Martha Driver and Sid Ray, 'Preface: Hollywood knights', in Driver and Ray (eds), *The Medieval Hero on Screen: Representations from Beowulf to Buffy* (London: McFarland, 2004), pp. 5–18 (p. 5). See also David Williams, who describes medieval films as 'not quite a genre', Williams, 'Medieval movies', *The Yearbook of English Studies*, 20 (1990), 1–32 (1); and John Ganim (Chapter 8 below), who also defines medieval film as a genre, while arguing for the overlap between this genre and film *noir*.

3 Richard Burt, 'Getting schmedieval: of manuscript and film prologues, para-

texts, and parodies', *Exemplaria*, 19:2 (Summer 2007), 217–42 (219); Tison Pugh and Lynn T. Ramey, 'Introduction: filming the "other" Middle Ages', in Tison Pugh and Lynn T. Ramey (eds), *Race, Class and Gender in 'Medieval' Cinema* (New York: Palgrave Macmillan, 2007), pp. 1–12 (p. 1). See also Robin Blaetz, 'Cecil B. DeMille's *Joan the Woman*', in Kathleen Verduin (ed.), *Medievalism in North America*, Studies in Medievalism VI (Cambridge: Brewer, 1994), pp. 109–22 (p. 112).

4 Pugh and Ramey, 'Introduction', p. 1.

5 Arthur Lindley, 'The ahistoricism of medieval film', *Screening the Past*, 3 (online journal, no pagination). Christian Kiening agrees that medieval films depict the Middle Ages to be outside historical continuity, but limits this to American films: 'For European film, the Middle Ages are history; for American film, they are ancient or even pre-history', Kiening, 'Mittelalter im Film', in Christian Kiening and Heinrich Adolf (eds), *Mittelalter im Film* (Berlin: De Gruyter, 2006), pp. 3–101 (p. 12), our translation.

6 Lindley, 'Ahistoricism', no page.

7 *Ibid.*, no page.

8 *Ibid.*, no page.

9 Susan Aronstein, *Hollywood Knights: Arthurian Cinema and the Politics of Nostalgia* (New York: Palgrave Macmillan, 2005); Roberta Davidson, 'The reel Arthur: politics and truth claims in *Camelot, Excalibur*, and *King Arthur*', *Arthuriana*, 17:2 (Summer 2007), 62–84; Kathleen Coyne Kelly, 'Hollywood simulacrum: *The Knights of the Round Table* (1953)', *Exemplaria*, 19:2 (Summer 2007), 270–89. See also Casey King, 'Abolitionists in American cinema: From *The Birth of a Nation* to *Amistad*', in Timothy Patrick McCarthy and John Stauffer (eds), *Prophets of Protest: Reconsidering the History of American Abolitionism* (New York: New Press, 2006), pp. 268–93 (p. 268).

10 See Marcia Landy, Chapter 5 below.

11 Arthur Lindley, 'Once, present and future kings: *Kingdom of Heaven* and the multitemporality of medieval film', in Pugh and Ramey (eds), *Race, Class and Gender*, pp. 15–29 (p. 26).

12 Lindley, 'Ahistoricism', no page.

13 *Ibid.*, no page.

14 For a critical use of the juxtaposition of history and memory see Katharine Hodgkin and Susannah Radstone, 'Introduction: contested pasts', in Hodgkin and Radstone (eds), *Contested Pasts: The Politics of Memory* (London: Routledge, 2003), pp. 1–21; Raphael Samuels, *Theatres of Memory* (London: Verso, 1994), p. x; cf. Ruth Evans, 'Chaucer in cyberspace: medieval technologies of memory and *The House of Fame*', *Studies in the Age of Chaucer*, 23 (2001), 43–69 (49).

15 David Matthews, 'Medieval studies and medievalism', in Ruth Evans, Helen Fulton and David Matthews (eds), *Medieval Cultural Studies: Essays in Honour of Stephen Knight* (Cardiff: University of Wales Press, 2006), pp. 9–22 (12–13).

16 Cathy Carruth, *Unclaimed Experience: Trauma, Narrative and History* (Baltimore: Johns Hopkins University Press, 1996); Eric L. Santner, *Stranded Objects: Mourning, Memory, and Film in Postwar Germany* (Ithaca: Cornell University Press, 1990).

17 Philip Rosen, *Change Mummified: Cinema, Historicity, Theory* (Minneapolis: University of Minnesota Press, 2001), p. 20.

18 *Ibid.*, p. 20.

19 See also David Herlihy, who notes about historical films: 'As eyewitnesses, [viewers] also become contemporaries with those happenings, react to them, and to this extent participate in them', in Herlihy, 'Am I a camera? Other reflections on film and history', *The American Historical Review*, 93:5 (December 1988), 1186–92 (1187).

20 Laura Mulvey, *Death 24x a Second: Stillness and the Moving Image* (London: Reaktion, 2006), p. 12.

21 *Ibid.*, p. 8.

22 *Ibid.*, p. 9.

23 Andrew Higson (Chapter 9 below) highlights the extent to which the time of filming and the circumstances of production and marketing influence a film's representation of the past, too.

24 Aron Gurevich, 'Au Moyen Age: conscience individuelle et image de l'au-delà', *Annales (Economies, Sociétés, Civilisations)*, 2 (1982), 255–75, English translation by S. C. Rowell as 'Perceptions of the individual and the hereafter in the Middle Ages', in Gurevich, *Historical Anthropology of the Middle Ages*, ed. Jana Howlett (Cambridge: Polity, 1992), pp. 65–89 (p. 83). See also Karl Lamprecht, *Einführung in das historische Denken* (Leipzig: Voigtländer, 1912); p. 10; Jo Tollebeek, ' "Renaissance" and "fossilization": Michelet, Burckhardt, and Huizinga', *Renaissance Studies*, 15:3 (2001), 354–66; and Bettina Bildhauer (Chapter 2 below) on film theorists' perception of medieval time as static.

25 Charles Homer Haskins, *The Renaissance of the Twelfth Century* (Cambridge, MA: Harvard University Press, 1927), p. 4.

26 Janet Coleman, *Ancient and Medieval Memories: Studies in the Reconstruction of the Past* (Cambridge: Cambridge University Press, 1992), and Otto Gerhard Oexle, ' "Die Statik ist ein Grundzug des mittelalterlichen Bewusstseins": die Wahrnehmung sozialen Wandels im Denken des Mittelalters und das Problem ihrer Deutung', in Jürgen Hietke and Klaus Schreiner (eds), *Sozialer Wandel im Mittelalter: Wahrnehmungsformen, Erklärungsmuster, Regelungsmechanismen* (Sigmaringen: Thorbecke, 1994), pp. 45–70.

27 For a critique of this view, see Jacques Le Goff, 'For an extended Middle Ages', in Le Goff, *The Medieval Imagination*, trans. Arthur Goldhammer (Chicago: Chicago University Press, 1988), pp. 18–23.

28 Mary Carruthers, *The Craft of Thought: Meditation, Rhetoric, and the Making of Images, 400–1200* (Cambridge: Cambridge University Press, 2006 [1998]), p. 101.

29 Mary J. Carruthers, *The Book of Memory: A Study of Memory in Medieval Culture* (Cambridge: Cambridge University Press, 1992 [1990]), p. 259.

30 Evans, 'Chaucer in cyberspace', 46–7. See also Gayle Margherita, *The Romance of Origins: Language and Sexual Difference in Middle English Literature* (Philadelphia: University of Pennsylvania Press, 1994), esp. pp. 5–6.

31 Evans, 'Chaucer in cyberspace', 47.

32 *Ibid.*, 67.

33 See also Kathleen Biddick, *The Shock of Medievalism* (Durham, NC: Duke University Press, 1998), esp. pp. 1–16.
34 See Sarah Salih (Chapter 1 below) on spolia as another medieval model of thinking history differently that is used in medieval film; Richard Burt (Chapter 7 below) on manipulations of time in the Bayeux tapestry as shown in medieval film; and Carol O'Sullivan (Chapter 3 below) on how medieval film uses language to signal temporal difference.
35 See also Alexander Kluge, *Der Angriff der Gegenwart auf die übrige Zeit: Abendfüllender Spielfilm, 35mm, Farbe mit s/w Teilen, Format: 1 : 1,37: Drehbuch*, Taschenbücher Syndikat EVA, 46 (Frankfurt am Main: Syndikat, 1985), pp. 107–8.
36 See also Kiening, 'Mittelalter im Film', pp. 69–86.
37 See Alison Walker, Chapter 6 below.
38 Kathleen Davis, 'Time behind the veil: the media, the Middle Ages, and Orientalism now', in Jeffrey Jerome Cohen (ed.), *The Postcolonial Middle Ages* (New York: Palgrave, 2001), pp. 105–22. David Elridge, *Hollywood's History Films* (London: I. B. Tauris, 2006), pp. 16–17, notes the similarities between the premodern period and the Middle East's depiction on film. See also John Ganim, *Medievalism and Orientalism: Three Essay on Literature, Architecture and Cultural Identity* (New York: Palgrave Macmillan, 2005). Anke Bernau (Chapter 4 below) shows a parallel association of the Middle Ages with the backward Southern United States.

1

Cinematic authenticity-effects and medieval art: a paradox

Sarah Salih

Authenticity, agreed to be an impossible goal, still haunts discussion of films about the past. As Richard Burt argues, the critical consensus has decisively rejected the 'fidelity model'.[1] In the wake of the linguistic turn it has become apparent that historical films are not academic histories, and that academic histories are not themselves the past, but representations of it governed by certain discursive conditions. Historical films are, likewise, constructed according to their own generic requirements. Examining the points of contact and divergence between these two modes of representing the past can be most informative, but their purposes and criteria for success are quite different.[2] Academic historians and literary critics who comment on historical film recognise, as Paul Halsall puts it, that they do not own the past, and that their past is not the only one.[3] Historical film is of the category of representation of the past which Pierre Nora distinguishes from the professionalised discipline of history as 'memory', 'embodied in living societies and as such in permanent evolution, subject to the dynamic of remembering and forgetting, unconscious of the distortions to which it is subject, vulnerable in various ways to appropriation and manipulation'.[4] Memory is a practice common to medieval and to modern popular culture's uses of the past: it continually reshapes the past to answer the shifting questions put to it by the present.

And yet, as David Williams argues, 'the demand for authenticity, for the real thing, works subtly in the minds of all watchers of film'.[5] *King Arthur* (2004), for example, was advertised as 'The Untold True Story That Inspired The Legend', a self-deconstructing slogan which begs the question of how such an untold story might have been accessed.[6] A kind of authenticity may be expected even of films with overtly fantastic settings, such as the adaptations of J. R. R. Tolkien's *Lord of the Rings* (2001–3).[7] The desire for authenticity may recur in the very academic discourse which has apparently banished it. John Aberth, for example, cites Robert Rosenstone to caution that 'movies occupy a world apart from the historical, and if historians trespass onto that realm, they should acknowledge the different rules of the game', but nevertheless goes on to castigate the 'historical blunders' and 'sheer historical nonsense' of certain medieval films.[8] Although authenticity may not be a reasonable criterion to apply to historical film, academics and audiences continue to register the failure or absence of authenticity effects, those conventions of representing the past which, though arbitrary, are established signifiers of period. As Jonathan Rosenbaum says: 'It doesn't matter if the historical details of the film are authentic. They just have to look authentic to the audience.'[9] None of us knows what the Middle Ages looked like: our perceptions of authenticity relate, both positively and negatively, to representations of the period with which we are already familiar. As William F. Woods argues: 'Our feeling for the authentic can be sustained by what seems typical, the kinds of clothes, gestures, and so forth that we expect of medieval reality.'[10]

However, medieval films have a period-specific difficulty with producing an effect of authenticity. If, as Natalie Zemon Davis argues, the effect of authenticity is 'most frequently ... a matter of the "look" of the past ... "the period look", "period props" and "period costume"', the medieval is troubled by its lack of a secure visual identity.[11] Hence medieval films are not, on the whole, heritage film, this being the subgenre of films about the past which invests most thoroughly in producing a period look. Heritage films take part in what Andrew Higson identifies as a museum aesthetic, in which 'the *mise-en-scène* ... is crammed with period artefacts plundered from the nation's heritage archives', to produce the illusion that the camera has captured the past as it really looked.[12] The heritage film is so named because it belongs to the same discourse of representations of the past as the heritage industry of historical sites, museums and souvenirs. It requires periods to be recognisable, and thus indicates them with a set of visual codes familiar enough to be deciphered with ease. If ancient Romans, as Roland Barthes famously noted, can be recognised by the 'Roman fringe' – an arbitrary sign, unrelated to historical practice, which nevertheless functions as a period marker and sign of *Romanitas* in certain films set in ancient Rome – British history has its own period signifiers.[13] Elizabethan films are populated with people wearing ruffs in wood-panelled rooms, Regency films by empire-line dresses and striped wallpaper. Such objects simultaneously specify the historical period and the mode of its representation within the generic conventions of the heritage film, which signify authenticity. The strategy is museum-like in that it assembles a selection of period objects and displays them enclosed in the film as in a vitrine, insulating the objects from the contaminating touch of other periods, and especially from the present-day of the viewer.

This strategy, however, is not the normal mode of representation of the medieval. It has been argued more than once that the period is typically the vehicle, but not the content, of medieval films. Rather than attempt to apprehend medieval alterity, films use the period to allegorise contemporary concerns.[14] *Kingdom of Heaven* (2005), for example, revisited the crusades at a moment when relations between the West and the Middle East were again a pressing issue, linking past and present in its closing caption, 'the Kingdom of Heaven is still not at peace'. Considerable popular interest in the medieval coexists with a lack of precise information about it, so that its image is multiple, fragmentary and visually unclear. Umberto Eco famously subdivided the plethora of contemporary manifestations of the medieval into 'ten little Middle Ages', and commentators on medievalism regularly generate further lists: the four cinematic approaches to the period analysed by David John Williams; Valerie Lagorio's seven modes of modern Arthurianism; Arthur Lindley's five functions of the medieval.[15] The Middle Ages are, indeed, extremely multiple: the term can cover a millennium of European and near-Eastern history as well as several fantasy domains. If the same period can be identified by its piety and its violence, its barbarism and its courtliness, then its profile is too fragmented for it to have a secure identity in modern culture. Hence there is no single style of representing the medieval on film, but a variety of looks, from the monochrome murk of the medieval scenes of *The Navigator: A Medieval Odyssey* (1988) to the bright palette and sharp detail of *A Knight's Tale* (2001).

We know the medieval, through its extant material culture, in the form of fragments. In Britain the period is distanced by the political upheaval of the Reformation and its material consequences. Margaret Aston argues that the presence of the ruins of former monastic buildings throughout British landscapes following the Dissolution produced a 'visible rupture with the past' through which the medieval became irrevocably associated with inaccessibility and ruination.[16] Ruins continue to signify the medieval. Heritage sites regularly display reconstructions of post-medieval interiors, but medieval sites are more commonly left in the ruined state which thus comes to be felt to be proper to them. Conservation may involve maintaining them at just the right pitch of ruination. The remains of Fountains Abbey (Yorkshire), for example, are still viewed in their eighteenth-century state, 'landscaped ... as a picturesque folly', according to the Abbey's website; and a plaque at the remains of Bury St Edmunds Abbey (Suffolk) forbids 'damaging the ruins'.[17] Reformation iconoclasm also ensured that insular medieval religious art typically survives in mutilated or fragmentary forms, as headless figures or glass scraps. The survival rate of medieval secular art is even lower. The heritage industry thus does not foster the kind of instant visual recognition of the Middle Ages as a living environment on which a medieval heritage film would depend. Medieval art and architecture in contemporary Britain are almost always visibly marked by the passage of time.

Even when medieval artefacts survive more or less intact, their non-mimetic style is often an obstacle to the non-expert viewer, as Williams argues: 'The art of the period is a natural source of images for the historical film-maker intent on realism, but the stylization of much medieval art is a special obstacle.'[18] It may be true, as Raphael Samuel writes, that 'the Bayeux tapestry ... is probably most people's idea of the Norman Conquest', but the tapestry's stylisation would not transfer easily to film.[19] That the tapestry has in fact been cited in film proves the point, for it functions as a 'metaphor ... for the inability of filmed history to represent the past accurately and convincingly', as Richard Burt shows.[20] One of the few medieval films to refer explicitly to the art of the period, *Perceval le Gallois* (1978), uses it to construct a non-mimetic aesthetic.[21] The uncertain visual identity of the Middle Ages means that the period is resistant to many forms of realism. The anti-mimetic *Monty Python and the Holy Grail* (1975), in which various modes of the illusory medieval – chivalric glamour, earthy squalor, quotations of medieval forms – jostle with the rude interruptions of modernity, may be the paradigmatic medieval film, and is certainly a favourite of many medievalists.

It is, then, problematic for film-makers to connote the Middle Ages by putting medieval art-works on screen. Instead they have recourse to representational strategies which they share with the Middle Ages. Medieval artists and viewers would have found the 'Roman fringe' an entirely comprehensible signifying system. It is not, in principle, different from the strategy adopted by the illustrator of the presentation

manuscript of John Lydgate's *Life of St Edmund* for marking Viking
invaders by putting them in oriental headgear.[22] Their turbans, like
the Roman fringe, or indeed like the horned helmets which twentieth-
century cinematic Vikings were to adopt, do not need any relation
to historical practice to carry symbolic and connotative value. In a
period when narratives moved between textual and visual media as
routinely as they do today, pictorial artists faced the same questions of
adaptation as do modern film-makers. They needed to make manifest
a material world about which a text may remain silent. Umberto Eco,
commenting on the film adaptation of his novel *The Name of the Rose*,
remarked: 'It is one thing to say, "They ate off wooden plates", but ... a
film-maker wants to know the exact dimensions of those plates.'[23] Likewise, it was one thing for Thomas Malory to imply that one hundred
and fifty knights could sit at the Round Table, but it fell to the illuminators of Arthurian narratives to attempt to visualise such an extraor-
dinary piece of furniture.[24] Medieval illustrative cycles thus regularly
added information to their textual sources, information which might
itself then become part of the tradition.

The remainder of this chapter examines the contrasting uses, or non-
uses, of medieval art objects in two medieval films and assesses how
they contribute to the films' overall authenticity-effects. Both films are
based on twentieth-century novels which share a knowing approach to
the past, patching overt anachronism with real and apparent samples
of medieval text. *Camelot*, directed by Joshua Logan and released in
1967, was based on the 1960 Broadway musical, which in turn was
freely adapted from T. H. White's Arthurian tetralogy *The Once and
Future King*, written in 1939–41. White's main source was Malory's
fifteenth-century version of the Arthurian cycle, *Morte d'Arthur*,
which itself synthesised a wide range of earlier French and English
sources. *The Name of the Rose*, directed by Jean-Jacques Annaud and
released in 1986, was adapted from a single source, but a very complex
one. Eco's philosophical-historical thriller, published in Italian in 1980
and translated into English in 1983, is a polyphonic novel, which Linda
Hutcheon took to be one of the defining examples of postmodernist
'historiographical metafiction.'[25]

These two quite different films both tend to confirm Lindley's
argument that audiences of medieval films 'automatically privilege
the current signified over the medieval signifier', and can be read as
encoded examinations of the time and place of their making. Lindley
himself sketches such a reading of *The Name of the Rose*, involving

'Benedictines as Blackshirts, Fraticelli as the Brigate Rosa, Adso and William as compromised liberals.'[26] Alan Lerner, the librettist of *Camelot*, felt that Arthurian legend had to be 'stripped of its ... medieval trimmings and trappings' if it was to realise its potential as a treatment of the 'Brotherhood of Man'.[27] White's narrative was given a democratic makeover to mark its transplantation to the US, and Arthur became a meritocratic monarch, aligning the legend with the phenomenon identified by Susan Aronstein and Nancy Coiner as 'a peculiarly American Middle Ages: the Middle Ages of Democratic Possibility.'[28] Its contemporary resonances were soon to become much more specific. The association of the stage version of *Camelot* with the Kennedy presidency was begun by Jacqueline Kennedy herself, who, in her first interview after her husband's assassination, recalled: 'At night, before we'd go to sleep, Jack liked to play some records; and the song he loved most came at the very end of this record. The lines he loved to hear were: Don't let it be forgot, that there was once a spot, for one brief shining moment[,] that was known as Camelot.'[29] The association of Kennedy with Arthur was thus even at its inception posthumous and nostalgic, combining idealisation of the past with anxiety for the present.[30] The film of *Camelot* continued and tweaked this use of Arthurian legend as a vehicle for contemporary American politics. Aronstein persuasively reads it as a conservative response to the 1960s counter-culture, which celebrates maturity, self-discipline and established order.[31] It shares with *The Name of the Rose*, then, a much-mediated relationship with the medieval, which both films treat as a pretext for modern concerns.

The visual codes which they use to signify medievalness, and in particular their uses of medieval artefacts, are, however, revealingly and utterly different. The reception of *The Name of the Rose* indicates that the film, at least on its initial release, succeeded in producing an effect of authenticity, and even acquired a reputation for devotion to historical accuracy. The medieval historian Jacques le Goff was employed as a historical adviser. Eco contributed to the perception of the film's accuracy, commenting that 'Annaud made philological demands. He wanted to reproduce the period in all its details.'[32] Few of these details, however, are attached to medieval artefacts. The novel makes extensive reference to medieval art, and its ekphrastic set-pieces showcase its author's (and translator's, in the English translation I am quoting) expertise and virtuosity. The description of the door of the abbey church occupies six pages, and the marginalia of a psalter, a sculpted Madonna and an illuminated apocalypse are also described in detail.[33] These artefacts are crucial to the novel, either as clues to its crime plot or as the exempla of its exploration of semiotics. The descriptions are themselves cinematic in their reproduction of visible movement, animated by the imagination of Adso, the narrator, who sees, for example, 'twenty-four ancients ... in ecstasy, faces turned towards the Seated One, whose praises they were singing, their limbs also twisted ... not in wild fashion, however, but with movements of ecstatic dance', on the tympanum of the abbey's church.[34] The visual slips easily into the visionary. Following the novel's success, Eco published *Reflections on* The Name of the Rose, identifying and reproducing images of some of the medieval artefacts which were the originals of those described.[35]

The film thus had available a ready-made set of visual references, but chose to use medieval artefacts very sparingly. They are not wholly absent. Ecclesiastical treasures and vestments – the abbot's pectoral cross, the golden reliquaries in the abbey's treasury, the robes of the papal envoys – occasionally relieve the darkness of the film with flashes of light and colour. At the church doorway Adso studies grotesque carvings; and in the library he looks at an illuminated treatise on embryology. More typical, and more telling, however, are the film's departures from the visual texture of the novel. Eco himself commented on the difference between authenticity and authenticity-effects in depictions of the medieval visual environment: 'I believe the period can be better represented by reproduction. Take church doorways: these used to be painted, but today they are colourless and covered with the patina of time.'[36] However, the church doorway and interior in the film reproduce the modern appearance of such buildings: they are, anachronistically, the austere grey stone which many modern viewers take to be the natural colour of old churches (see Figure 3). Medieval observers, such as the author of *Mandeville's Travels*, thought a church 'withouten peynture' unusual enough to require comment and explanation.[37] In the film an authentically polychromatic church would have worked as an anti-authenticity-effect, and have disrupted the dominant browns and greys of the film's colour scheme.[38] The colourless church silently represents not only the medieval but also a modern perspective on it, made material in the visual effect of the intervening centuries. Other shots appear to show a more systematic resistance to medieval art even when it is the object of the plot's or characters' attention. When William examines Adelmo's

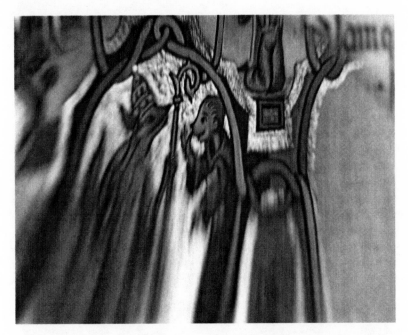

2 Distorted manuscript illuminations in *The Name of the Rose* (1986)

comic manuscript illuminations, the camera looks at them unsteadily, through the distortion of William's spectacles, as if to demonstrate this film's inability to see medieval iconography (Figure 2). The blurred pictures then require the supplement of William's spoken explanation of their content and significance: the audience are prevented from reading the pictures themselves. The film follows the novel in using Ubertino's meditation on a statue of the Virgin and Child to dramatise monastic misogyny. In the novel this artefact is clearly, appropriately for its setting in 1327, envisaged as being in the International Gothic style, 'carved in the modern fashion, with an ineffable smile and prominent abdomen, wearing a pretty dress with a small bodice, the child on her arm', but the film, equally clearly, shows a massive Renaissance Madonna which must have been dropped in from some two centuries later.[39] The anachronism is utterly unnecessary; a Gothic Madonna would have served equally well. It is, however, consistent with the film's thoroughgoing rejection of the museum aesthetic.

The film's authenticity-effect was not, then, produced by the museum aesthetic, and depended as much on the film's paratext as it did on

what was on screen. The *Guardian* admired Annaud's 'obsessive attention to historical authenticity, from specially-woven monks' habits to
having all fillings and crowns removed from his actors' mouths'.[40] That
detail of the teeth is cited so regularly that it evidently functions as the
film's leading authenticity-effect.[41] While it is quite true that medieval
teeth did not have fillings and crowns, to use this as a sign of medievalness is not a neutral choice. Nor did ancient Roman or Regency teeth
have fillings or crowns, and yet it would be difficult for tooth decay
to signify either of those periods. Medieval people would have been
accustomed enough to decayed teeth to be unmoved by the sight: they
become significant only through a modern gaze. However, dental decay
does not fully permeate the world of *The Name of the Rose*. In a dental
variant on Anne Hollander's classic observation that the principals of
any historical film can be recognised by their present-day hair, Sean
Connery as William of Baskerville and Christian Slater as Adso of
Melk have present-day, indeed film-star-perfect, teeth.[42] Medieval

3 Medieval teeth and an unpainted church interior in
The Name of the Rose (1986)

teeth, meanwhile, are most visible in characters who embody what the film takes to be medieval traits, such as the erotic mystical fervour of Ubertino and the monstrous simplicity of Salvatore (see Figure 3). Watching the teeth, we have a film about two modern persons adrift in an alien era of credulity, superstition and primitive dentistry.

The authenticity-effect of *The Name of the Rose*, then, is largely produced by non-mimetic techniques, and consists of the representation of a dark, dirty and downtrodden medieval, which appears to be both revisionist and familiar. Its evocation of squalor and suffering can be received as a realistic correction to the glamorised Middle Ages of chivalric romance, though it is of course no less stylised. For Williams the film is a prime example of the 'dirty school' of medieval cinema, a style of representation which persuades because it accords with so many discourses on the medieval.[43] This is the Middle Ages of Reformation and Enlightenment rhetoric, darkened by religious ignorance and awaiting the light of Protestant truth or of reason. This is the Middle Ages already mediated through the eighteenth- and nineteenth-century Gothick medievalisms which construct the period as the location of darkness, superstition and horror. This tradition was already among the intertexts of the novel, and underlies the horror films which provide a ready-made cinematic equivalent to the novel's allusions. The teeth are a synecdoche of all the other signs of medieval murk and monkishness, taking their place amongst the shadows, cowls, hunchbacks, rats, corpses, sinister figures lurking behind creaking doors, ravens perching on freshly dug graves, looming castles and other venerable horror film phenomena which make up *The Name of the Rose*'s coherent aesthetic. The scattered clusters of medieval artefacts which are the exceptions to its resistance to a heritage aesthetic all confirm the mood by contributing to the ideological representation of the medieval as superstitious, fearful and dominated by an exploitative church which claims a monopoly even on decoration and colour.

Camelot is an entirely opposite example. It probably never intended to produce an effect of authenticity, and certainly did not achieve one in the opinion of medievalists, as Stuart Airlie observes:

> At a symposium devoted to the reception of the Middle Ages ... medievalists reeled in horror at screened excerpts from such Hollywood monstrosities as *The Knights of the Round Table* (1953) and *Camelot* (1967), lamenting such films' concerns for mere trappings such as costumes at the expense of a specific feel for period and of any sense of the otherness of the past.[44]

Medievalists still enjoy reeling at *Camelot*, and at the lavish spectacle of its 'mere trappings'. Not only does the film not look like the Middle Ages; it looks like no time that has ever existed. It looks like a genre, not a period: it looks, unmistakably, like a 1960s Hollywood musical populated by actors in spangled tights and stage make-up. Its successful production of a generically correct look was rewarded with Oscars in 1968 for art direction and costume design. Its Camelot is that which Monty Python were to skewer as 'only a model' and 'a silly place'; its knights indeed 'do routines and chorus scenes / with footwork impeccable'. Williams comments that 'Guinevere and Arthur live in an apartment in sixties style, clean and tastefully barbaric, with a sunken seating area, animal skins, and scatter-cushions'.[45] Vanessa Redgrave, as Guinevere, is costumed throughout the film in 1967 fashions and presides over a Maying scene that looks like a 'hippie picnic', in Aronstein's words.[46] When her preposterous fairy-tale coach stops in a drift of artificial snow, she asks for a cup of tea, an anachronism very much in the spirit of White's book, in which the knights 'were drinking Metheglyn, not Port, but by mentioning the modern wine it is easier to give you the feel'.[47]

Clearly we are not even in hailing distance of mimesis and the museum aesthetic: the film makes no attempt to create the illusion that this is what the past looked like. It is instead a prime example of what Alice Grellner describes as 'sparkle' and Williams as a 'clean' Middle Ages, in which 'people are wounded and die, but they shed little visible blood; the sun shines as on a May morning, and the colourful costumes seem to be of a stuff that repels dirt'.[48] Martha Driver perceptively likens such representations of the medieval to the medieval's own idealised representations of itself in elite media such as the calendars of Books of Hours, where 'the costumes of the peasants are brightly coloured, the women's aprons crisply white and clean'.[49] The fantastic, Technicolor Middle Ages of *Camelot* is quite consistent with the gilded fantasy of aristocratic life which was illuminated in luxury manuscripts. For both genres, visual appeal and conspicuous luxury are more important criteria than historical correctness.

The non-realist and non-historicist aesthetic of *Camelot* is thus continuous with the medieval tradition of Arthurian writing and imagery. Arthurianism, lacking a secure historical location, is a special category of medievalism. The legend has always been adapted to contemporary concerns: anachronism is its very essence.[50] White imagined Malory writing the *Morte* as 'a man in 1470 describing events attributed to

479 (?) as if they had taken place in the 12th century.'[51] White's own Arthurian period weaves details taken from the twelfth through to fifteenth centuries into an overtly fictive chronology, in which Arthur succeeds 'Uther the Conqueror, 1066 to 1216', and leaps to White's present day as the Arthurian world comes to an end, with its nemesis, Mordred, aligned with Hitler.[52] White's temporal overlaps imitate those of Malory, whose Mordred suddenly introduced 'grete gunnes' to a world previously innocent of such technology.[53] In both texts the Arthurian world is destroyed by the encounter with modernity. Malory was thoroughly incoherent about the historical difference between his age and Arthur's, which functions sometimes as a nostalgically idealised past and at others as a version of the present. Medieval visualisations of Arthurian scenes generally preferred to represent them as contemporary rather than to attempt to indicate historical distance.[54] Arthurian texts regularly gesture towards history, but the era is not located in history: it is – and always has been – a multi-temporal, or extra-temporal, zone of fantasy. Arthurianism is an infinite sequence of variants, but with no origin.

Nevertheless, the film furnishes its fantasy Arthurian era with versions of several recognisable late-medieval artefacts. The castle-on-the-hill shots resemble, as they often do, the calendar scenes of the Duc de Berry's *Très Riches Heures*. The map hanging in Arthur's chamber has been simplified and scaled up from Matthew Paris's map

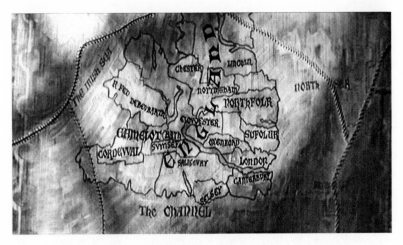

4 An imitation of Matthew Paris's map in *Camelot* (1967)

of Britain; a pavement rather like the cosmati-style pavement of West-minster Abbey is laid in his throne-room; his round table is the object which is now kept at Winchester. White's novel is full of visual texture, and is alert to the semiotics of clothes, furnishing and heraldry. The objects in the film, however, are not derived from the novel: in a move-ment fundamentally opposite to the script's modernisation of the legend they have been drawn directly from medieval sources. Their meanings are affected by the translation. The map in Arthur's chamber is based on one which is placed at the beginning of an abbreviation of Matthew's chronicle, in BL Cotton Claudius D.vi (Figure 4).[55] It has thus been shifted from a clerical, Latinate, written context to a secular one. However, the setting is not inappropriate, for Henry III displayed world-maps in his great chamber at Westminster and in the great hall of Winchester Castle.[56] The film naturalises the nation state by placing a map of the realm in place of the map of the world, and also secularises it, replacing Matthew's multiple networks, including trading routes and monastic sites, with a division of the realm into administrative units much like British counties or American states. The change mini-mises historical difference: while a medieval world-map would show a startlingly alien world, the innovations of Matthew's map, such as northern orientation and representation of Britain as a discrete unit, are, fortuitously, those which have become conventional.[57] Neverthe-less, its use by the king as an instrument of monarchy is true to medi-eval practice.

The Westminster pavement in its original setting was an immensely complex symbolic cosmology, speaking of the interdependence of monarchical and ecclesiastical powers, and the philosophical dimen-sion of kingship.[58] Here it, too, is secularised, moved from a cathedral to a royal hall (Figure 5): *Camelot's* world has one source of power and authority, the monarchy, not the dual powers of lordship and church of medieval history. The Winchester Round Table is perhaps the most interesting of the objects, for it is an artefact which neatly encapsulates the multiple media and times of Arthurianism. It was probably made in the late thirteenth century for an Arthurian-themed festivity in Edward I's court, and was repainted in the early sixteenth century, with the face of Arthur bearing a distinct resemblance to the then monarch, Henry VIII.[59] It was a replica used for courtly re-enactments of the Arthurian past which would have been quite as fanciful as anything in *Camelot*, and yet its presence in Winchester was cited by Caxton as a proof of the truth of Malory's Arthurian narrative.[60] The table is

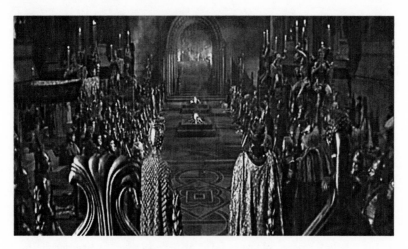

5 Visual hybridity in *Camelot* (1967)

a paradoxical object, a representation of the past which nevertheless functions as a token of the reality of the past, both in its medieval existence and in the film. Taken together, these artefacts make an ideological claim about the glamour of power and its continuity.

The presence of these objects on screen, however, does not make *Camelot* a heritage film, nor does it produce authenticity-effects. The medieval artworks share screen space with later ones, such as the abstract stained glass around the round table and a wall-hanging at the entrance to the great hall, both of which are clearly 1960s, and some Rodinesque sculpture inside. The mise-en-scène of *Camelot* is indeed monstrous, as Airlie had called it, or hybrid. The film thus rejects the period segregation of the museum aesthetic in favour of alternative methods of displaying the past and its artefacts. The museum vitrine which classifies and separates objects by type and date may be the standard modern mode of displaying the past, but it is not the only one. *Camelot's* juxtaposition of artefacts of different kinds and periods is more like older fashions in display, such as the early modern curiosity cabinet or indeed the medieval church treasury. The treasuries fulfilled some of the functions of the modern museum; as Nancy Netzer writes: 'the church took on the role of a repository or the material expression of a community's collected memory and of an exhibition hall where objects were both used and displayed for contemplation and admiration.'[61] One of the greatest of medieval treasuries, that of the abbey of

Saint-Denis, was a miscellany of riches: it included, for example, the sword of Charlemagne, an antique cameo of the Emperor Claudius, an early medieval chess-set, the hair of St Margaret and a unicorn's horn.[62] Saint-Denis's treasury was exceptional in its scale and value, but not in its chronological range or its mixture of objects of historical, spiritual, aesthetic and natural interest.

Camelot and *The Once and Future King* are more like treasuries than museums, heaping up disparate citations of medieval art and texts for cumulative effect. However, the film's visual juxtaposition of different periods is perhaps most like one of the key aesthetic principles of medieval approaches to the past, the reuse of architectural, artefactual and textual spolia. Spolia are ancient artefacts which are appropriated or excerpted and put to work in a different context, a practice which combined thrift and philosophy. The theoretical origin of this aesthetic principle is located in Exodus, when the departing Israelites steal the treasures of the Egyptians.[63] St Augustine allegorised this incident in *De doctrina Christiana* to argue that Christians were justified in taking treasures – that is, the goods, knowledge, science and literature of classical culture – and stripping them of overt paganism to adapt them to their own purposes:

> Like the treasures of the ancient Egyptians, who possessed ... vessels and ornaments of silver and gold and cloths, which on leaving Egypt the people of Israel, in order to make better use of them, surreptitiously claimed for themselves ..., similarly all the branches of pagan learning contain not only false and superstitious fantasies ... but also studies for liberated minds which are more appropriate to the service of the truth, and some very useful moral instruction, as well as the various truths about monotheism to be found in their writers. These treasures – like the silver and gold ... which were used wickedly and harmfully in the service of demons must be removed by Christians ... and applied to their true function, that of preaching the gospel.[64]

Appropriation and hybridity are thus identified as prime tools of Christian culture. Medieval Europe was full of buildings and objects, many of them of high status, produced using spolia. In Britain, at the outermost edge of the Roman Empire, Roman stonework frequently survives embedded into medieval buildings.[65] Such recycling could produce very complex objects, which set up visual dialogues between past and present. 'Spolia', in modern scholarship, is a primarily architectural term, but there are plenty of examples of the principle in medieval art, religion and literature: Augustine's argument is itself an allegorical appropriation of a historical narrative. To take just one example: the Herimann Crucifix is an eleventh-century bronze crucifix built around an antique jewel, a head of the Roman empress Livia carved from lapis lazuli. This object is used as the head of Christ, attached to a body which is quite different in style and material.[66] The ancient head is treasured not by insulating it from the present as in a vitrine display but by incorporating it into the present: thus an originally pagan artefact is appropriated to Christian devotional practice. Past and present are both hybridised: the present is made multi-temporal, and the ancient object made to bear meanings foreign to its original context.

Camelot, I suggest, treats its medieval objects as spolia, ancient treasures which are all the better for being put in a bright new setting. The underlying logic of the practice is also similar. Though to a twenty-first-century viewer the Herimann Crucifix may look post-modern, made up, like Adso's rescued library at the end of *The Name of the Rose*, of 'disiecta membra', its intent was quite otherwise.[67] It intended, we can presume, to tell a grand narrative of the supersession of paganism by Christianity. The appearance of European medieval objects in *Camelot* tells a comparable narrative of *translatio imperii* from the Old World to the New. The things have, conceptually, been shipped across the Atlantic, bringing their symbolic power with them. In a continent which is not full of medieval ruins, the medieval can be reconstituted as intact. In appropriating Arthurian symbolism, Jacqueline Kennedy was, knowingly or not, following the example of Edward I and Henry VIII. She attributed to her husband a concept of history 'full of heroes', which was entirely consistent with medieval uses of Arthurian tradition.[68]

Medieval film, as Williams says, is 'not quite a genre': the category is more interesting to moonlighting medievalists than to critics of film.[69] Though the multiplicity of the cinematic medieval militates against its becoming a coherent genre, it is possible that medieval films might indeed have some specifically cinematic characteristics which distinguish them from films set in other periods of the past. This chapter makes only one, tentative contribution to a list of such characteristics: that the fragmented visual profile of the medieval makes medieval authenticity-effects particularly troublesome to produce. Davis calls on films about the past to complicate their truth claims.[70] I doubt that *Camelot* was what she meant, but it does complicate its truth claims by presenting a visual surface which combines medieval and post-medieval elements. Though the effect is not authentically medieval, the process, paradoxically, has much in common with medieval modes of understanding and representing the past. The cinema does not have its own patron saint, but it seems reasonable to suppose that the medium might be included with Clare of Assisi's patronage of television.[71] That a medieval visionary should oversee this modern technology is appropriate, for both enable visions beyond mundane realism.

Notes

This chapter is based on a paper delivered at the Middle Ages on Film Conference, St Andrews, 7–9 July 2005. Thanks to the conference organisers and to all who attended.

1 Richard Burt, 'Introduction: getting schmedieval: of manuscript and film prologues, paratexts, and parodies', *Exemplaria*, 19:2 (Summer 2007), 217–42 (218).

2 See Robert A. Rosenstone, 'History in images/history in words: reflections on the possibility of really putting history onto film', *American Historical Review*, 93:5 (1988), 1173–85; Hayden White, 'Historiography and historiophoty', *American Historical Review*, 93:5 (1988), 1193–9.

3 Paul Halsall, 'Thinking about historical film', http://www.crusades-encyclopedia. com/thinkingabouthistoricalfilm.html, accessed 15 October 2007, pp. 4–5.

4 Pierre Nora, 'Between memory and history', in Nora (ed.), *Realms of Memory: Rethinking the French Past, vol. 1: Conflicts and Divisions*, trans. Arthur Goldhammer (New York: Columbia University Press, 1996), pp. 1–20 (p. 3).

5 David Williams, 'Medieval movies', *Yearbook of English Studies*, 20 (1990), 1–31 (3).

6 See www.imdb.com/title/tt0349683/taglines, accessed 26 October 2007.

7 David Salo, 'Heroism and alienation through language in *The Lord of the Rings*', in Martha Driver and Sid Ray (eds), *The Medieval Hero on Screen: Representations from Beowulf to Buffy* (Jefferson: McFarland, 2004), pp. 23–37.

8 John Aberth, *A Knight at the Movies: Medieval History on Film* (New York: Routledge, 2003), pp. ix, 296, 298.

9 Quoted in Martha Driver, 'Writing about medieval movies: authenticity and history', *Film and History*, 29:1–2 (1999), 5–7 (6).

10 William F. Woods, 'Authenticating realism in medieval film', in Driver and Ray (eds), *Medieval Hero on Screen*, pp. 38–51 (p. 47).

11 Natalie Zemon Davis, '"Any resemblance to persons living or dead": film and the challenge of authenticity', *Yale Review*, 76:4 (1987), 457–82 (461).

12 Andrew Higson, *English Heritage, English Cinema* (Oxford: Oxford University Press, 2003), pp. 39–40: see also Claire Monk, 'The British heritage-film debate revisited', in Monk and Amy Sergeant (eds), *British Historical Cinema: The History, Heritage and Costume Film* (London: Routledge, 2002), pp. 176–98.

13 Roland Barthes, 'The Romans in films', in Barthes, *Mythologies* (St Albans:

Paladin, 1973), pp. 26–8 (p. 26); see also Vivian Sobchak, 'The insistent fringe: moving images and the palimpsest of historical consciousness', www.latrobe.edu. au/screeningthepast/firstrelease/fr0499/vsfr6b.htm, accessed 15 October 2007.

14 Arthur Lindley, 'The ahistoricism of medieval film', www.latrobe.edu.au/ screeningthepast/firstrelease/fir598/ALfr3a.htm, accessed 15 October 2007; Williams, 'Medieval movies', 6.

15 Umberto Eco, 'Dreaming of the Middle Ages', in Eco, *Travels in Hyper-Reality*, trans. William Weaver (London: Picador, 1986), pp. 61–72 (pp. 68–72); David John Williams, 'Looking at the Middle Ages in the cinema: an overview', *Film and History*, 29:1–2 (1999), 8–19 (11); Valerie M. Lagorio, 'King Arthur and Camelot, USA in the twentieth century', in Bernard Rosenthal and Paul E. Szarmach (eds), *Medievalism in American Culture* (Binghamton: Medieval and Renaissance Texts and Studies, 1989), pp. 151–69 (p. 160); Lindley, 'Ahistoricism of medieval film'.

16 Margaret Aston, 'English ruins and English history: the Dissolution and the sense of the past', *Journal of the Warburg and Courtauld Institutes*, 36 (1973), 231–56 (232).

17 www.fountainsabbey.org.uk/estate/theabbey1d.html, accessed 15 October 2007.

18 Williams, 'Medieval movies', 7.

19 Raphael Samuel, *Theatres of Memory: Past and Present in Contemporary Culture* (London: Verso, 1994), p. 28.

20 *Exemplaria* Special Cluster 'Movie Medievalism', Richard Burt, 'Re-embroidering the Bayeux Tapestry in film and media: the flip side of history in opening and end title sequences', *Exemplaria: A Journal of Theory in Medieval and Renaissance Studies*, 19:2 (2007), 327–50 (341).

21 See Leslie Abend Callahan, '*Perceval le Gallois*: Eric Rohmer's vision of the Middle Ages', *Film and History*, 29:3–4 (1999), 46–53.

22 *The Life of St Edmund, King and Martyr: A Facsimile of British Library MS Harley 2278*, intro. A. S. G. Edwards (London: British Library, 2004), e.g., fol. 39r.

23 Gideon Bachman, '*The Name of the Rose*: interview with Umberto Eco', *Sight and Sound*, 55:2 (1986), 129–31 (130).

24 Thomas Malory, *Works*, ed. Eugène Vinaver (Oxford: Oxford University Press, 1971 [1929]), p. 60; see Beate Schmolke-Hasselmann, 'The Round Table: ideal, fiction, reality', *Arthurian Literature*, 2 (1982), 41–75, for various visualisations of the table.

25 Linda Hutcheon, *A Poetics of Postmodernism: History, Theory, Fiction* (New York: Routledge, 1988), p. 113.

26 Lindley, 'Ahistoricism of medieval film'.

27 Alan J. Lerner, *The Street Where I Live: The Story of* My Fair Lady, Gigi *and* Camelot (London: Hodder and Stoughton, 1978), p. 174.

28 Susan Aronstein and Nancy Coiner, 'Twice knightly: democratizing the Middle Ages for middle-class America', in Kathleen Verduin (ed.), *Medievalism in North America* (Cambridge: Brewer, 1994), pp. 212–31 (p. 213).

29 Quoted in Lerner, *The Street Where I Live*, p. 221.

30 See also Pamela S. Morgan, 'One brief shining moment: Camelot in Washington, D.C', in Verduin (ed.), *Medievalism in North America*, pp. 185–211.

31 Susan Aronstein, *Hollywood Knights: Arthurian Cinema and the Politics of Nostalgia* (Basingstoke: Palgrave Macmillan, 2005), pp. 89–98.

32 Bachman, 'Name of the Rose', 130.

33 Umberto Eco, *The Name of the Rose*, trans. William Weaver (London: Picador, 1984), pp. 40–5, 76–8, 48, 230, 174–5.

34 Eco, *Name of the Rose*, p. 42.

35 Umberto Eco, *Reflections on* The Name of the Rose (London: Secker and Warburg, 1985).

36 Bachman, 'Name of the Rose', 130.

37 *Mandeville's Travels, Edited from MS. Cotton Titus C. XVI in the British Museum*, ed. P. Hamelius, EETS os 153 (London: Oxford University Press, 1919), p. 36.

38 Williams, 'Medieval movies', 4.

39 Eco, *Name of the Rose*, p. 48.

40 Andrew Pulver, 'Adaptation of the week no. 44: *The Name of the Rose*', *The Guardian* (5 February 2005).

41 See also comments on www.imdb.com/title/tt0091605/usercomments, accessed 12 August 2006, for example, 'I actually enjoyed seeing the filth, the rotted teeth, the dirty hands, the deformity.'

42 Anne Hollander, *Seeing through Clothes* (Berkeley: University of California Press, 1975), p. 310.

43 Williams, 'Medieval movies', 8.

44 Stuart Airlie, 'Strange eventful histories: the Middle Ages in the cinema', in Peter Linehan and Janet L. Nelson (eds), *The Medieval World* (London: Routledge, 2001), pp. 163–83 (p. 164).

45 Williams, 'Medieval movies', 15.

46 Aronstein, *Hollywood Knights*, p. 93.

47 T. H. White, *The Once and Future King: The Complete Edition* (London: HarperCollins, 1996), p. 4.

48 Alice Grellner, 'Two films that sparkle: *The Sword in the Stone* and *Camelot*', in Kevin J. Harty (ed.), *Cinema Arthuriana: Twenty Essays* (Jefferson: McFarland, 2002), pp. 118–26; Williams, 'Medieval movies', 7–8.

49 Martha Driver, 'What's accuracy got to do with it? History and authenticity in medieval film', in Driver and Ray (eds), *Medieval Hero on Screen*, pp. 19–22 (p. 20).

50 Rebecca A. Umland and Samuel J. Umland, *The Use of Arthurian Legend in Hollywood Film: From Connecticut Yankees to Fisher Kings* (Westport: Greenwood Press, 1996), p. 95.

51 Elizabeth Brewer, *T. H. White's* The Once and Future King (Cambridge: Brewer, 1993), p. 198.

52 White, *Once and Future King*, p. 207.

53 Malory, *Works*, p. 707.

54 Muriel Whitaker, *The Legends of King Arthur in Art* (Cambridge: Brewer, 1990), p. 35.

55 P. D. A. Harvey, 'Matthew Paris's maps of Britain', in P. R. Coss and S. D. Lloyd (eds), *Thirteenth-Century England IV* (Woodbridge: Boydell, 1992), pp. 109–21 (p. 109).

56 Daniel Birkholz, *The King's Two Maps: Cartography and Culture in Thirteenth-Century England* (New York: Routledge, 2004), p. xxv.

57 Suzanne Lewis, *The Art of Matthew Paris in the* Chronica Majora (Aldershot: Scolar, 1987), p. 365; Birkholz, *The King's Two Maps*, p. 82.

58 Richard Foster, *Patterns of Thought: The Hidden Meaning of the Great Pavement of Westminster Abbey* (London: Cape, 1991).

59 Martin Biddle, 'The making of the Round Table'; Pamela Tudor-Craig, 'Iconography of the painting', in Biddle, *King Arthur's Round Table: An Archaeological Investigation* (Woodbridge: Boydell, 2000), pp. 337–92, pp. 285–333.

60 Malory, *Works*, p. xiv.

61 Nancy Netzer, 'Collecting, re/collecting, contextualizing and recontextualizing: devotion to fragments of the Middle Ages', in Netzer and Virginia Reinburg (eds), *Fragmented Devotion: Medieval Objects from the Schnütgen Museum, Cologne* (Boston: McMullen Museum of Art, 2000), pp. 17–30 (p. 19).

62 Blaise de Montesquiou-Fezensac, *Le Trésor de Saint-Denis: Inventoire de 1634,* avec la collaboration de Danielle Gaborit-Chopin, 3 vols (Paris: Picard, 1973 and 1977), inventory items 111, 34, 101, 344, 165.

63 Exodus 3:21–2, 12:35–6.

64 Augustine, *On Christian Teaching*, trans. R. P. H. Green (Oxford: Oxford University Press, 1997), Book II, chapter 40/60/145, pp. 64-5.

65 Tim Eaton, *Plundering the Past: Roman Stonework in Medieval Britain* (Stroud: Tempus, 2000).

66 Andreas Petzold, *Romanesque Art* (London: Weidenfeld and Nicolson, 1995), p. 141.

67 Eco, *Name of the Rose*, p. 500.

68 Lerner, *The Street Where I Live*, p. 221.

69 Williams, 'Medieval movies', 1.

70 Davis, 'Any resemblance', 478.

71 David Hugh Farmer, *The Oxford Dictionary of Saints* (Oxford: Oxford University Press, 1987 [1978]), p. 89.

2

Forward into the past:
film theory's foundation in medievalism

Bettina Bildhauer

While most chapters in this book are concerned with medieval film in the sense of films about the Middle Ages, this chapter shows that *all* films have been considered medieval by a surprisingly large number of influential film theorists. The argument they put forward is that film is so radically different and new that it is no longer just part of modern culture, but instead, in an apparent paradox, medieval again. With film, a new period after modernity begins, which is never called postmodern in these theories, but instead appears as a return to the Middle Ages.

This conceptualisation of film as medieval in its production, transmission, aesthetics or reception, as I shall argue, originates with the earliest attempts to come to terms with the new medium and underlies many influential film theories of the twentieth century and even the most recent media theories. Hugo Münsterberg's *The Photoplay* (1916), for instance, usually considered to be the first major book on film theory, makes a brief comparison between film and medieval art. The most prominent film theories until the 1950s came from critics and thinkers who had been shaped by the Weimar Republic and a German intellectual pedigree in philosophy, sociology and art history, among them Béla Balázs, Walter Benjamin, Siegfried Kracauer and Erwin Panofsky. They all enthusiastically elaborated on the link (or contrast) between film and the Middle Ages.[1] The central idea of early film studies – that (silent) film is a purely visual medium that opens up a new way of seeing – was based on the analogous assumption of medieval art as another totally visual medium that provided a historical precedent. The 'realist' debates of the 1950s, which are in particular associated with André Bazin, continue this tradition of seeing film as a regeneration of a medieval aesthetics. With apparatus theory and the emergence of film studies as an independent discipline since the

1970s, the (early modern) Renaissance rather than the Middle Ages became the period most commonly compared to the era of film. But the medieval continued to be important in what now became a separate discipline and tradition: the wider field of media studies as inaugurated by Marshall McLuhan. If read through the lens of the Middle Ages, unacknowledged continuities and unlikely alliances between these different film theories thus become apparent.

The reliance of film theory on medievalism has never been acknowledged by film scholars or medieval scholars. This is symptomatic of the traditional divide between medieval and modern studies, where the continuities and influences of medieval thought, art and culture on modernity are rarely researched. Throughout this chapter, my concern is not to what extent film theories provide a representation of medieval mentality which would be considered accurate by contemporary historians. Instead I am interested in the ways in which preconceived notions of the Middle Ages filtered into and were influenced by film theory throughout the twentieth century; and to what extent film theory relies on knowledge about the Middle Ages for its basic principles. In the following I shall not trace the trajectory of the chronological development of film theory, but shall structure my argument around the recurrent ideas about the Middle Ages it articulates. There are three major related imaginings of medieval mentality and of film put forward by film theorists. Firstly, the idea of medieval mentality as visual and as uniting body and mind, in particular as exemplified by medieval painting. This was believed to be revived in film especially by those arguing that film teaches us to see material reality afresh. Secondly, the idea of medieval mentality as collective, a worldview which is perceived to be embodied by the cathedral, and again seen to be revived in film particularly by those emphasising a collective authorship and audience of films. Finally, I shall turn to theories which conflate the Middle Ages and modernity into a single period, characterised by a view of the cosmos as static and enclosed. This outlook, they maintain, was finally ended by the advent of film.

Visuality and holism: film as medieval painting

The conception of film as a medieval medium is as old as film theory. As early as 1916, Hugo Münsterberg, a German experimental psychologist at Harvard, attempted to establish film (or the photoplay, as he calls it) as a radically new art form, worthy of academic attention because of its unprecedented way of stimulating the mind through vision. He argued that only purely visual material had a place in film, while the use of written intertitles in the silent film of his time seemed imperfect to him in a manner he compared to medieval artistic technique:

> Some religious painters of medieval times put in the picture itself phrases which the persons were to speak, as if the words were leaving their mouths. But we could not imagine Raphael and Michelangelo making use of a method of communication which is so entirely foreign to the real spirit of painting. Every art grows slowly to the point where the artist relies on its characteristic and genuine forms of expression ... The photoplay of the day after tomorrow will surely be freed from all the elements which are not really pictures.[2]

Münsterberg here presents both film and medieval painting as essentially visual media, but as still contaminated in comparison to the entirely pictorial post-medieval art that was produced by Raphael (1483–1520) and Michelangelo (1475–1564) and that will, according to him, be achieved again in the film of the future. Italian Renaissance art, as is usual in the German intellectual tradition, no longer counts as medieval for Münsterberg, whereas the technique of scrolls within pictures stands in for all medieval art, irrespective of exact date, genre, medium and place of origin. In several ways this displays the well-known basic tenets of early, formalist film theory: an orientation towards the future potential rather than existing achievements of film; the strong value judgments attached to this in a prescriptive manner; and the ideal of film as an entirely visual medium, to which intertitles and later sound should be secondary or even alien; all to the end of establishing film as a new art form in its own right. It is less well known that the comparison of film to medieval art was an equally typical element of these early theories.

But Münsterberg is an exception in his characterisation of medieval art as not entirely visual. That the Middle Ages were a time in which the visual rather than the verbal dominated thought, mentality and art was a much more widespread idea in the first decades of the twentieth century, most famously propagated by Johan Huizinga in his hugely successful *Autumn of the Middle Ages* (1919).[3] For writers like Béla Balázs, the comparison of film to the visuality of medieval art and perception became a cornerstone of film theory. In his first review column for the Viennese newspaper *The Day*, in 1922, he formulates programmatically and succinctly how film will completely revolutionise modern society by a return to the visual Middle Ages:

But crucially, film is a fundamentally new kind of art of an emerging new culture ... A means of mental expression that will influence humankind so widely and so deeply due to the unlimited accessibility of its technology must be of similar significance as Gutenberg's technological invention was for its time. Victor Hugo once wrote that the printed book assumed the role of the medieval cathedrals. The book became the carrier of the people's spirit and shredded it into millions of little opinions. The book broke the stone: the one church into a thousand books. Visible spirit became readable spirit, visual culture became conceptual. We probably need to say no more about how this changed the face of human society. But today, another machine is at work to give human society a new spiritual shape. The many millions of people who sit every night and watch images, *wordless images*, which represent human feelings and thoughts – these many millions of people are learning a new language: the long forgotten, now *newly emerging (and indeed international) language of facial expressiveness* ... Perhaps we are standing on the threshold of a new visual culture?[4]

In order to show the entirely innovative nature of film, Balázs here suggests a history of the world with two major turning points: the invention of the printing press and that of the cinematograph. The invention of print changed medieval visual culture into a modern society of reading and writing, and the invention of cinema then turns modern literary culture back into a visual one. The medieval period is characterised by cathedrals, unity and visibility; the modern by books, fragmentation, conceptuality and readability; and the 'postmodern' one by film and, again, by unity and visibility. Balázs, betraying a scepticism towards writing that Jacques Derrida later saw as typical of Western thought, follows in the footsteps of Victor Hugo's Romanticism. He clearly prefers the allegedly immediate visuality of the Middle Ages to the cultural modes of his own time. But this view of the Middle Ages as a radically different, superior past is here curiously combined with a future-oriented embrace of the new art and technology of film, which is seen to herald a return to the visual language of the Middle Ages and to its unified spirit. While this may seem a strange juxtaposition of nostalgia and progressiveness, it is born out of a consistent belief in radical change: the belief that the world was revolutionised through the fundamental shift from medieval to modern, and that a similarly revolutionary rupture will be made possible again through film. The future is thus imagined as a period that is *chronologically* postmodern, in the sense that it follows modernity, but *culturally* post-medieval, in that it will reinstitute medieval mentality: film takes us not back to the future, but forward into the past. Balázs develops this idea throughout his many influential critical writings, quoting the above-cited passage almost verbatim two years later in his book *The Visible Human* (1924) as well as his 1945 volume *Theory of the Film*.[5] Only grudgingly modi-fied to accommodate sound film, the hope that film will teach people to see again and affect a new period of visual orientation forms the core of Balázs's film theory.

Balázs's distinction of three eras – one pre-Gutenberg ('medieval') period, one ('modern') period from Gutenberg to Edison characterised by the book, and one ('postmodern') post-Edison period, defined by film – is common to Weimar film theory. For example, Adolf Behne (a writer and critic who, like many of his contemporaries, also published theoretical musings on film) echoes this division in 1926:

> Film is something fundamentally new, film is really essentially the litera-ture of our time ... Film is the simple, direct and legitimate sequel of the book – Edison is the new Gutenberg ... The audience is no longer interested in books? But every night it sits in front of the modern book and learns to see, think, feel through film – the book which millions read and nobody 'owns'.[6]

For Behne as for Balázs, film will teach its audience to 'see' again rather than to read books. But according to Behne, this development will not lead to a major shift in mentality for two reasons. First, both book and film are simply media that transport arguments (*Transportmittel*); the way in which they do so is of little importance. Besides, even in so far as style and imagery matter, visuality had already been present in books before the advent of film, in the shape of images or figurative language. Written images are no longer able to compete with cinema's superior way of transmitting images and are therefore gradually disap-pearing from the latest writing. Visuality will simply move its outlet from book to film; it is not a new phenomenon. So, while presenting the formalist belief in film as a radically new medium, Behne does not ascribe to it the potential to change the whole of society by way of a return to a pre-Gutenberg bliss.

Like Balázs and Behne, Sergei Eisenstein emphasises the ideal visu-ality of film, famously arguing that meaning in film is created mostly through the visual juxtaposition and composition of images. It is less often acknowledged that, for him, this visual technique is prefigured in medieval and Renaissance painting. In *The Film Sense* (1943) Eisen-stein refers to the multiple vanishing points and perspectives which combine in the multifocal (but not fragmented) works of Albrecht Dürer, Leonardo da Vinci, Jan van Eyck and El Greco.[7] Film, Eisenstein demands, should strive to similarly provide multiple points of focus. He also compares the way in which the eye is guided through each image of his own film *Alexander Nevsky* (1938) to the use of a visual path 'at an earlier stage of graphic art', citing as his examples 'the most dramatic (and cinematic) of all illuminated manuscripts ... the Greek manuscript of the sixth century known as the Vienna Genesis' as well as works from the 'era of perspective' by Dirk Bouts, Domenico Ghirlandaio and Hans Memling.[8] Like in Balázs's writing, early art here figures as an illustration for the visuality that cinema ought to achieve: guidance of the eye, provided in sixth- and fifteenth-century art by painting a path which the viewer's gaze can follow; and in twentieth-century film by attracting the eye to a sequence of focal points. So, like Balázs, Eisenstein advocates cinema's return to medieval representational techniques, but he posits the rupture in representation later than Balázs, and later than most theorists. The development of pictorial techniques that create an illusion of three-dimensional perspective is usually postulated as the beginning of a modern, post-medieval period. This periodisation was established in Erwin Panofsky's seminal study 'The perspective as symbolic form' (1927), where medieval flatness ends and modern perspective begins with the Renaissance or Quattrocentro, associated with artists like Leonardo da Vinci and his *camera obscura*, or Diego Velázquez (1599–1660).[9] But for Eisenstein the crucial break does not come between the medieval and the modern, but later in modernity. The tradition of guiding the gaze, according to Eisenstein, lasts into the 'era of perspective' and into modernity, too, and breaks off only in the recent past. However, he believes again that it will be reignited in film, as pioneered by *Alexander Nevsky* (which is – not coincidentally – set in the thirteenth century).

Later film theory, however, came to associate the art of da Vinci and his contemporaries clearly with the post-medieval Renaissance; and with a representation of the world not from multiple perspectives but from a centred, single viewpoint: the eye of the beholder. According to apparatus theorists like Christian Metz, Jean Baudry and Daniel Dayan, and media theorists like Marshall McLuhan, the single eye of the Renaissance viewer is in traditional cinema emulated in the subject-position of the spectator, following the 'eye' of the camera.[10] This encourages fantasies of dominance and omnipotence of the viewing subject. Though Metz, Baudry and Dayan do not mention the medieval alternative, they criticise the alleged Renaissance view of the world provided by traditional cinema, and thus continue not only to analyse film from a historical angle but also to criticise and deconstruct the modern worldview from this position. Marshall McLuhan is more explicit in his postulation of the premodern worldview as an alternative to the modern privileging of the eye, in a way that revisits Balázs's criticism of modernity; Balázs's view that the medium matters at least as much as the message; and his timeline of Western history as defined through media of communication. McLuhan adds to the standard tripartite temporal framework – antiquity, Middle Ages, modernity – an extra, initial period, beginning his chronology with a tribal period that he sees characterised by pre-alphabetic, oral communication. This is then followed by the 'medieval' (and ancient) era of manuscripts, the 'modern' one of print, and finally the 'postmodern' one of new media like the telephone, television and film.[11] Like Balázs he values the era before print (even after the invention of the alphabet) positively as more holistic than the following era of print, which is characterised by the narrow, linear logic of the printed word. McLuhan differs from Balázs and agrees with apparatus theory in so far as he allocates visuality to the 'modern' era of print, when the eye is dominant, rather than the medieval period, where all senses are still involved in reading practices (for instance, when manuscripts are read out, or carved letters retain tactility). Accordingly, he judges the point of a return to a more holistic, premodern culture to be the invention not of the camera, with its continued emphasis on the visual, but of the telegraph. Nevertheless, he shares the idea of a more holistic Middle Ages and the utopian hope of a better world to come, enabled by 'postmodern' technology.

Balázs's emphasis on medieval visuality, however, remained influential elsewhere. His hope that film would be able to restimulate medieval visuality is one of the founding formulations of realist or phenomenological film theory. André Bazin, the best-known promoter of this school, which proposes that film should recapture reality and make everyday material objects visible again by focusing the viewer's attention on them, frames his analysis of film in terms of the medieval. Bazin has become infamous for claiming that film can represent objective reality as opposed to subjective perception. But the fact that he compares this to holistic medieval modes of representation suggests that he means more than a superficial realism that merely records what is visible to the eye in a way independent of the perceiver.[12] In his 1945 essay 'The ontology of the photographic image',

Bazin builds on Balázs's idea that film can bring back the lost unity of medieval art and reality. While, according to Bazin, medieval art was able to show what mattered spiritually and physically, albeit in a naive manner, the technical discovery of how to represent perspective forced artists to decide whether outer or inner likeness was more important to them, since they were now unable to represent both at the same time (presumably because they could no longer express symbolic or transcendental relations spatially, but had to follow realist conventions in depicting scale and position). It is thus only since the fifteenth century, Bazin claims, that Western painting and sculpture have been torn between the two conflicting desires to represent either the spiritual essence or the outer likeness of an object, while medieval art could effortlessly combine both:

> Medieval art never passed through this crisis; simultaneously vividly realistic and highly spiritual, it knew nothing of the drama that came to light as a consequence of technical developments. Perspective was the original sin of Western painting. It was redeemed from sin by Niepce and Lumière. In achieving the aims of baroque art, photography has freed the plastic arts from their obsession with likeness.[13]

Medieval art here appears as radically different from modern art, and film as radically different yet again. The invention of photography by Nicéphore Niepce (c. 1826), and of film by Auguste and Louis Lumière, redeemed art not only by providing a perfect outer likeness, thereby leaving painting and sculpture free to convey the spiritual or inner essence of its objects, but also by managing to represent outer, objective likeness and the essence or 'being' of an object simultaneously. This implies that film is in some unspecified way able to achieve once more what medieval art did: it shows both inside and outside to perfection. While situating this argument in the new debate about film's potential objectivity and realism, Bazin merely repeats Balázs's holistic view of the Middle Ages and film.

Bazin argues that the seismic shift from medieval to modern modes of representation is constituted by the discovery of perspectival representation in painting. For Balázs, on the other hand, medieval visuality was possible not because there was no difference between modes of *representing* inside and outside but because, even in reality, there was no gap between outside and inside, face and character, body and mind of each human being. As he explains in *The Visible Human*: 'Artists were allowed to paint soul and spirit without becoming "literary", because soul and spirit were not stuck in the realm of ideas, but could become entirely embodied.'[14] This unit of body and soul, then, is not just a feature of art, but is based on a unity of actual people's bodies and minds. The medium of film, Balázs hopes, will reunite body and mind in the same way to create fully integral human beings by teaching people to understand humans on the silent screen purely through their facial expressions and gestures. This will enable them to read each other's body language as well, so that the body will regain the ground it has lost to verbal communication: the modern rift between body and mind will be healed.

Balázs here cites the widespread idea, most famously formulated by Jacob Burckhardt, that the mind–body split and therefore the self-conscious individual only emerged in the Renaissance, or in the Enlightenment (especially with René Descartes), which makes this fragmentation a historically situated phenomenon and therefore more open to reversal. The Middle Ages thus emerge as a time when the holistic ideal actually existed, and when the body still played an important role. This is a view famously endorsed by medievalists like Mikhail Bakhtin and still prevalent in much medieval scholarship as well as popular thought.[15] This emergence of the split individual is often linked to media developments, in particular the representation of individuals in portrait painting and self-reflexive biographical writing. It is also still propagated in film theory. The utopian vision of a world returned to a holistic, medieval, non-written state through the power of film articulated by the influential feminist film theorist Heide Schlüpmann in 1998 strongly echoes Balázs's enthusiastic prophecies. She hypothesises a medieval culture of 'productive philosophy', 'love and laughter', 'woman and imagination' along the lines that she finds described in Friedrich Nietzsche's work, particularly in *The Birth of Tragedy*.[16] Schlüpmann believes that the written word has repressed this medieval culture since the Renaissance and Enlightenment, corrupting and making scientific its philosophy. But a third, 'postmodern' era starts with the arrival of film at the same time when Nietzsche dialectically, through writing, rediscovers what writing has repressed: 'at his time a medium developed which, from the bottom of "low culture", of fairs and pleasure grounds, would shape up to become a new aesthetic culture: the photographic medium of film'.[17] Film will be able to heal the corruption of philosophy and return contemporary culture to holism. According to Schlüpmann's convoluted argument, writing has led to a split between mind and body. Unlike Balázs she does not explain how writing causes this separation – presumably by abstracting concepts or signifiers from the material existence of that which is signified. Film 'enacts this split', probably by showing the body and the world visually rather than representing them abstractly, thereby making the viewer conscious of their separation elsewhere.[18] In this way film for Schlüpmann 'allows the lifting of the repression, and the flowering of visual pleasure, rescuing the powers of ecstasy': a return to the unrepressed, pre-rationalised, holistic culture of the Middle Ages.[19]

Collectivity: Cinema as medieval cathedral

Schlüpmann's neo-Nietzschean and neo-Romantic fantasy of a holistic Middle Ages postulates a unity not just of body and soul but also of 'the people' as a whole, in both the Middle Ages and in a future culture influenced by film. She assumes a Middle Ages characterised by an 'Occitan culture of laughter, a folk culture [*Volkskultur*] of fairs and feasts', as described by Nietzsche, Mikhail Bakhtin and the historian Marie-Odile Métral.[20] Likewise, as mentioned, film for her comes from the 'the bottom of "low culture", of fairs and pleasure grounds' to revolutionise society from below.[21] Again this is characteristic of a commonly held view of the Middle Ages as a more communal time, a view already implicit in Burckhardt's idea of the emergence of the individual only in modernity.

While Schlüpmann sees this collective orientation of the Middle Ages embodied in the 'low' culture of markets and feasts, the cathedral as 'high art' is also frequently invoked as a prime example of this communal medieval mindset.[22] Art historians from Erwin Panofsky to Norbert Nussbaum have highlighted the collective nature both of cathedral construction, with its anonymous architects and builders, and of the buildings' reception by believers united in faith.[23] In current film studies film is also predominantly presented as collectively produced and received. In a reaction to earlier auteur debates, film scholars now emphasise that any film gaining cinematic release is rarely the product of one person or 'auteur' (however useful this concept may be), but involves the collaboration between, for instance, a producer, director, actor, distributor and programmer. Not only the production but also the reception of films in the cinema is usually characterised as communal. Both the collective reception and the production by a (small) group of people suggest to many thinkers that film is in essence a popular medium, expressing ideas widely present in a culture rather than individual authors' views. Apparatus theory in the 1970s and more recent studies of Hollywood cinema in particular have followed Behne's characterisation of cinema as a popular and democratic medium. It may come as no surprise that the collective nature of production and reception of both films and medieval cathedrals have often been compared to each other. In his summary of the theoretical debates about authorship and collectivity, Gilbert Perez notes that the medieval cathedral was a favoured image for the collaboration of 'many hands' by those opponents of auteur theory who propagate a positive view of the communal nature of film production: 'Many hands are sometimes viewed approvingly (as in the selfless group of artistry of a medieval cathedral) but more often disapprovingly (as in the soulless fabrication on an assembly line).'[24] The medieval cathedral appears here as the model for idealised collective production in contrast to vilified alienated labour in assembly-line style.

Although Perez does not specify the source of this image, it can be traced back to Balázs's texts quoted above. For Balázs this allegedly unified 'spirit of the people' in the Middle Ages had found its ultimate expression in the cathedral.[25] Fragmented by modernity's print culture, this *Volksgeist* would re-emerge intact through film. Cinema for Balázs has already become the only genuinely popular form of art, emerging from the masses and bringing together all classes, following the neo-Romantic fantasy that 'every seamstress and every princess' is able to understand the embodied language of film.[26] This cinematic community is furthermore envisaged as international, because silent film is able to transcend the barriers of national (verbal) languages.[27] For Balázs this nostalgia for a distinctive medieval visuality, holism and community thus seamlessly fits in not only with his high hopes for social change to be brought about by film but also with his communist ideals of a radically transformed society: proletarian, unalienated and international.

The association of cinema with the cathedral, combining popular accessibility with high art, helped to emancipate cinema from its origins in the variety show and the Nickelodeon as 'cinema of attraction'.[28] New York's Roxy Theatre even called itself 'The Cathedral of the Motion Picture' at its opening in 1927.[29] Moreover, the comparison of cinema with the cathedral, a favourite topic of Weimar art history, adds credibility to Balázs's proposal that film was a form of art, and as such worthy of serious study.[30] Even Robert Musil, who in his 1925 critique of Balázs's film theory challenges many of his utopian hopes, agrees that 'film has become the *Volkskunst* of our time', and compares it to the church: 'And the churches and places of worship of all religions have not in millennia covered the world with such a dense web as the cinema did within three decades.'[31] Bernd Eichinger, producer of *The Name of the Rose* (1989), still shares this view of the medieval abbey as a 'melting pot for personalities and scholars coming together from all over the world', which he sought to recreate in the international co-production and casting of actors for this medieval film.[32]

In his 1948 essay 'Adaptation or the cinema as digest', André Bazin similarly holds up the collective nature of medieval art (if not solely that of cathedrals) as a positive model to which film ought to return. He describes it as an alternative to modern ideas of individual authorship, in order to defend filmic adaptations of books:

> The ferocious defense of literary works is, to a certain extent, aesthetically justified; but we must also be aware that it rests on a rather recent, individualistic conception of the 'author' and of the 'work', a conception that was far from being ethically rigorous in the seventeenth century and that started to become legally defined only at the end of the eighteenth. In the Middle Ages, there were only a few themes, and they were common to all the arts. That of Adam and Eve, for instance, is to be found in the mystery plays, painting, sculpture, and stained-glass windows, none of which were ever challenged for transferring this theme from one art form to another ... You may perhaps observe that those days are over and that it would be aesthetic nonsense to want to anachronistically reverse the revolution of the relationship among the creator, the public, and the work of art. To this I would respond that, on the contrary, it is possible that artists and critics remain blind to the birth of the new, aesthetic Middle Ages, whose origin is to be found in the accession of the masses to power (or at least their participation in it) and in the emergence of an artistic form to complement that accession: the cinema.[33]

Again, the Middle Ages are radically set up as a visual, collective time, completely different from a following literary, individualistic period. Film is once more construed as being able to bring about a new Middle Ages, a new, paradisiacal era of collective, popular production. Again Balázs's neo-Romantic view of medieval collectivity is thus incorporated into Bazin's new critical argument about the role of the filmmaker as an individual artist.

In his famous 1934 essay 'Style and medium in the motion pictures', Erwin Panofsky also used the medieval cathedral as a model for the collective production of film. However, he returns to Münsterberg's critical view of both the Middle Ages and film when he claims that both were still imperfect, preliminary stages, not only because film employs intertitles as medieval painters and illuminators used scrolls of words, but also precisely because of their collective mode of production. He presents cinema as art for the masses, 'originally, a product of genuine folk art', satisfying the crude desires of the people for sadism, pornography, retributive justice and base humour.[34] This collective nature of film is now compared to that of the medieval cathedral not with regard to a shared expression of a Romantic unified people's spirit, but in terms of their production: 'It might be said that a film, called into being by a co-operative effort in which all contributions have the same degree of permanence, is the nearest modern equivalent of a medieval cathedral.'[35] Panofsky illustrates this claim by elaborating on the corresponding roles of producer and bishop, director and architect, and several other pairings down to technicians and 'woodsmen', each of whom believes 'with perfect bona fides, that his is really the most important job – which is quite true to the extent that it is indispensable.'[36] But the likeness of cinema and cathedral stops for him when it comes to finance:

> This comparison may seem sacrilegious, not only because there are, proportionally, fewer good films than there are good cathedrals, but also because the movies are commercial. However, if commercial art be defined as all art not primarily produced in order to gratify the creative urge of its maker, but primarily intended to meet the requirements of a patron or buying public, it must be said that non-commercial art is the exception rather than the rule, and a fairly recent and not always felicitous exception at that.[37]

Panofsky's slightly patronising tone here suggests that film and medieval architecture, with their plethora of self-important collaborators and little good output, are only ever second best in comparison with (post-medieval) Renaissance art, which he goes on to praise in the rest of the article. More importantly in our context, the Middle Ages remain for him an island of pre-commercial, communal production. He ignores that most medieval art fits his definition of commercial – that is, being produced for a patron rather than out of the spontaneous creative urge of an artist – and instead goes on to cite the works of the Renaissance artists Albrecht Dürer and William Shakespeare as great examples of commercial art. Panofsky's hopes for the future of film lie in its gradual development away from medieval modes of production (as a result of capitalist market forces), rather than in its revolutionary return to the Middle Ages.

Movement: movies against medieval stasis

Theorists like Walter Benjamin, Siegfried Kracauer and Vilém Flusser, on the other hand, contrast rather than compare film with the Middle Ages with regard to the alleged enclosed cosmos of the Middle Ages, which is usually seen as shattered rather than imitated by film. The idea that the Middle Ages imagined the cosmos as limited, bounded, geocentric and uniform is a well-established historiographical cliché.[38] Béla Balázs, for instance, depicts the medieval world as a united whole, citing the example of medieval mystery plays, in which heaven, earth and hell were staged simultaneously.[39] For him this is repeated in Erwin Piscator's plays, which use stacked platforms and film projections to represent the whole world – this time, that of the socialist worldview. The unity of medieval art is here still a model, rather than that from which modernity needs to break away. When talking more specifically about film, however, Balázs does refer to the liberated movement of the camera, which, he argues, opens up the world for viewers, rather than presenting them with yet another 'closed world'.[40] Walter Benjamin and Siegfried Kracauer, on the other hand, construct a timeline along which a period characterised by a limited worldview (encompassing the Middle Ages and modernity) comes to an end with the arrival of film, which brings about a new era. In his brief piece 'About the Middle Ages' (1916), Benjamin had characterised the worldview of medieval people as enclosed and limited.[41] In his much-quoted essay 'The work of art in the age of its mechanical reproducibility' (1935), he sees this medieval spirit subsisting into the modern period, where works of art still always retain their aura as unique artefacts with ritual or cultic meaning. The real innovation comes only in the recent past, with the invention of film, which allows the images of objects to be reproduced and transported. For Benjamin this means that the objects themselves become mobile. He mentions that the cathedral can escape the static limitations of a building thanks to the invention of photo-graphy: 'The cathedral leaves its place to find a reception in the studio of the art lover.'[42] While all art produced before the advent of film ('medieval' and 'modern' alike) was united by the fact that it had an aura, the reproducibility of film rings in a new era. For Benjamin film broke away from the static and claustrophobic enclosure of previous times when it 'exploded this world of dungeons'.[43] The paradigmatically contemporary film is characterised by a liberation of space and time – camera and projection free up and stretch space and time and make them mobile. Despite his famous calls for an innovative historiography, Benjamin's representation of the Middle Ages as static and limited relies on an entirely conventional model.[44]

Even more explicitly than Benjamin, Siegfried Kracauer suggests that film breaks out of medieval limitations in his late work *Theory of Film: The Redemption of Physical Reality* (1960). While defining the reinstatement and re-presentation of physical, visible reality as the key innovation of film, along the lines set out by Balázs and Bazin, Kracauer believes that film achieves this through its ability to construct seemingly endless worlds, making us aware of the boundless spatial possibilities of modern reality. Kracauer contrasts the endlessness of filmic space (in which the camera moves through a space imagined to be infinite) with actual historical locations, which are reconstructible only to a limited extent, and therefore necessarily not endless. He mentions especially the enclosed cosmos of the Middle Ages, which he sees as having a static and narrow view of space and time, too, in opposition to the modern 'flow of life'.[45] Films about the Middle Ages therefore distort both the period and the medium – they wrongly present the Middle Ages as open, and do not do the medium's boundlessness justice. For Kracauer our limited access to the past, which can only ever be recreated partially, thus merges with an alleged self-perception and reality of the past – and especially of the Middle Ages – as limited: it is not simply that we can no longer access or reconstruct the limitless space as it was in the Middle Ages, but space in the Middle Ages had never been limitless, and was never perceived to be so. This becomes clear when he explains his theory, using the example of Carl Theodor Dreyer's film *Day of Anger* (1943):

> This remarkable film obviously rests upon the sensible premise that the experience of spatial and temporal endlessness is a relatively modern experience and that therefore the attempt to reproduce the declining Middle Ages in terms of a nineteenth-century medium constitutes a violation of historical truth. When the Inquisition tried and burned witches, the world was stationary rather than dynamic, thinly populated rather than crowded, there was not yet the sensation of dizzying physical movement and the amorphous masses were still to come. It was essentially a finite cosmos, not the infinite world of ours.[46]

According to Kracauer as well as Benjamin, then, film takes leave of this postulated limited and static worldview of the past and gives material, physical reality back to people, teaching them to see afresh, through an emphasis on materiality, endlessness and movement. This view is still current in media studies, although now often perceived less positively. Vilém Flusser contrasts the static images of premodern times (for which he quotes the stone age of the Lascaux cave paintings and the 'Florence of the Medici' during the 'Early Renaissance' as examples) with the 'flood' of moving images of today.[47] Unlike Kracauer and Benjamin, Flusser does not see film as breaking out from a negatively valued enclosed world, but as an overwhelming dissolution of boundaries.

I hope to have shown, then, the longevity of certain ideas concerning both film and the Middle Ages, which are either compared to each other with respect to their perceived collective, visual and holistic character, or set up in opposition to one another, with film being defined as representing a rupture with an allegedly limited, medieval cosmos which commanded limited representational techniques. It is time to acknowledge film theory's reliance on medievalism. For film scholars, this means realising the importance of the Middle Ages as a point of contrast and comparison for many of the most influential film theories. For medievalists, it means becoming aware of stereotypes about the Middle Ages that still inform medievalist scholarship and are so influential outside the discipline.

Notes

1 Béla Balázs, 'Kinokritik!', in Balász, *Schriften zum Film* (Munich: Hanser, 1982–84 [1922]), 2 vols, vol. 1, pp. 5–6; Balász, *Der sichtbare Mensch oder, Die Kultur des Films*, ed. Helmut H. Diederichs (Frankfurt am Main: Suhrkamp, 2001 [1924]), esp. pp. 9–23, selected passages in Balázs, '*Visible Man, or the Culture of Film* (1924)', trans. Rodney Livingston, introduction Erica Carter, *Screen*, 48:1 (2007), 91–108; Balász, *Iskusstvo Kino* (Moscow: Goskinoizdat, 1945), in English as *Theory of the Film: Character and Growth of a New Art*, trans. Edith Bone (New York: Dover, 1970), pp. 39–40; Balász, *Der Geist des Films* (Frankfurt am Main: Suhrkamp, 2001 [1930]), esp. p. 74; Walter Benjamin, 'Das Kunstwerk im Zeitalter seiner technischen Reproduzierbarkeit', in Benjamin, *Gesammelte Schriften*, ed. Rolf Tiedemann and Hermann Schweppenhäuser, 7 vols (Frankfurt am Main: Suhrkamp, 1972–89 [1935]), vol. I.2 (1974), pp. 431–508, in English as 'The work of art in the age of its technological reproducibility second version', in Benjamin, *Selected Writings*, ed. Marcus Bullock and Michael W. Jennings, 4 vols (Cambridge, MA: Belknap Press of Harvard University Press,

1996-2003), vol. 3 (2002), pp. 101–33; Siegfried Kracauer, *Theory of Film: The Redemption of Physical Reality* (Princeton, NJ: Princeton University Press, 1997 [1960]), pp. 71, 78–82; Erwin Panofsky, 'Style and medium in the motion pictures', in Gerald Mast *et al.* (eds), *Film Theory and Criticism* (New York: Oxford University Press, 1992 [1934/1947]), pp. 233–48.

2 Hugo Münsterberg, 'The photoplay: a psychological study', in Allan Langdale (ed.), *Hugo Münsterberg on Film: The Photoplay: A Psychological Study and Other Writings* (New York: Routledge, 2002 [1916]), pp. 45–162 (p. 143).

3 Johan Huizinga, *The Autumn of the Middle Ages*, trans. Rodney J. Payton and Ulrich Mammitzsch (Chicago: University of Chicago Press, 1996); first German translation 1924.

4 Balázs, 'Kinokritik!', pp. 5–6; emphasis in original. All translations from German are mine. See also Gustav Frank, 'Musil contra Balázs: Ansichten einer "visuellen Kultur" um 1925', *Musil-Forum*, 28 (2003/4), 105–52; Sabine Hake, *The Cinema's Third Machine: Writing on Film in Germany, 1907–1933* (Lincoln: University of Nebraska Press, 1993), pp. 212–46; Massimo Locatelli, *Béla Balázs: Die Physiognomik des Films*, Beiträge zur Film- und Fernsehwissenschaft, 54 (Berlin: Vistas, 1999); Gertrud Koch, 'Béla Balázs: the physiognomy of things', trans. Miriam Hansen, *New German Critique*, 40 (Winter 1987), 167–77.

5 Balázs, *Der sichtbare Mensch*, pp. 16-17, Balázs, 'Visible man', 96; Balázs, *Theory of the Film*, pp. 39–40; Balázs, *Der Geist des Films* (Frankfurt am Main: Suhrkamp, 2001 [1930]), esp. p. 74. He also compares the film detective to St George (*Der sichtbare Mensch*, p. 101; *Geist des Films*, pp. 153–4). The partial English translation Balázs, 'Visible man', leaves out this and most other instances of Balázs's medievalism. See also references to Balázs below.

6 Adolf Behne, 'Die Stellung des Publikums zur modernen deutschen Literatur', in Anton Kaes (ed.), *Kino-Debatte: Texte zum Verhältnis von Literatur und Film 1909–1929* (Munich: Deutscher Taschenbuch Verlag, 1978 [1926]), pp. 160–3 (p. 162).

7 Sergei Eisenstein, *The Film Sense*, ed. and trans. Jay Leyda (London: Faber and Faber, 1986 [1943]), pp. 83–8.

8 *Ibid.*, pp. 148–50.

9 Erwin Panofksy, *Perspective as Symbolic Form*, trans. Christopher S. Wood (New York: Zone, 1991 [*Die Perspektive als symbolische Form*, 1927]); cf. Carl Landauer, 'Erwin Panofksy and the renascence of the Renaissance', *Renaissance Quarterly*, 47 (1994), 255–81.

10 E.g., Christian Metz, *The Imaginary Signifier: Psychoanalysis and the Cinema*, trans. Celia Britton (Bloomington: Indiana University Press, 1982); Jean-Louis Baudry, 'Ideological effects of the basic cinematographic apparatus', trans. Alan Williams, in Leo Braudy and Marshall Cohen (eds), *Film Theory and Criticism: Introductory Readings* (Oxford: Oxford University Press, 2004, [1970]), pp. 355–65 (p. 357); Daniel Dayan, 'The tutor-code of classical cinema', in Braudy and Cohen, *Film Theory* [1974], pp. 106–17 (pp. 111–12); Marshall McLuhan, *The Gutenberg Galaxy: The Making of Typographic Man* (London: Routledge & Kegan Paul, 1962); Marshall McLuhan, *Understanding Media: The Extensions of Man* (London: Routledge & Kegan Paul, 1964), esp. p. 288.

11 McLuhan, *Gutenberg Galaxy*; McLuhan, *Understanding Media*, esp. pp. 284–96.

12 For a critical summarising evaluation of Bazin and the realist debates see, for example, Philip Rosen, *Change Mummified: Cinema, Historicity, Theory* (Minneapolis: University of Minnesota Press, 2001), pp. 3–41.

13 André Bazin, 'The ontology of the photographic image', in Bazin, *What Is Cinema?*, ed. Hugh Gray (Berkeley: University of California Press, 1967–71 [1945]), 2 vols, vol. 1, pp. 9–16 (p. 12; also pp. 10–11).

14 Balázs, *Der sichtbare Mensch*, pp. 16–17 (not translated in Balázs, 'Visible man').

15 Mikhail Bakhtin, *Rabelais and His World*, trans. Hélène Iswolsky (Cambridge: MA: MIT Press, 1968 [1965]).

16 Heide Schlüpmann, *Ein Detektiv des Kinos: Studien zu Siegfried Kracauers Filmtheorie* (Basel: Stroemfeld, 1998), pp. 123–43 (pp. 138–9). The relevant chapter had previously appeared in an English translation by Ishbel Flett as Schlüpmann, 'Re-reading Nietzsche through Kracauer: towards a feminist perspective on film history', *Film History*, 6:1 (1994), 80–93; similar ideas are repeated in Schlüpmann, *Abendröthe der Subjektphilosophie: Eine Ästhetik des Kinos* (Basel: Stroemfeld, 1998), esp. p. 139.

17 Schlüpmann, *Detektiv*, p. 139.

18 *Ibid.*, p. 139.

19 *Ibid.*, p. 139.

20 *Ibid.*, p. 142.

21 *Ibid.*, p. 139, cited above.

22 See Bettina Bildhauer, 'Zeiträume: Das Mittelalter als Innenraum – Kosmos, Kathedrale, Kino', in Hans-Jochen Schiewer *et al.* (eds), *Innenräume: Anglo-deutsche Arbeitstagung* (Berlin: de Gruyter, 2008).

23 Abbot Suger, *On the Abbey Church of St Denis and Its Art Treasures*, ed. Erwin Panofsky (Princeton, NJ: Princeton University Press, 1979 [1946]), pp. 19–20; Norbert Nussbaum, *German Gothic Church Architecture*, trans. Scott Kleager (New Haven: Yale University Press, 2000 [1985]), e.g., p. 112.

24 Gilberto Perez, *The Material Ghost: Films and Their Medium* (Baltimore: Johns Hopkins University Press, 1998), p. 4.

25 Balázs, 'Kinokritik!', pp. 5–6, quoted above.

26 Balázs, *Der sichtbare Mensch*, p. 22 (not translated in Balázs, 'Visible man').

27 This is a widespread view, echoed, for instance, in Carlo Mierendorff, 'Hätte ich das Kino' [1920], in *Kino-Debatte*, pp. 139–46 (p. 145).

28 See Tom Gunning, 'The cinema of attraction: early film, its spectator and the avant-garde', *Wide Angle*, 8:3–4 (1986), 63–70.

29 Quoted in Ben M. Hall, *The Best Remaining Seats: The Golden Age of the Movie Palace* (New York: Da Capo, 1988), p. 82. Joseph Roth had already likened a visit to the cinema to attending mass: Roth, 'The conversion of a sinner at Berlin's UFA palace', in Roth, *What I Saw: Reports from Berlin 1920–1933*, trans. Michael Hofmann (New York: Norton, 2003), pp. 167–9.

30 For a critical description of Panofsky's contrasting use of film to legitimise his idealist theory of art see Thomas Levin, 'Iconology at the movies: Panofsky's film theory', *Yale Journal of Criticism*, 9:1 (1996), 27–55.

31 Robert Musil, 'Ansätze zu neuer Ästhetik: Bemerkungen über eine Dramaturgie des Films', in Musil, *Gesammelte Werke 2: Prosa und Stücke, Kleine Prosa, Aphorismen, Autobiographisches, Essays und Reden, Kritiken* (Reinbek: Rowohlt, 1978 [1925], pp. 1137–54 (p. 1138).

32 'Interview mit Bernd Eichinger', in *Kino*, 1 (1987), 12–14 (14).

33 André Bazin, 'Adaptation or the cinema as digest' (1948), in *Bazin at Work: Major Essays and Reviews from the Forties and Fifties*, trans. Alain Piette and Bert Cardullo (New York: Routledge, 1997), pp. 41–51 (pp. 46–7). Medieval images of paradise are more critically compared to film by Siegfried Kracauer, who admonishes mainstream Weimar film for depicting high society as so idealised that it 'shines like the paradise of medieval pictures'; Kracauer, 'Film 1928', in Kracauer, *Das Ornament der Masse: Essays* (Frankfurt am Main: Suhrkamp, 1977 [1928]), pp. 295–311 (p. 298); Kracauer, 'Film 1928', in Kracauer, *The Mass Ornament: Weimar Essays*, trans. Thomas Y. Levin (Cambridge, MA: Harvard University Press, 1995), pp. 307–20 (p. 310).

34 Panofsky, 'Style and medium', p. 233.

35 *Ibid.*, p. 244.

36 *Ibid.*, p. 244.

37 *Ibid.*, p. 244.

38 E.g., Horst Fuhrmann, *Germany in the High Middle Ages, c. 1050–1200*, trans. Timothy Reuter (Cambridge: Cambridge University Press, 1986 [1983]). McLuhan, on the other hand, sees the medieval cosmos as fragmented into separate spaces, rather than unifiable and representable by a single map.

39 'Reine Kunst, unreine Ästhetik', in Balázs, *Schriften*, vol. 2, pp. 224–6; also 'Vom politischen Sinn des Bühnengerüstes', in Balázs, *Schriften*, vol. 2, pp. 257–8.

40 Balázs, *Geist des Films*, pp. 14–15.

41 Walter Benjamin, 'Über das Mittelalter' [c. 1916], in Benjamin, *Gesammelte Schriften*, vol. II.1 (1977), pp. 132–3 (p. 133).

42 Benjamin, 'Das Kunstwerk', p. 438; 'The work of art', p. 103. Siegfried Kracauer similarly argued that cathedrals are mobilised and become independent of subjective viewpoints through photography, which 'takes the crockets and figures down from the Gothic cathedrals'; 'Die Photographie' [1927], in Kracauer, *Ornament der Masse*, pp. 185–203 (p. 202); 'Photography', in Kracauer, *Mass Ornament*, pp. 47–63 (p. 62). Benjamin's interlinking conceptions of modernity, film and space and their reception in film theory have been well researched, e.g., Tom Gunning, 'The exterior as intérieur: Benjamin's optical detective', *boundary 2*, 30:1 (Spring 2003), 105–29; Miriam Hansen, 'Benjamin and cinema: not a one-way street', in Gerhard Richter (ed.), *Benjamin's Ghosts: Interventions in Contemporary Literary and Cultural Theory* (Stanford: Stanford University Press, 2002), pp. 41–73 [1999]; Susanne Radstone, 'Cinema/memory/history', *Screen*, 36:1 (1995), 34–47; Gertrud Koch, 'Cosmos in film: on the concept of space in Walter Benjamin's "Work of Art" essay', *Qui parle*, 5:2 (1992), 61–71; Anne Friedberg, 'Les flâneurs du mal(l): cinema and the postmodern condition', *PMLA*, 106 (1991), 419–31; Miriam Hansen, 'Benjamin, cinema and experience: "The Blue Flower in the Land of Technology"', *New German Critique*, 40 (1987), 179–224; David Frisby, *Fragments of Modernity: Theories of Modernity*

in the Work of Simmel, Kracauer and Benjamin (Cambridge: Cambridge University Press, 1985), pp. 207–65.

43 Benjamin, 'Kunstwerk', p. 461 (Benjamin, 'Work of art', p. 117).

44 Benjamin's characterisation of the cathedral as not designed for an individual, subjective vantage-point ('certain sculptures on medieval cathedrals are invisible to the spectator on the ground') can, however, be read against itself to demonstrate that the cathedral already has the potential of opening up non-'Renaissance', multiple viewpoints: Benjamin, 'Kunstwerk', p. 443 (Benjamin, 'Work of art', p. 106).

45 Kracauer, *Theory of Film*, pp. 71, 78–82. Much has been written about Kracauer's view of modern space as unbounded, e.g., Anthony Vidler, 'Agoraphobia: spatial estrangement in Georg Simmel and Siegfried Kracauer', *New German Critique*, 54 (Fall 1991), 31–45; Miriam Hansen, 'Decentric perspectives: Kracauer's early writings on film and mass culture', *New German Critique*, 54 (Fall 1991), 47–76.

46 Kracauer, *Theory of Film*, p. 81. He had already formulated the problem with historical film's attempts to represent 'eras which are, in distinction from ours, static' in 1940, using Carl Th. Dreyer's *The Passion of Joan of Arc* (1928) as one example of this; see Siegfried Kracauer, 'Der historische Film' [1940], in Kracauer, *Kino: Essays, Studien, Glossen zum Film*, ed. Karsten Witte (Frankfurt am Main: Suhrkamp, 1974), pp. 43–5 (pp. 43–4).

47 Vilém Flusser, 'Bilderstatus', in *Lob der Oberflächlichkeit: Für eine Phänomenologie der Medien* (Cologne: Bollmann, 1995 [1991]), pp. 133–46.

3

A time of translation: linguistic difference and cinematic medievalism

Carol O'Sullivan

The question of language is at once perennially present and strangely absent within film studies, which has tended as a discipline to think of film *as* language, rather than as a medium which incorporates language as an expressive resource.[1] This chapter is part of a larger project discussing the problems posed to film, since the advent of sound film, by foreign language (that is, language not native to the viewer) – problems which relate as much to questions of mimesis and representation as to the international circulation of film. The problem of foreign language in filmic representations of the Middle Ages would seem *a priori* to pose itself on three fronts: in relation to the temporal distance from the viewer, as the languages of the period are no longer spoken; in relation to the co-existence of languages, particularly Latin and the vernaculars, in medieval society; and, above all, in relation to the widespread cinematic depiction of the Middle Ages as a time of high mobility and intercultural contact. The present chapter will explore to what extent medieval film engages with questions of language, and to what extent these engagements may be distinctive.[2] Three principal sites of activity are identified: extra-diegetically speaking, subtitles constitute a key authenticity-effect. They also participate in distinctive forms of textual and visual play. Diegetically speaking, in its representations of situations of language contact and translation, it is argued here that popular medieval film shares contemporary cinematic concerns about intercultural communication in a global society.

Sternberg and film's mimetic challenge

In relation to the treatment of language, the most significant feature of medieval film might at first sight seem to be its globalising geographies.

In *A Knight's Tale* (2001) the cosmopolitanism of the knightly life and the international jousting circuit are called up for us with comic grandiloquence by Chaucer, played by Paul Bettany, in his presentation of 'Sir Ulrich von Liechtenstein from Gelderland':

> I first met him atop a mountain near Jerusalem, praying to God, asking his forgiveness for the Saracen blood spilled by his sword. Next, he amazed me still further in Italy when he saved a fatherless beauty from the would-be ravishings of her dreadful Turkish uncle. In Greece he spent a year in silence just to better understand the sound of a whisper.

Ridley Scott's *Kingdom of Heaven* (2005) offers us what Roger Ebert has called 'the 12th-century equivalent of GPS [global positioning system]' in the directions to Jerusalem given by Godfrey of Ibelin to his son Balian: 'Go to where they speak Italian, and then keep going.'[3] Maps are frequently used indexically to depict the long journeys involved; in *King Arthur* (2004) the map is used to emphasise how far Arthur's Sarmatian knights are from their homeland; and in *The 13th Warrior* (1999) the map is superimposed on footage of rolling landscapes and a dialogue track listing the many peoples encountered by Ibn Fadlan on his way from Arabia to the Volga.

The boundary crossing which such globetrotting narratives entail might be expected to confront film with 'a formidable mimetic challenge: how to represent the reality of polylingual discourse through a communicative medium which is normally unilingual', as Meir Sternberg put it in a seminal 1981 article.[4] In film as in literature, this challenge proves less formidable in practice than in theory. Nevertheless, medieval film provides us with much material for reflection on, in Sternberg's words, 'the interlingual tension between language as represented object ... and language as representational means'.[5] These relationships between film, language and representation may be more clearly delineated with the help of the model outlined by Sternberg.

For Sternberg there are three representational stances possible in narrative in relation to language. He calls the first 'referential restriction'. This 'consists in confining the scope of the represented world to the limits of a ... community whose speech patterns correspond to those of the implied audience'.[6] This is by definition inapplicable to much historical film, including films set in the medieval period. The two other, polar practices outlined by Sternberg are of greater relevance to us. 'Vehicular matching' suits 'the variations in the representational medium to the variations in the represented object' by representing, for instance, English through English and French through French in *Henry V* (dir. Laurence Olivier, 1944; dir. Kenneth Branagh, 1989).[7] In films aimed at monolingual audiences, diegetic interpreting or subtitles are likely to be required. By contrast 'homogenizing convention' 'retains the freedom of reference while dismissing the resultant variations in the language presumably spoken by the characters as an irrelevant, if not distracting, representational factor'.[8] In cinema this manifests as the imperialist arrogance of which Ella Shohat and Robert Stam write in *Unthinking Eurocentrism*:

> Hollywood proposed to tell not only its own stories but also those of other nations, and not only to Americans but also to the other nations themselves, and always in English. In Cecil B. de Mille epics, both the ancient Egyptians and the Israelites, not to mention God, speak English.[9]

Both homogenisation and vehicular matching are extreme approaches which are rarely entirely adhered to.[10] Few films can afford to risk alienating their audience by shooting entirely in an archaic or obsolete language, *pace* Mel Gibson's *The Passion of the Christ* (2004). At the same time relatively few films opt for entirely crude homogenisation. Rather, Sternberg identifies a number of intermediate procedures which may be more readily incorporated into representational strategies: 'selective reproduction', 'verbal transposition' and 'conceptual reflection'. 'Selective reproduction' is the 'intermittent quotation of the original heterolingual discourse'.[11] We might identify the sporadic use of Latin, the presumed lingua franca of all characters except Salvatore, in *The Name of the Rose* (1986) as an example of such selective reproduction. 'Verbal transposition' is defined by Sternberg as 'the poetic or communicative twist given to what sociolinguists call bilingual interference', in other words, the use of forms of expression which evoke an underlying foreign language.[12] These can be syntactic forms or turns of phrase. In cinema accent is frequently called upon to play this role. 'Conceptual reflection' retains 'not so much the verbal forms of the foreign code as the underlying socio-cultural norms, semantic mapping of reality, and distinctive referential range, segmentations and hierarchies'.[13] Here we might think, for instance, of the jousting terminology used by King Bruno the Questionable in *Jabberwocky* (1977).

These strategies offer a framework within which to situate language usage and language strategies in medieval film. More often than not, the mimetic challenge posited by Sternberg is resolved through fairly unproblematised homogenisation – something which medieval film has in common with medieval romance, whose authors, according to Marianne Kalinke,

> appear to be blissfully ignorant of linguistic borders – and their heroes immune to linguistic unintelligibility ... the fictional Gahmuret, father of Parzival, sets out from his native Anjou to traverse Baghdad, Morocco, Persia, Damascus, Aleppo, Alexandria, Seville, and Toledo, apparently without benefit of languages other than his native tongue, to judge by Wolfram von Eschenbach's silence in this matter.[14]

Similarly William Thatcher and his friends can travel through France and to England in *A Knight's Tale*, or Robin of Locksley escape from the Holy Land with a Moorish fellow-prisoner in *Robin Hood: Prince of Thieves* (1991), without ever needing or encountering any language but late twentieth-century English. But while many medieval films adhere cheerfully to the homogenising convention, a significant subset engages to a greater or lesser extent with language difference in a variety of ways and to such a degree as to suggest that language is indeed one of the abiding concerns of medieval film.

The '-ethness' of medieval film

Before proceeding with a discussion of foreign language proper, we should pause a moment on the best-known acoustic manifestation of medieval difference, the set of mimetic clichés which we might call the '-ethness' of medieval film. Alongside the proliferation of visual codes which signify the medieval on screen, viewers are accustomed to hearing 'the surface markers of a linguistic alterity (*-eth, thee, ye*) [which function as] iconic metonyms for the whole historical otherness of the medieval world', as Richard Osberg and Michael Crow observe.[15] Effects of distance can also be achieved by accent, as in Vincent Ward's time-travel film *The Navigator: A Medieval Odyssey* (1988), in which the medieval characters affect a strong Cumbrian accent, though the Middle Ages are more often associated with standard English or attempted standard English, as in the sometimes strained efforts of actors such as Christian Slater in *Robin Hood: Prince of Thieves* or Heath Ledger in *A Knight's Tale*. Register, lexis and morphology are used as an inexpensive way of dressing the medieval set in films as different as *Excalibur* (1981) and *Army of Darkness: The Medieval Dead* (1992). Such linguistic difference can also signal the alienness of the medieval transplanted into the modern, as in *Les Visiteurs* (1993), or vice versa, as in *Black Knight* (2001).

Morphological markers of the medieval have long been detached from their grammatical functions. -Eth and -st have achieved long and happy afterlives as suffixes to an eclectic range of parts of speech, as epitomised in the opening vignette of Woody Allen's *Everything You Always Wanted to Know About Sex ...* (1972), entitled 'Do Aphrodisiacs Work?':

> QUEEN: Ay, well, I do confess a thirst. Bringst to me.
> JESTER: Yest, wouldst grab some of this potion before the fizz goes out. Isn't it wonderful?
> ...
> QUEEN: It bubbleth greatly.
> JESTER: Wolfst 'em down, milady.
> QUEEN: Cheerst!

This feature is not unique to anglophone film; the enormously successful French time-travel comedy *Les Visiteurs* similarly abuses stray morphemes to achieve a medievalised vocabulary. 'Il ne s'est point laissé accornardir!' exclaims King Louis VI Le Gros of his faithful vassal Godefroy, Count of Montmirail, who has saved his life in battle. 'De sa brave épée il a abroyé le crâne d'un anglois abominatif!' 'Cornard' (cuckold) and 'broyer' (to crush) are given archaising prefixes; older forms are preferred such as 'anglois' for 'anglais' and 'point' for 'pas'; back-formation gives us 'abominatif' for 'abominable'. The ludic impulse at work in these treatments of language, and their treatment in subtitles, is one to which I will return later in this chapter.

'Subtitles embed us': deconstructing the authenticity effect

Perhaps the most obvious encounter with foreignness in the medieval film is that mediated by subtitles. The subtitles of medieval film immediately engage our understanding of how subtitles function in a wider audiovisual context. Subtitles are thought of as an afterthought to the production process, as fulfilling a fundamentally supplementary or paratextual function.[16] A clear distinction is assumed between an unsubtitled source text and the subtitled target text. Such a perspective is not applicable to the subtitles I will discuss here, which are as a rule appended to part of the dialogue only and are planned from an early stage in the film's production. Rather than having a supplemental function, these subtitles constitute an integral element of filmic medievalism.

Because subtitles are experienced as mediating a pre-existing original, they act as an assurance to the viewer that *something* lies behind them, that something has been translated to the present – an important resource for medieval film, in a medium haunted by the inaccessibility of the past. Within the lively debates about the relative merits of subtitling and revoicing which preceded the scholarly development of audiovisual translation studies, subtitling stands for authenticity, for an ethical and outward-looking interest in other cultures and subjectivities. Such attitudes persist today, underpinned by the cultural capital still invested in the notion of the 'foreign film'. For Robert Kilborn subtitles are a palimpsest where 'the original text remains intact beneath the subtitled overlay'.[17] Subtitles, with their multiplication of sign systems, require a certain processing effort of the spectator, who is rewarded with access to the source text which nevertheless remains in some essential way unchanged.

As a result subtitles generate a powerful sense of *presence*. They at once support and give the lie to David Lowenthal's generalisation that 'movies … plunge us into a vivid past … seemingly without mediation'.[18] In overwriting the past on screen, subtitles make our visual experience of the diegetic world an incomplete one. Yet by partially blocking it from our view they only evoke an underlying past still more strongly.[19] We may thus conclude that subtitles plunge us into a vivid past precisely *because* they mediate, illustrating the intimate relation outlined by Jay David Bolter and Richard Grusin between immediacy, which strives for an effect of unmediated transparency, and hypermediacy, by which the medium deliberately calls attention to itself.[20]

The authenticity-effect provided by subtitles is put to good use in several films whose primary purpose is what Gil Bartholeyns terms the 'realization of the medieval universe'.[21] One such film is *The Name of the Rose*, a film whose preoccupations oscillate between historical accuracy and apparent authenticity.[22] The film selectively reproduces the Latin which would have acted as a lingua franca in the period. The use of Latin in Jean-Jacques Annaud's film, reflecting the polyglossia of the source novel, exceeds the usual ecclesiastical ornamentation or musical settings to encompass relatively lengthy quotations and even the odd incidental remark by a minor character. The film also features the crazed macaronic speech of the ex-heretic Salvatore. Most, though not all, of the Latin is subtitled; the effect of the obviously compressed subtitles is to hint at a cultural universe of which the spectator is only given a glimpse.

Subtitles may also be pressed into service in films that portray themselves as 'rewriting' the medieval past. An example may be found in the short scene in *Braveheart* (1995) in which William Wallace first meets the French princess, played by Sophie Marceau. During their interview, the Princess's adviser Hamilton attempts to communicate privately with her in Latin:

WALLACE: Oh, Longshanks did far worse the last time he took a Scottish city.
HAMILTON: Sanguinarius homo indomitus est,
[SUBTITLE: He is a bloody murdering savage]
HAMILTON: et semper dicens mendacium.
[SUBTITLE: and he's telling lies.]
WALLACE: Ego numquam pronunciare [*sic*] mendacium. Sed ego sum homo indomitus.
[SUBTITLE: I never lie. But I am a savage.]
WALLACE: Ou en français, si vous préférez?
[SUBTITLE: Or in French if you prefer?]

The bid for authenticity represented by the use of subtitled 'original' languages in this scene is masked by its comic effect and its ostensible purpose of allowing Wallace to score points off his enemies and reveal himself to the princess as an educated man, which will have repercussions for the plot. Interestingly, although there are scant signs of vernacular languages in *Braveheart*, in a piece of possibly revisionist marketing during the promotional work on his subsequent film, *The Passion of the Christ* (2004), it was suggested that Gibson had at one time discussed the idea of making *Braveheart* in the languages of the period.[23] In fact the use of subtitled language in a film which has a problematic and contested relationship to history (the director Gibson admits on the DVD audio commentary to this scene that the meeting is a piece of 'cinematic whimsy' as the princess would have been a child at the time it was supposed to have taken place) can now be seen as a rehearsal for *The Passion of the Christ* and Gibson's subsequent *Apocalypto* (2006), which share in *Braveheart*'s 'surface authenticity'.[24]

As Atom Egoyan puts it: 'subtitles offer a way into worlds outside of ourselves. They are a unique and complex formal apparatus that allows the viewer an astounding degree of access and interaction. Subtitles embed us.'[25] Subtitles in the historical film function almost as a mode of time travel, translating the past into the present. The irony is, of course, that the reverse is the case. Each of these instances of translation is in fact on multiple levels a translation of the present into the past. This reverse translation process is comically illustrated in season seven, episode five of *Buffy the Vampire Slayer* ('Selfless'). The episode provides some back-story for the more than thousand-year-old ex-demon Anya, which includes two subtitled scenes set in AD 880 in the invented Norse village of Sjornjost. This is in no way the kind of studiedly authenticising Middle Ages discussed above. This medieval setting happily flaunts the inaccuracies typical of medieval film including cheap costumes and stilted dialogue.[26] The characters speak lines translated from the original English script into a phoneti-cally learned and semi-recognisable modern-day Swedish. The English subtitles are marked by a degree of bilingual interference which we might also name 'translationese', characterised by unusual lexical and syntactic choices which appear to reflect traces of a source linguistic substratum, a phenomenon very similar to Sternberg's 'verbal trans-position'. The translatedness of the dialogue is also conveyed through spurious cultural references ('conceptual reflection', in Sternberg's terms), as in the fleeing villagers' cries of 'Run, save your babies and your beadwork!', or Olaf's protest: 'I have no interest in this Rannveig. Her hips are large and load-bearing like a Baltic woman. Your hips are narrow, like a Baltic woman from a slightly more arid region.' An anachronistic use of sepia tones in these scenes, alongside a grainy, flickering quality to the picture, supplements the stiltedness of the language and the distancing effect of the subtitles to differentiate the medieval from the present-day frame story. In a nice touch the commentary track by episode writer Drew Goddard and director David Solomon specifies that the special film stock for the Sjornjost scenes had to be imported from Europe, from the 'old world'. But any vestigial sense of the distance or presence of the past is forestalled by the contemporary turns of phrase and the fact that the scenes in the past are full of references to the characters as we know them in the present. The patent inauthenticity of the scenes refuses any attempt on the part of the viewer to read the subtitles as transmitting verbal material from the past.

To subtitle the Middle Ages on screen is to recognise not only that the process involved is one of pseudotranslation, rather than transla-tion, but that, in fact, a *reverse* process of translation is taking place.[27] At the most pragmatic level of this process, film scripts are written in English and translated (or improvised) in the foreign language, mirroring the fact that the preoccupations of medieval film – as with historical film in general – tend to be not the historical vicissitudes of the past but the narrative, representational and/or political concerns of the present.[28]

'This outrageous accent': *Monty Python* and the abusive subtitles

Perhaps one of the most recognisable instances of subtitling in a medieval film occurs in *Monty Python and the Holy Grail* (1975). For an audience in the 1970s the entertaining mock-Swedish subtitles which grace the film's credits not only commented on the general untrustworthiness of subtitles and subtitlers but also recalled the 'translated' medieval aesthetic enshrined in art cinema by European auteurs such as Eric Rohmer (*Perceval ou le Conte du Graal*, 1965), Robert Bresson (*Lancelot du Lac*, 1974) and, pre-eminently, Ingmar Bergman (*The Seventh Seal*, 1957; *The Virgin Spring*, 1960). As Donald Hoffman observes, though the subtitles are still funny to an audience today, 'they are [now] funny without resonance, or, at least, without a specific resonance', because, with the declining prestige of foreign-language art film, their audience is no longer one which associates subtitles with the Middle Ages.[29] This loss of relevance might explain the re-subtitling of the whole film for the 'Ultimate Definitive Final' special edition DVD released in 2002. This includes in the '(unbelievably) Special Features': 'NEW! Subtitles For People Who Do Not Like The Film (taken from Shakespeare's *Henry IV, Part II*)'. These subtitles are a collage of phrases from Shakespeare's play taken out of context and assigned on a roughly semantic or syntactic basis, with each subtitle containing at least one element in common with the dialogue track.

If there is 'a new kind of fidelity, namely, of the DVD to the film', as Richard Burt sustains, then the Python team are having none of it.[30] At their most pertinent and impertinent, the *Henry IV, Part II* subtitles force us to question our every assumption about the film. From its opening scene, everything the subtitles say contradicts what Arthur says. The beleaguered King Arthur, who has at times great difficulty in persuading his listeners of his credentials (here we remember Dennis of the anarcho-syndicalist commune), finds himself undermined by his translated self at every turn:

> ARTHUR: I am Arthur, son of Uther Pendragon from the castle of
>   Camelot.
> [SUBTITLE: It is Robert Shallow, sir; a poor esquire of this country.][31]

ARTHUR: King of the Britons! Defeater of the Saxons!
[SUBTITLE: Duke of Norfolk! Archbishop of York!][32]
ARTHUR: Sovereign of all England!
[SUBTITLE: Most royal imp of fame!][33]

But belying the well-known and much-loved film dialogue, of course, the DVD merely adds another layer to the film's established tendency to undercut its own allusion, to paraphrase David Day.[34]

As a piece of inspired whimsy, these subtitles are on one level just another reflection of Monty Python's long-standing interest in the comic potential of translation. They function, however, on many levels. By recycling a text with a high cultural capital, the subtitles comment on the way in which subtitles add value to the film text. They re-enact the projection of the contemporary on to the past, which is characteristic of medieval film, by overwriting a purportedly tenth-century tale with fragments of a sixteenth-century retelling of fourteenth-century events. As an ostensible translation (or rather an instance of 'bound intertextuality', to use Theo D'haen's recent term) they illustrate the ways in which the Holy Grail textual material (and indeed the *(Monty Python and the) Holy Grail* textual material) has itself been renewed, rewritten and repackaged over time in a variety of media. We may even speak of a palimpsest effect: though these subtitles leave the original film text available to the viewer, that original is, as I will show, by no means intact.[35] At a distance of over thirty years from the film's original release, these 'remixed' subtitles also echo the film's own trajectory within popular culture and the way in which expressions and exchanges from the film have been widely quoted within fan communities and beyond.[36]

At their most successful, the subtitles appear to recuperate *underlying* meanings, perhaps most explicitly in the well-known scene at Castle Arrrghhh in which John Cleese, in the role of a member of the castle's French garrison, flings insults at Arthur and his knights:

> You don't frighten us, English pig-dogs! Go and boil your bottom, sons of a silly person. I blow my nose at you, so-called Arthur King, you and all your silly English k-nnnnniggets. Thpppppt! Thppt! Thppt! ... I don't wanna talk to you no more, you empty headed animal food trough wiper! I fart in your general direction! Your mother was a hamster and your father smelt of elderberries!

The speech is constructed around classic elements of the insult: explicit instruction, opprobrious epithet, references to antecedents. A popular perception that insults vary widely between languages and cultures allows the viewer of the unsubtitled scene to understand Cleese's dialogue as a series of imitations of translations from the French, albeit in an exaggerated form. Since we are accustomed to subtitles explaining, clarifying, illuminating the dialogue on screen, the new DVD subtitles function as a kind of back-translation: here, at last, are the originals which may shed light on those outlandish Gallic slurs. The French knight is revealed to have practised a degree of self-censorship in his translation from French to English. Where he calls the King an 'empty-headed animal food-trough wiper' the subtitles reveal that he had in fact called him 'thou whoreson little tidy Bartholomew boar-pig!' (II, iv). Where he says 'I fart in your general direction' what he had in fact said is 'I kiss thy neaf' (II, iv). The viewer may not be sure what 'neaf' means but it is without doubt both four-letter and Anglo-Saxon.[37] Perhaps most shockingly, the mild remark 'Go away or I shall taunt you a second time' turns out to be a positively bowdlerised translation of 'Away! Or I will ride thee o' nights like the mare' (II, iv). This effect of translational mise en abîme is perhaps best instantiated in the line 'Away, away, varletesses' from the scene at Castle Anthrax. The subtitle reads 'Away, varlets' (II, i), acknowledging Shakespeare's play as a source for the film's dialogue, and casting the subtitle as simultaneously original and translation.

The *Henry IV, Part II* subtitles are frequently, as we have seen, abusive in the literal sense. They may also be considered abusive in the translational sense. The 'abusive translation' (a term coined by Philip Lewis) 'values experimentation, tampers with usage, seeks to match the polyvalencies or plurivocities or expressive stresses of the original by producing its own.'[38] In a provocative essay Abé Mark Nornes introduces the concept of 'abusive subtitling' as an alternative to the 'corrupt', transparent subtitles currently standard in the industry. Corrupt subtitling prioritises unobtrusiveness, and in achieving it 'smoothes over its textual violence and domesticates all otherness while it pretends to bring the audience to an experience of the foreign.'[39] Abusive subtitling resists the corruption inherent in current subtitling practices by foregrounding the process of translation.

At its most straightforward, 'abusive subtitling' can be defined as 'the translator's attempt to experiment with language in ways that are analogous to the linguistic playfulness of the original scenario and its verbalization.'[40] *Les Visiteurs* offers us some fine examples of such abusive subtitling, where the deviations from standard language present in the source text are reflected by similar deviations in the target text. In dialogue from the film quoted earlier in this chapter, King Louis VI Le Gros declares of the film's protagonist that: 'Il ne s'est point laissé accornardir! De sa brave épée il a abroyé le crâne d'un anglois abominatif!' The VHS English subtitles to this segment read: 'His baldrick was nary stuckolded' / 'With his sword,' / 'He yslaked a scurvy English head.' A similar mixture of archaic and mock-archaic lexis and affixes is used to create a medievalising register corresponding to that of the original.

This would seem like a fairly unremarkable translational solution to the verbal play in the source text, were it not for the ingrained conservatism of subtitlers and subtitles. Partly owing to their association with literacy and partly owing to the disruptive effect on the viewer of apparent errors in subtitles, subtitles are expected to conform to a very standard form of the target language. This can result in a lack of flexibility vividly illustrated in an anecdote related by the film-maker Claire Denis. One scene from her film *Friday Night* (2002) features dialogue which is barely audible to the film's spectators. When subtitling the film, Denis asked the subtitler whether the subtitles could render the dialogue only partially, by omitting letters or words, in order to reflect this auditory quality, and was told that this was impossible. Instead, the characters' dialogue is fully rendered in the subtitles and the tension between inside and outside present in the unsubtitled sequence has been diminished.[41] It is understood that later releases of *Les Visiteurs* contained subtitles that were considerably less inventive and disappointed some viewers.[42]

Abusive subtitling seeks to make itself highly visible in a way which is antithetical to the doctrine of transparency which underpins subtitling practice. The Monty Python Shakespeare subtitles are inherently abusive in that they foreground the processes at work in textual transmission and rereading, and the instability of the categories of translation and original.

In different ways the subtitles to *Les Visiteurs* and the Shakespearean subtitles to *Monty Python and the Holy Grail* relate in innovative and temporally specific ways to their source texts. One final example may serve to reinforce the linguistic synergy suggested here between film comedy and the medieval. In the 1997 Disney comedy *George of the Jungle*, subtitling plays with 'medieval' typography. Towards the end of the film George, a comic-heroic Tarzan figure who speaks in the classic tongue-tied manner in English, is moved to thank his brothers,

My noble kinsmen, thou hast served me well.

6 George addresses the other apes in *George of the Jungle* (1997)

the apes, for their help in defeating the film's villain Lyle Vandergroot. He addresses the apes in a series of hoots and squeaks which are translated in subtitles (Figures 6 and 7). These subtitles stand out for several reasons: their illogicality, given that throughout the film George has spoken to the apes in English; their lexical and morphological archaisms; the inaccurate use of the latter according to the conventions of '-ethness' discussed earlier in this chapter; and most of all, their typographical form. Elaborate capitals are combined with vestiges of uncial script, particularly in regard to the letters *a*, *e* and *t*. The strikingly elaborate font contrasts with the sans serif fonts used elsewhere in the film's occasional subtitles.

George's subtitles extract humour from the implausibility of the notion of translating between ape and human. Their excessive elaborateness belies the absence of any meaningful source text, but at the same time they explicitly evoke the multiple intertextualities at work in the text. One element of this is the medievalising English widely used in colonial narratives to represent the speech of colonial subjects. In *Allan Quatermaine* Rider Haggard represents the fictitious African

Now thy work 'tis done, but behold, how Shep doth dispatch these villains.

7 The poachers come to a sticky end in *George of the Jungle* (1997)

language Zu-Vendi using 'fake medieval' English like 'Dost thou mean that thou wilt.'[43] This English can also be found in Rudyard Kipling's Indian stories. The notion of animal language has its origins in Edgar Rice Burroughs's Tarzan novels, which make much of Tarzan's ability to communicate with animals, and go so far as to supply some words of animal languages.[44] The *matière de Tarzan* also boasts a more traditionally medievalist ur-text in the form of Burroughs's early novel *The Outlaw of Torn*, an action adventure set in thirteenth-century England. As one critic has put it, 'Tarzan is Norman of Torn without the armour.'[45] All of these intertexts inform this moment of translation, which works well because of the established importance of language to the Tarzan narrative, and what is at first sight an arbitrary choice of ornamentation for the subtitles in fact reinscribes George within the translational transactions intrinsic to post-colonialism.[46]

From these three very different examples we may tentatively conclude that the filmic Middle Ages seem to prompt forms of linguistic play, extending the range of possible relationships between image and subtitle. In these looking-glass instances of translation, which exploit and experiment with the visual and morphological characteristics of language in the best tradition of abusive subtitling, lie some of the most innovative and ludic uses of subtitling in popular cinema.[47]

Medieval film and the politics of language

Problems of communication, whether acknowledged or ignored, underpin the narratives of the three films discussed in this final section. *The 13th Warrior* tells the story of an Arab ambassador who joins a band of Northmen to battle a mythical foe in Scandinavia; *Kingdom of Heaven* is a crusade narrative culminating in the capture of Jerusalem by Saladin in 1187; and *King Arthur* combines a saga of national origin with a retelling of Arthurian legend. For all these films language is an immediate and pressing issue which will be solved in very different ways, ways which reflect the current cultural capital of translation in popular film. At the same time the tension between representational pragmatism, political expediency and perceived authenticity will be shown to be a productive one, which can still create a space for compelling moments of cinematic multilingualism.

In previous sections I argued that subtitled foreign language use is characteristic of films whose primary preoccupation is authenticity (or the lack of it). Subtitles are, of course, by no means the only way of negotiating language difference. In facilitating the viewer's under-standing of foreign language dialogue, subtitles paradoxically elide translation; they deny the non-communication, the incomprehension which is the source of the translation imperative. In the opening skir-mish of Antoine Fuqua's *King Arthur* there is an early exchange between Arthur and a Pictish warrior who finds himself at Arthur's mercy, only to be released. Arthur speaks English, while the Pict speaks a subti-tled language purporting to be Pictish.[48] The two characters seem to understand each other perfectly, and the presence of the subtitles for the Pictish dialogue allows the viewer to ignore the linguistic-colonial realities which underpin the film's entire narrative, from the recruit-ment of cavalrymen from the subjugated Sarmatians to the defeat of the Saxons by the united force of Roman cavalry, Pictish warriors and presumably British peasants.

At the same time subtitles are inevitably ethnographising; they mark the subtitled speakers out as Other, as different. In the early part of *King Arthur* the Picts are the primary threat, represented as strongly Other: half-naked, speaking an indecipherable language and lurking in the forest setting traps for the Romans. In contrast, apart from some ecclesiastical Latin and a Germanic phrase or two, the languages of the Sarmatians, the Romans, the Britons and the Saxons are all represented by English throughout. With the news of the Saxon invasion, the political balance shifts. After the rescue of the Pictish princess Guinevere, daughter of Merlin, an alliance is created between the Romans and the Picts. From the moment of Guinevere's appearance the subtitles disappear, as both Merlin and Guinevere speak English, and no other Pictish characters are given lines. The resulting effect is one of accelerated linguistic homogenisation – a necessary preliminary, as Benedict Anderson has argued, to the formation of a nation, which is in fact the film's ultimate plot device.[49] In the film's final scene Merlin marries Arthur and Guinevere, establishing the unity of the island in opposition to external forces and declaring that 'from this day all Britons will be united in one common cause'.

On the surface linguistic diversity is selectively acknowledged in *King Arthur*, both through the use of subtitled Pictish and through accent effects which depend largely on the nationalities of the film's cast. Bishop Germanius, played by Ivano Marescotti, and the Roman settlers are played by Italians; the Saxons' Saxonness is conveyed by casting a Swede and a German (Stellan Skarsgård and Til Schweiger) as their leader Cerdic and his son Cynric. In fact, subtitles become effectively just another visual trope for otherness, and questions of translation and communication are de-emphasised to the point of absence.[50] To use Sukanta Chaudhuri's terms, *King Arthur* is a unilingual, though not a monolingual, film.[51]

Ridley Scott's *Kingdom of Heaven* very obviously belongs to a time when cinematic as well as political preoccupations are centred on a perceived incompatibility of world view between east and west. *Kingdom of Heaven* is a period film of the type described by Gil Bartholeyns in which

> history takes on board a cause that transcends that of the story being told and that of the diegesis. The author thus involves himself in a process of connecting past and present. His contemporaneousness is bound up with his consciousness of a historical (or mythical) past, which is thus thoroughly characterized by a sense of responsibility. This kind of film projects more than history itself and goes beyond 'mere' historical reconstruction by establishing a connection of intention between past and present.[52]

The early action of the film takes place in France, where Balian the smith meets his father, the crusader Geoffrey of Ibelin. Geoffrey leads a motley group of Crusaders from various language communities. Balian travels through France and Italy with Geoffrey, but language difference does not become an issue until the moment of Balian's arrival in the Near East, the sole survivor of a shipwreck. The first challenge of this foreign land is translation. An encounter with a pugnacious Syrian lord intent on seizing Balian's horse is mediated through Nasir (played by Alexander Siddig), who, though a man of importance in Saladin's circle, assumes the neutrality expected of an interpreter. Balian emerges victorious from the encounter and spares Nasir's life, an act which will earn him Nasir's gratitude and support. The scene underscores the gulf in understanding between the Near East and a linguistically undifferentiated Europe (in Nasir's initial address to the shipwrecked Westerner there is no indication as to which language might be being mimetically represented by English). This also reflects the increased awareness of the problem of translation which has arisen as a result of the events of 11 September 2001. In a narrative spanning many different speech communities, room is found for only one binary opposition; inevitably, in the light of the film's strongly implied use of the Crusades to comment on the current conflict in the Middle East and the invasion of Iraq, this opposition is between east and west.

It is perhaps worth clarifying that the reduction of the polyglot environments of thirteenth-century Europe and the Roman Empire to binary terms is of interest *not* inasmuch as it denies or obscures any assumed specificity of linguistic negotiations in those locations in those periods but inasmuch as it conforms to cinematic conventions and twenty-first-century schemata. John Ganim's observation that 'beneath its apparent stability as an idea, the Middle Ages repeatedly has been represented as both domestic and foreign, as both historical origin and historical rupture, as both native and "native"', not only makes a valuable point about shifting perceptions of the Middle Ages but also illustrates the rhetorical potency of the binary opposition between self and other which is illustrated by the linguistic polarities in these two films.[53]

It should not be thought, however, that mainstream film is unable or unwilling to engage with language difference: the spate of relatively recent films on the subject – from *Dances With Wolves* (1990) to *Amistad* (1997), *Lost in Translation* (2003), *The Last Samurai* (2003), *The Interpreter* (2005) and *Babel* (2006) – would immediately disprove such an idea. The final film to be discussed in this chapter can be classed among these films, in which the inclusion of multiple languages both stems from and promotes the consideration of precisely those problems of communication and misunderstanding that remind viewers they live in a world of competing languages and worldviews.

John McTiernan's *The 13th Warrior* is based on the popular novel *Eaters of the Dead* (1976) by Michael Crichton. It narrates the adventures of an Arab, Ibn Fadlan, who fights alongside a group of Vikings to defeat a supernatural enemy. The narrative presents itself in familiar terms as the tale of an effete aristocrat reluctantly recruited to a company of warriors. Alongside the conventions of the action movie, including the classic 'buddy' trope observable in the relationship between Ibn Fadlan and Herger the Joyous, and those of the Hollywood spectacular (exotic settings, a cast of hundreds and elaborately staged battle scenes which reflect the film's nine-figure budget), *The 13th Warrior* offers a nuanced portrayal of cultural contact which is most evident in the treatment of language in the film.

Eaters of the Dead draws on two medieval narratives, the story of *Beowulf* and a tenth-century travel narrative, the *Kitāb* by Ibn Fadlan, an Arabic ambassador to the tribes of northern Europe.[54] The portion of Ibn Fadlan's manuscript partially reproduced in the novel gives an account of the customs of a group called the Rūs. The origins of the Rūs are uncertain. They may have been of Viking origin, assimilated into the Slavic tribes of the Volga.[55] In Crichton's novel they become Vikings.

An unusually horizontal power relationship obtains between the two cultures in this film, which locates the Other not in the east but in the north, as Hugh Magennis has remarked in a perceptive review, and which ultimately shows both the Arab protagonist, played by Antonio Banderas, and his Viking companions in a positive light.[56] It is not the Middle Eastern but the Northern characters who embody the 'mythic, ritual, irrational, and pagan' Orientalist clichés as Ganim summarises them.[57]

In Crichton's source novel Ibn Fadlan's inability to speak the language of the Northmen is compensated for in their early encounters by interpreters travelling in his entourage and subsequently by the Northman Herger, 'by the grace of Allah ... a man of parts and knowing some of the Latin tongue.'[58] At no point in the novel do we 'hear' the tongue of the Northmen, which is condemned early on by the narrator as being 'ugly to the ear and difficult to comprehend.'[59] The novelist is able to take advantage of what Sternberg calls 'explicit attribution' – simply, the ability of a reader to read as if reading Latin, if told that such-and-such a character is speaking Latin.[60] Herger's and Ibn Fadlan's shared knowledge of Latin allows Herger to function as mediator between the Rūs and Ibn Fadlan.

The film steers a path between vehicular matching and homogenising, using the device of accelerated language learning. In their first encounter with the Northmen, at a raucous feast, Ibn Fadlan and his companion Melchisidek struggle to make themselves understood:

MELCHIS.:	[*to a passing Viking*] We seek your ...
	[*to Rethel*] We seek your headman, your, king ...
IBN FADLAN:	Try Greek.
MELCHIS.:	[*to Edgtho*] Hegemona humeteron. Basilea humeteron. Eh? [*Edgtho attracts Herger's attention by kicking him*]
	[*to Herger*] Hegemona humeteron. Basilea humeteron. [*Trying Latin*] ...uestrum regem.
HERGER:	Noster rex? Tabernaculum.
MELCHIS.	[*to Ibn Fadlan*]: He says their king is out there in that tent.
HERGER:	Non loquetur.
MELCHIS.:	He says the king will not speak to us.
HERGER:	Non loquetur, quia mortuus est!
MELCHIS.:	Apparently the king won't speak to us because he's dead.[61]

This exchange comes very close to Sternberg's vehicular matching, with the emphasis on the juxtaposition of multiple languages rather than philological specificity. The linguistic preparation for the film, as described by Juta Kitching, the film's language consultant, in an online interview, included provision not only for Latin and Greek but also for a few Arabic phrases for the ambassadors' entourage and some words in Klahoose, a First Nations language from British Columbia (where the film was shot), which was intended for the Wendol characters. The actors playing the Northmen initially speak modern Norwegian, except for the Danish actors who speak their own language variety.[62] The Norwegian is anachronistic, as modern Norwegian was not spoken until at least the sixteenth century, but any requirement for linguistic specificity here is mitigated by the fact that the Northmen have dual nationality, being both the Rūs of Ibn Fadlan and the warriors of *Beowulf*.[63]

Subsequent exchanges during the ambassador's stay among the Northmen are achieved through relay interpreting, including the following virtuoso moment of simultaneous cultural and linguistic translation, in which Herger translates the words of the King's funeral ceremony, dimly audible at a distance, into Latin, which Melchisidek in turn translates for Ibn Fadlan's benefit (at this point, English still represents Arabic):

CELEBRANT: [*faintly, at a distance*] Å, der ser jeg min far.
HERGER: Ecce patrem video.
MELCHIS.:   Lo, there do I see my father.
[*Herger continues to speak but Melchisidek's interpreting shifts from consecutive to simultaneous here and most of the Latin is inaudible.*]
HERGER: Ecce matrem et sorores et fratres video.
MELCHIS.:   Lo, there do I see my mother, my sisters and my brothers.
CELEBRANT: Å, der ser jeg mine forfedre ... tilbake til begynnelsen.
HERGER: [Ecce ibi genus mei populi video ... retro] ad initium.
MELCHIS.:   Lo, there do I see the line of my people back to the beginning.
CELEBRANT: Å, de kaller på meg.
HERGER: Ecce me vocant.
MELCHIS.:   Lo, they do call to me.
CELEBRANT: De ber meg om å ta min plass iblant dem sittende der i Valhalla.
HERGER: Sedens ibi in sede beatorum, in Valhalla.
MELCHIS.:   They bid me take my place among them in the halls of Valhalla where the brave may live forever.

The film takes the requirement of relay translation and shows how rhetorically successful it can be. The second time we will hear this invocation, again in English, it will be because Ibn Fadlan is saying it in the language of the Northmen – a testament to how open viewers are to mimetic strategies, but also a pleasing metaphor for the rapport which develops between the Arab and his Viking hosts: by half-way through the film they are, literally, speaking the same language.

Ultimately, of course, all this conscientious reproduction is still at the service of mimetic strategies: the pragmatic purpose of this long process of language learning is to facilitate a return to English, no longer representing Arabic but instead standing in for the language of the Northmen. To follow the novel Herger would have needed to continue to interpret for Ibn Fadlan for the rest of the film: a cumbersome task which would certainly prove unacceptable to most viewers (by the end of the novel even Herger has begun to tire of translation).

Instead Ibn Fadlan learns the language of his hosts. As the group journeys north Ibn Fadlan listens to the conversations around the fire in
the evening, which initially take place in a language which is strange
to him and to the non-Norwegian-speaking viewer. Close-ups of faces
and lip movements and repeated shots convey the attentiveness with
which Ibn Fadlan studies his companions' language. With the passage
of time, signified by changes in the weather and dissolves between
scenes, comprehensible (in other words, English) words begin to leap
out of the conversation, until finally Ibn Fadlan is spurred to intervene
in the conversation in response to an unflattering remark about his
mother. After Ibn Fadlan finally reveals his linguistic knowledge to his
companions, English, standing in for Norse, becomes the language of
the rest of the film.

It is not surprising that this scene was singled out by critics for
its verisimilitude, though clearly considerable poetic licence has
been used in this portrayal of accelerated, total-immersion language
learning.[64] Linguistic competence by no means guarantees Ibn Fadlan's
understanding of his hosts' culture, but at least they now share a
common language in which he can ask questions. The sequence offers
a thoughtful portrayal of the problems of intercultural communication
and a demonstration that language is a necessary, though not sufficient,
condition for learning about a foreign culture – and by extension, about
the Middle Ages themselves: our introduction to the world of Buliwyf
takes place largely through Herger's explanations to Ibn Fadlan. By
the end of the film, Ibn Fadlan will be equipped to write down the tale
of Buliwyf's deeds, in a satisfying piece of sleight-of-hand collapsing
the two medieval narratives, *Beowulf* and the *Kitāb*, and casting Ibn
Fadlan as the notional author of *Beowulf*.

Although the elaborate sequence of linguistic negotiations which
make up the first quarter of an hour of the film exists only because the
explicit attribution of language possible in prose fiction is impossible
to duplicate on film, the cumulative result is the construction of one
of the most thoughtful representations of a multilingual environment
existing in popular film. It may fairly be said that, paradoxically, in this
example at least, a strategy which ultimately marginalises language
difference incidentally reinforces its importance for the viewer,
suggesting that there is still space for compelling moments of cinematic multilingualism, even at the heart of hegemonic film practices.

Notes

1 This understanding of film goes back to the era of silent film, to D. W. Griffith's famous affirmation of film as the universal language. For a useful account of the semiotic understanding of film as language see James Monaco, *How to Read a Film: The Art, Technology, Language, History and Theory of Film and Media* (Oxford: Oxford University Press, 2000 [1981]), pp. 152–227.

2 Medieval film has been defined in a number of ways, and potentially covers an enormous range of films engaging with medieval history, texts, characters and/ or themes; see, e.g., Martha W. Driver and Sid Ray, 'Preface: Hollywood knights' in Driver and Ray (eds), *The Medieval Hero on Screen: Representations from Beowulf to Buffy* (Jefferson, NC: McFarland, 2004), pp. 5–18 (p. 5); and William D. Paden, 'I learned it at the movies: teaching medieval film', in Richard Utz, Jesse G. Swan and Paul Plisiewicz (eds), *Postmodern Medievalisms* (Cambridge: Brewer, 2004), pp. 79–98 (p. 79); and the introduction to this volume. My use of the term 'medieval film' here is a convenient shorthand, and does not assume the coherence or conceptual usefulness of the category. It should also be specified that I treat this category as including both film and television treatments of the Middle Ages.

3 Roger Ebert, review of *Kingdom of Heaven*, rogerebert.suntimes.com/apps/ pbcs.dll/article?AID=/20050505/REVIEWS/50426001/1023, accessed 16 October 2007.

4 Meir Sternberg, 'Polylingualism as reality and translation as mimesis', *Poetics Today*, 2:4 (1981), 221–39 (222). Sternberg is referring largely to print literature, but the presence of cinematic examples invites the extension of his model to film.

5 *Ibid.*, 222.

6 *Ibid.*, 223.

7 *Ibid.*, 223.

8 *Ibid.*, 224.

9 Ella Shohat and Robert Stam, *Unthinking Eurocentrism: Multiculturalism and the Media* (London: Routledge, 1994), pp. 191–2.

10 Sternberg, 'Polylingualism', 223.

11 *Ibid.*, 225.

12 *Ibid.*, 227.

13 *Ibid.*, 230.

14 Marianne Kalinke, 'The foreign language requirement in medieval Icelandic romance', *Modern Language Review*, 78 (1983), 850–61 (850).

15 Richard H. Osberg and Michael E. Crow, 'Language then and language now in Arthurian film', in Kevin J. Harty (ed.), *King Arthur in Film: New Essays in Arthurian Cinema* (Jefferson, NC: McFarland, 1999), pp. 39–66 (p. 59).

16 See e.g. Zoé de Linde and Neil Kay, *The Semiotics of Subtitling* (Manchester: St Jerome, 1999), p. 17; Ian Balfour, 'Afterword: filming translation (the most exemplary film)', in Atom Egoyan and Ian Balfour (eds), *Subtitles: On the Foreignness of Film* (Cambridge, MA: Alphabet City, 2004), pp. 531–2 (p. 531).

17 Robert Kilborn, ' "They don't speak proper English": a new look at the dubbing

and subtitling debate', *Journal of Multilingual and Multicultural Development*, 10:5 (1989), 421–34 (426). See also Robert Kilborn, 'Speak my language: current attitudes in television subtitling and dubbing', *Media, Culture and Society*, 15 (1993), 641–60 (646).

18 David Lowenthal, *The Past Is a Foreign Country* (Cambridge: Cambridge University Press, 1985), p. 367.

19 On the authenticising effect of language difference in itself see David Salo, 'Heroism and alienation through language in *The Lord of the Rings*', in Driver and Ray (eds), *The Medieval Hero*, pp. 23–37 (p. 27).

20 Jay David Bolter and Richard A. Grusin, *Remediation: Understanding New Media* (Cambridge, MA: MIT Press, 2000).

21 Gil Bartholeyns, 'Representation of the past in films: between historicity and authenticity', *Diogenes*, 48:1 (2000), 31–47 (34).

22 Gideon Bachmann, '*The Name of the Rose*', *Sight and Sound*, 55:2 (1986), 129–31 (130). This interview offers a striking contrast between the account of Annaud's insistence on extreme 'fidelity', as in casting actors whose nationality corresponded to that of their characters, and Umberto Eco's remark that 'authenticity may be more readily achieved by faking' (130). See also Sarah Salih's close reading of the film's visuals in Chapter 1 above.

23 Todd McCarthy, 'What language did they speak in Sodom?'; posted 4 March 2004 at www.variety.com/article/VR1117901223?categoryid=5&cs=1, accessed 16 October 2007.

24 Quoted in Vivian Sobchack, 'The insistent fringe: moving images and historical consciousness', *History and Theory*, 36:4 (1997), 4–20 (7).

25 Atom Egoyan and Ian Balfour, 'Introduction', in Egoyan and Balfour (eds), *Subtitles*, pp. 21–30 (p. 30).

26 See, e.g., David Day, '*Monty Python and the Holy Grail*: madness with a definite method', in Kevin J. Harty (ed.), *Cinema Arthuriana: Twenty Essays* (Jefferson, NC: McFarland, 2002 [1991]), pp. 127–35 (p. 130).

27 For discussions of the notion of pseudotranslation, where an 'original' text is deliberately presented as a translation, see, e.g., Susan Bassnett, 'When is translation not a translation?' in Bassnett and André Lefevere (eds), *Constructing Cultures: Essays on Literary Translation* (Clevedon, PA: Multilingual Matters, 1998), pp. 25–40 (pp. 27–8). To identify the processes around medieval subtitling as pseudotranslation is not, of course, to deny that medieval film itself often constitutes the result of a complex series of translations, adaptations and retellings of source material.

28 See also, for instance, Arthur Lindley, 'Scotland saved from history: Welles's *Macbeth* and the ahistoricism of medieval film', *Literature/Film Quarterly*, 29:2 (2001), 96–100; Danièle Gasiglia-Laster, '*Les Visiteurs du soir*: une date peut en cacher une autre', *Cahiers de l'Association Internationale des Etudes Françaises*, 47 (1995), 79–98; Bartholeyns, 'Representation'.

29 Donald Hoffman, 'Not dead yet: *Monty Python and the Holy Grail* in the twenty-first century', in Harty (ed.), *Cinema Arthuriana*, pp. 136–48 (p. 137).

30 Richard Burt, 'Getting schmedieval: of manuscript and film prologues, paratexts, and parodies', *Exemplaria*, 19:2 (Summer 2007), 217–42 (228).

31 *Henry IV, Part II*. Act III, sc. ii.
32 *Henry IV, Part II*. Act IV, sc. i. The Archbishop is a character in the play.
33 *Henry IV, Part II*. Act V, sc. v.
34 Day, '*Monty Python and the Holy Grail*', p. 131.
35 See Richard Burt's discussion of the ways in which the paratexts of the original film engage extensively with medieval textual practices; 'Getting schmedieval', 13–14.
36 Greg M. Smith, ' "To waste more time, please click here again": Monty Python and the quest for film/CD-ROM adaptation', in Smith (ed.), *On a Silver Platter* (New York: New York University Press, 1999), pp. 58–86 (pp. 65–6).
37 S/he might be disappointed to discover that it means 'hand'.
38 Philip E. Lewis, 'The measure of translation effects', in Joseph F. Graham (ed.), *Difference in Translation* (Ithaca, NY: Cornell University Press, 1985), pp. 31–62 (p. 41).
39 Abé Mark Nornes, 'For an abusive subtitling', *Film Quarterly*, 52:3 (Spring 1999), 17–34 (18).
40 *Ibid.*, 30.
41 'Outside myself: Claire Denis interviewed by Atom Egoyan', in Egoyan and Balfour (eds), *Subtitles*, pp. 69–76 (pp. 74–5).
42 See, for instance, the customer review by 'Therobbie1 "Sci-Fi Fanatic" ', 'Why the difference in translations between VHS and DVD versions?', 21 April 2006, available at www.amazon.com/gp/product/customerreviews/B00005NB9Z/ ref=cm_cr_dp_synop/103-17159137314218?ie=UTF8&m=ATVPDKIKX0DE R&n=130&s=dvd&customer-reviews.start=1#R89VGTE6ME4QM.
43 Quoted in Bassnett, 'When is translation', p. 37.
44 Walt Morton, 'Tracking the sign of Tarzan: trans-media representation of a pop-culture icon', in Pat Kirkham and Janet Thumim (eds), *You Tarzan: Masculinity, Movies and Men* (New York: St Martin's, 1993), pp. 106–25 (pp. 107–9).
45 Stan Galloway, 'The Greystoke connection: medievalism in two Edgar Rice Burroughs novels', in Kathleen Verduin (ed.), *Medievalism in North America* (Cambridge: Brewer, 1994), pp. 100–8 (p. 103).
46 On the relationships between translation and post-colonialism see, e.g., Susan Bassnett and Harish Trivedi (eds), *Postcolonial Translation: Theory and Practice* (London: Routledge, 1999); Eric Cheyfitz, *The Poetics of Imperialism: Translation and Colonization from* The Tempest *to* Tarzan (London: Oxford University Press, 1991).
47 See Nornes, 'For an abusive subtitling', 18.
48 Some lines of reconstructed Pictish were provided for the film by Caitlin Matthews, see John Matthews, 'A knightly endeavour: the making of Jerry Bruckheimer's *King Arthur*', *Arthuriana*, 14.3 (2004), 112–15 (114).
49 See Benedict Anderson, *Imagined Communities: Reflections on the Origin and Spread of Nationalism* (London: Verso, 1991 [1983]), esp. pp. 37–46 and 67–82.
50 One effect of the lack of linguistic difference in the film is to undermine badly the subplot of the return home, which relies on a sense of the distance between Britain and Sarmatia. The ageographicality (the film was shot entirely in Ireland)

and discursive levelling which characterises the representation of the two spaces and speech communities militates against the spectator's empathising with the knights' nostalgia.

51 See Sukanta Chaudhuri, *Translation and Understanding* (New Delhi: Oxford University Press, 1999), pp. 72–3. Chaudhuri defines monolingualism as 'the literal state of knowing or using only one language', and unilingualism as 'a mindset or ethos that operates in terms of only one language'. She argues that 'unilingualism is entirely compatible with knowledge, even deep knowledge, of several languages; indeed, it is often seen at its most entrenched and intolerant in multilingual situations'.

52 Bartholeyns, 'Representation', p. 32.

53 John M. Ganim, 'Native studies: orientalism and medievalism', in Jeffrey Jerome Cohen (ed.), *The Postcolonial Middle Ages* (Basingstoke: Palgrave, 2001), pp. 122–34 (p. 131).

54 In fact, only the first three chapters of the novel reproduce the *Kitāb*, but the novel deliberately blurs the dividing line between the source texts, casting the whole narrative as an edition of a single manuscript, and buttressing this with paratextual apparatus including a detailed introduction and copious footnotes.

55 James Montgomery, 'Ibn Fadlān and the Rūsiyyah', *Journal of Arabic and Islamic Studies*, 3 (2000), 1–25 (23).

56 Hugh Magennis, 'Michael Crichton, Ibn Fadlan, fantasy cinema: *Beowulf* at the movies', *Old English Newsletter*, 35:1 (2001), 34–8. The even-handedness of the portrayal of both cultures in the film may be partly related to Ibn Fadlan's *Kitāb*, a 'consciously restrained narrative' containing 'passably "ethnographic" observation', as Montgomery argues ('Ibn Fadlān', 25). It could, of course, be argued that the film merely displaces otherness on to the Wendol, whom the novel describes as Neanderthal and who are portrayed in the film as being without intelligible language. 'These are not men', one character says of them.

57 The phrase used by Ganim in relation to John Selden's 'De Diis Syriis'; see Ganim, *Medievalism and Orientalism: Three Essays on Literature, Architecture and Cultural Identity* (New York: Palgrave Macmillan 2005), p. 71.

58 Michael Crichton, *Eaters of the Dead* (London: Arrow, 1997), p. 49.

59 *Ibid.*, p. 36.

60 Sternberg, 'Polylingualism', 231. The language consultant on the film, Juta Kitching, also had to work with an explicitly attributive script, as she explains: 'The script was often noncommittal in that it could for example give such vague directives as "*mutters under his breath in Norwegian*", or "*pronounces a magic spell in Norse*" or "*enquires about such-and-such in Latin*". In other words, there was no text supplied to be translated, so I had to make it up, to create the discourse and then translate' (at http://eaters.ifrance.com/interviews/kitching.htm, accessed 16 October 2007). Though not unknown, this device is extremely uncommon on screen, though the English subtitles for the DVD of *The 13th Warrior* make a spirited effort to achieve it, telling us confidently that the Latin through which Herger and Melchisidek communicate in the early scenes at the funeral is Greek.

61 I am indebted to Juta Kitching of the University of British Columbia, who very kindly supplied extracts from her translations for the film and provided enormously helpful and comprehensive answers to my many questions. I am also indebted to Dr Claire Thomson for clarification on Nordic-related issues. It goes without saying that any errors are my own.

62 As Kitching explains in the interview on http://eaters.ifrance.com, Norwegian was chosen over Swedish, which would have been appropriate to represent an eastern Scandinavian language variety, because Swedish intonation patterns are perceived in the US as odd.

63 Lars S. Vikør, *The Nordic Languages: Their Status and Interrelations* (Oslo: Novus, 1993), p. 51.

64 John Aberth, *A Knight at the Movies: Medieval History on Film* (London: Routledge, 2003), p. 60; Martha W. Driver, ' "Stond and delyver": teaching the medieval movie', in Driver and Ray (eds), *The Medieval Hero*, pp. 211–16 (p. 211).

4

'Poison to the infant, but tonic to the man': timing *The Birth of a Nation*

Anke Bernau

As well as causing political controversy from the moment of its release, D. W. Griffith's *The Birth of a Nation* (1915) was hailed as a milestone in cinema history. Endorsed on a political level by President Woodrow Wilson – whose scholarship on the American Civil War was explicitly referenced in the film's intertitles – it was also praised by film critics and viewers alike for its innovative style and use of technology.[1] *The Birth of a Nation* was three hours long; its production had involved six weeks of rehearsals, nine weeks of filming, three months of editing and had cost a 'record-breaking' $100,000.[2] All of this has prompted critics to see it as 'one of the most popular turning-point films of all time', as well as a 'national allegory'.[3] This 'national allegory' also claimed to be setting the historical record straight, to be teaching Americans their own history. It did this by drawing on a conjunction of contemporary ideas concerning nation, history and race, all of which, I argue, participated in popular and academic constructions of the medieval.[4]

Griffith's film, based on two novels by the popular preacher and author Thomas Dixon, is divided into two parts and tells the story of two white families, the Stonemans from the North and the Camerons from the South, against the backdrop of the American Civil War and Reconstruction era in the South. The families are united by their children's friendship, as well as by the romance that develops first between the eldest Stoneman son, Phil, and Margaret Cameron and, later, between the eldest Cameron son, Ben, and Elsie Stoneman. While Austin Stoneman, the club-footed father of Elsie and Phil, is a powerful figure in Northern political circles, represented as a misguided and fanatical proponent of racial equality, the Camerons are plantation owners, whose whole way of life is idealised as ensuring an organic social harmony. After the assassination of Abraham Lincoln, the Stonemans travel to Piedmont, South Carolina, in order to oversee Reconstruction policy. This brings them into conflict with the Camerons and other white families, who are shown to be oppressed by carpetbaggers, freedmen and ex-slaves as well as black militia. In the film's narrative climax, the youngest Cameron daughter, Flora, dies as she tries to escape the sexual advances made by Gus, an ex-slave. In desperation, she throws herself off a cliff and, holding the Confederate flag, dies in her brother Ben's arms. Ben Cameron, who has founded a local branch of the Ku Klux Klan in order to restore white supremacy, avenges Flora's death with his Klan comrades by abducting and executing Gus. A black militia is ordered to arrest the Klan members, and a battle ensues for control of Piedmont, which the Klan wins in a series of spectacular, action-packed scenes. The film ends with the double honeymoon of Elsie and Ben and Margaret and Phil, with both couples symbolising the reunification of North and South.

The film's popularity was enabled to a great extent by the cinematic medium itself. Its ability to reach a vast audience was recognised early on, both by those who saw in film a potent medium for propaganda and by those who feared this potential. As one critical reviewer of *The Birth of a Nation* wrote in 1915: 'What makes matters worse is that it is not a question of dealing with a single theatrical production, for the film can be duplicated so that the objectionable performance may be going on in forty or more cities at the same moment.'[5] If, as Benedict Anderson has argued so influentially, a nation is an imagined community, the imagining of which he links to such media as print, then film represented a newly powerful medium through which a national collectivity could be reached to a previously undreamt-of extent.

Alongside such self-consciously progressive constructions of nationhood, however, North America also followed the trajectory of European nationalisms which, from the late eighteenth to the early twentieth century, looked to the medieval past to provide them with originary moments. Scholars in emerging academic disciplines such as history, philology and anthropology claimed to be applying properly modern 'objective' and 'scientific' methods to their objects of study, which then enabled them to propose ideal forms of national government for the present and the future.[6]

While the US could not claim a medieval origin in the ways that European nations did, it still looked to the Middle Ages to provide a foundation for what was presented by many until the First World War as the most 'original' American identity: that of the Anglo-Saxon.

Thomas Jefferson's (unrealised) plan to depict the legendary warriors Hengist and Horsa on the Great Seal of the United States of America exemplifies his belief that Saxon laws were the 'foundation of American democracy'.[7] Unsurprisingly, therefore, Jefferson was also an ardent proponent of teaching early medieval history, law and Anglo-Saxon at the newly emerging universities of North America.[8] Underlying such views of the early medieval – specifically Anglo-Saxon – origin of American institutions was the 'germ theory', proposed in the 1880s by the historian Herbert Baxter Adams, under whom both Woodrow Wilson and Thomas Dixon studied at Johns Hopkins University. As a 'by-product of Darwinism', germ theory, as summarised by Henry Bragdon, posited that

> American political institutions were the result of a slow organic growth that began with the village organization of the Angles and Saxons carried across from Germany in the fifth century. Over the centuries these 'primordial cells of the body politic' developed into higher institutions. To understand the present, therefore, one must dig into the origins of government, especially local government, in England and America.[9]

For supporters of this theory America was not only the inheritor of the Anglo-Saxon past but the truest fulfilment of its historical destiny. This theory, as Laura Kendrick has pointed out, 'constructed a Middle Ages in which "Anglo-Saxons" replayed the period from 300 to 1500 and, in so doing, "rectified" the errors of European history', a view that was promulgated by, for instance, Woodrow Wilson.[10] Such attempts represent what Stephen Nichols has called 'past-oriented modernism'.[11] For its proponents History and Modernity were viewed not as opposed or conflicting forces; rather, the former was necessary to the success of the latter.

This focus on the past, however, existed within a context that increasingly privileged the present moment. The development of new technologies (such as the telephone, wireless and telegraph) in the late nineteenth and early twentieth centuries meant that the ways in which temporality was experienced and thought about changed, leading for many, according to Stephen Kern, to a sense that 'space and time' had been 'annihilated'.[12] Kern argues that the cinema represented another form of technology that 'expanded the sense of the present', specifically citing Griffith's innovative use of parallel-editing – which shows the viewer different yet simultaneously unfolding plotlines – in *The Birth of a Nation* and *Intolerance* (1916) as examples.[13] At the same time *The Birth of a Nation*, along with film more generally, was hailed for its development of cinematic narrative, characterised by a commitment to 'linear continuity', as Richard Maltby puts it.[14] Cinema's relationship to temporality was therefore multiple, as was modernity's more generally: it increasingly focused on a linear form of narrative, even while it offered the audience 'a sense of temporal displacement' – an 'escape from historical time', in Maltby's words.[15] In this it can also be compared to the temporalities available through medievalism, which variously placed the Middle Ages within a linear, teleological historical narrative, or used them as a free-floating signifier that could stand either for the present or even for a possible future.

Cinematic medievalism: past or future?

The Middle Ages were one locus of the past that proved popular in film from its earliest days.[16] Cinematic medievalism participated in and drew on a wider cultural and political preoccupation with the Middle Ages. As well as being present in academic and political discourse, medievalism was prevalent in the realm of artistic and literary endeavour. Romanticism, in reaction to what it perceived as modernity's obsession with function and sterile rationalism, posited the Middle Ages as an alternative, utopian realm promising creative and political possibility.[17] While the Romantic version of the Middle Ages has tended to be categorised (or dismissed) as straightforwardly 'antimodern', the reality was more complex. Artists, architects and other thinkers recognised the potential of combining the medieval and the modern, drawing, in turn, on information gleaned from the work of English and Continental medievalists.[18]

In popular culture the Middle Ages were often imagined in a spectacular mode – a mode they shared with 'historical realism' and cinematic technology.[19] Robin Blaetz notes that one of the things that made the Middle Ages particularly attractive to film producers and cinema audiences alike was precisely this potential for spectacle.[20] It is here that modernity's ambivalent relationship with the medieval becomes particularly evident, for film frequently drew on spectacle in order to depict the Middle Ages as desirable and familiar as well as abject and alien. Spectacle also, as I will show later, disrupts the linear structure of historical narrative, which complicates the truth claims of films such as *The Birth of a Nation*.

Medievalism and scientific racialism were linked through the syntax of spectacle which resulted in an association of the European Middle

Ages with contemporary (nineteenth- and twentieth-century) non-Western locales, particularly with the indigenous cultures of colonies, as John Ganim has shown.[21] In the lavish displays of the nineteenth- and early twentieth-century World Fairs in Europe and North America, for instance, visitors could marvel at reconstructions of European medieval towns and villages alongside similar scenes of contemporary life in the colonies. Such exoticised cultural scenes – both medieval and oriental – stood in contrast to technological exhibits, which triumphantly displayed Western progress and modernity. In films both the medieval and the 'foreign' were depicted as alluringly or disturbingly exotic.[22] As Kathleen Davis argues, the implied analogy between the medieval and the non-Western

> points to a double reliance by Westernizing/globalizing rhetoric upon the concept of the Middle Ages, which supplies both the image of the common past necessary for a sense of cohesion among modern nations in the present, as well as an alterior, static mode of existence against which claims of modernity can define themselves.[23]

In the latter version of the Middle Ages as alterior, the medieval could be understood as representing the 'childhood' of modern – now 'adult' – Western nations, thereby laying claim to a historical continuity between them, as well as being so *unlike* modernity that it was comparable to alien cultures.[24] This, in turn, offered a justification of imperialistic ambitions by suggesting that the cultures thus colonised were still in their infancy and, like children, needed the benign parental guidance of modern, 'adult' nations. Both medievalism and racialism drew on the trope of 'childhood', often using the mode of spectacle to depict that against which national and racial superiority could be asserted.

Just as some nineteenth-century historians argued for the 'germ theory' in relation to the development of political institutions, others applied evolutionary models to their theories of memory. Thus, the idea of 'organic memory', put forward in the second half of the nineteenth century by Henry Maudsley and Ewald Hering, located memory in the human body itself, arguing that each generation of cells carried within it the 'memory of the experience of the entire series of its parent cells and even those of former generations'. In addition to this bodily, cellular memory, psychological theories of memory posited that childhood was the time of life during which the most important memories were formed – these early memories were also the most deeply rooted in the individual's psyche.[25] Individual cells and individual humans were shaped by memories and memory traces that would determine their present and future behaviours. While these theories emphasise the individual life rather than the collective, their focus on the persistent relevance of past events echoed the views of those who saw history as crucial to an understanding of the present and the future. The association of the medieval with childhood, as well as its originary status in nationalist narratives, locates medievalism as a memory place of Western culture. But what truth was it perceived to offer? Was the medieval a 'memory' to be cherished or expelled? Film arguably offered an escape from this dichotomy; because the temporality of film – whether it purports to show past or future events – is always the 'continuous present'; its form, which insists of necessity on the immediacy that increasingly marked modernity, engaged with history in ways that extricated it from its context, rolling up its linearity into an ongoing here and now.[26]

As Bettina Bildhauer (Chapter 2) shows, the 'medieval' also operated for some thinkers as a model with which a radically new future could be envisioned and theorised. Thus early film theorists saw the cinematic medium as 'so radically and different and new that it [was] no longer just part of modern culture, but instead, in an apparent paradox, medieval again'.[27] In this understanding, the medieval was *more* than modern even as the Middle Ages also signified utter incompatibility with progress and modernity. At the heart of these differing understandings of the 'value' of the medieval for the modern world lay the question of which role history, memory and the past should play in the organisation of the present and the future. Griffith's epochal *The Birth of a Nation* participates in the wider culture's engagement with questions concerning the role of history, origin, nationalism and race – all of which are articulated in relation to ideas of temporality. These issues are then complicated by the film's formal and technological modernity as well as its implicit engagement with medievalism, which are drawn on in order to promote a particular racial and national narrative.

Historical time

From its earliest days film was regarded by some as a valuable educational tool, particularly also for teaching history, not least national history. Certainly Thomas Dixon was 'intensely excited by the new [cinematic] medium, especially as a tool for mass education', according to Cary D. Wintz; and Griffith was deeply concerned with what he saw as the necessity for historical authenticity and veracity in his films.[28] To authorise his historical vision in *The Birth of a Nation*, Griffith makes it clear that many of his intertitles are quotations taken from Woodrow Wilson's *History of the American People* (1902). Film's emotional directness, and its capacity for making the past visible, were believed to herald a thrilling pedagogical revolution. Proponents of this approach saw film as an 'objective' medium: it would take historical facts and events and recreate them for the benefit and edification of the audience. Film would function as a transparent window on to the past, thus helping also to illuminate the present and possibly even the future.

The Birth of a Nation signals its own historical authority from the outset, particularly in the first part and through its intertitles. The film's opening intertitles remind the audience of specific moments in American history that are presented as momentous: the beginning of the slave trade, the demands made by nineteenth-century Abolitionists, and the rise of the fictional politician Austin Stoneman

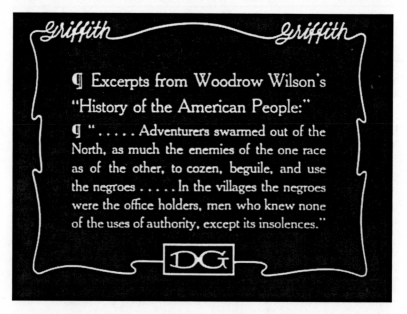

8 Griffith's use of Woodrow Wilson's *History of the American People* as authenticating source for *The Birth of A Nation* (1915)

(generally agreed to represent Thaddeus Stevens) in 1860. They then refer to specific Civil War battles (such as the Battle of Bull Run) and the events leading up to – and including – the assassination of President Lincoln 'on the fated night of April 14, 1865'. As the first part unfolds along a linear and teleological trajectory, the intertitles display a growing emphasis on historical time. Thus, while the beginning of the slave trade is not precisely dated, by the time we get to Lincoln's assassination succeeding intertitles offer an almost hourly countdown to his death. The effect is one of bringing historical events into ever sharper focus, of highlighting their causal impact on the national narrative – but also of asserting the film's ability to record them and represent them with precision.

This process positions and interpellates the audience twice over, both as immediate witnesses to a historical moment (the assassination, for instance) and to recognise themselves as being affected by the events they are watching unfold (as postwar Americans). Chronologically the audience is simultaneously in the past and the present – both the momentary and the narrative impact of history are enacted. Like Elsie and Phil Stoneman, the audience of *The Birth of a Nation* is sitting in a theatre of sorts, watching a historic moment. Like the film's protagonists, the film's audience is implicated in the events that unfold: 'we' (that is, Americans) are made aware that 'our' history is connected to theirs within the structure of national destiny. By offering viewers a detailed and lengthy representation of Lincoln's assassination the film does not only include them in Elsie and Phil's experience but addresses them as superior viewers because of their posteriority – the film's audience already knows what happens whereas the audience in the film does not. While 'they' are watching a stage production, 'we' are watching a film: watching history on films is shown to be *more* authentic than being there in the first place. Thus the film's production of analogous audience positions (theatre versus film) in relation to the historical moment articulates film's superiority over the role of the eyewitness, by aligning the latter with theatrical rather than cinematic vision. Here, the medium of film states that it can offer an authoritative – because more complete – experience of the past, while offering the more knowing audience the immediacy of the lived moment.

The emphasis on historical precision and time is not replicated in the second part of the film. Whereas the opening intertitle announces that this part is concerned with Reconstruction, it adds two further lines which suggest a more ambiguous timeframe:

Second part – Reconstruction.
❡The agony which the South endured that a nation might be born.
❡The blight of war does not end when hostilities cease.

The second part moves from specific historical events and historical time to a context in which what are presented as timeless truths are foregrounded. While specific events are highlighted as foundational, this is primarily done so that these values can emerge more emphatically. These, in turn, are made relevant to the present time of the audience, and are opened out into an open, undelineated future with which the nation must concern itself.

As these two temporalities (historical time and timelessness) alternate, historic and artistic spectacle merge and spectacle itself emerges as the film's preferred technique for signalling its most historically and nationally significant moments. The Civil War battle scenes, the assassination of Lincoln, the ride of the Ku Klux Klan: these sequences are the most spectacular of the film, as well as the most politically potent. They are both excessive and necessary.[29] While the purported aim of *The Birth of a Nation* is to offer a 'true' account of history to national memory, the cinematic spectacle also supersedes in authenticity the historical moment – the past-as-spectacle is thereby dislocated from linear narrative at the same time as history and spectacle are shown to be synonymous in nationalist and cinematic terms. Just as the discipline of history claimed to uncover the medieval origins of the present through modern methodology, so cinema could claim to bring those origins into the present through modern technology. Yet while on the one hand the film's intertitles privilege a historical (and national) narrative that is strictly linear (signalled by years, dates, hours), they also suggest that some events – those singled out as milestones in national history – are timelessly relevant, always existing in the 'now' of national self-consciousness and the 'now' of the audience's viewing experience. This split temporality, as Homi Bhabha among others has shown, is central to the narrative of nationhood.[30] In *The Birth of a Nation*, however, the split temporality of nationhood is further complicated by the unstable temporalities of race and medievalism that are drawn on to authorise this narrative.

Racial time

It has been argued that the American South was particularly enamoured of things medieval, with its neo-medieval tournaments, its 'plantation aristocracy' and its self-styled 'Chivalry', as well as in its search for historical examples that would help underpin its own slavery-dependent social organisation. The historians' organic, agrarian (and feudal) medieval social order, with its clear hierarchies and its Christian worldview, seemed to offer a respectable and authorising precedent. As a result, according to some Southern thinkers, slaveholders were the 'rightful heirs to the best in the Middle Ages'.[31] This view is at the forefront of Dixon's two novels on which *The Birth of a Nation* is based: *The Leopard's Spots* (1902) and the best-selling *The Clansman* (1905). Both explicitly reference the medieval numerous times, for instance when the latter states that a gathering of the Ku Klux Klan offered 'a picture such as the world had not seen since the Knights of the Middle Ages rode on their Holy Crusades'.[32]

It was this fascination with the medieval that critics of the South frequently invoked as evidence of its resistance to modernity. Mark Twain famously argued that if it weren't for the 'Sir Walter Scott disease the character of the Southerner ... would be wholly modern, in place of modern and mediaeval mixed, and the South would be fully a generation further advanced than it is'.[33] In this discourse, which, as Carolyn Dinshaw has shown, survives today, the South itself becomes associated with the negative qualities otherwise attributed to the Middle Ages: backwardness, brutality, feudalism, barbarism.[34] This familiar and enduring trope opposed the North and South, associating the former with progress, modernity, industrialisation and money; the latter with traditional values, agrarianism, religiosity and racism. Like the medieval for modernity, the South can function either as America's most 'echt', comforting version of itself or as its troublesome, sinister other.

This oppositional view of the South – as caught between antimodernism and progress – was one that many Southerners in the late nineteenth and early twentieth centuries had of themselves. Elizabeth Fox-Genovese and Eugene D. Genovese's detailed study of the South's interest in medievalism shows that its most influential thinkers shared their contemporaries' ambiguous relationship to the Middle Ages, as well as an intense concern with the role of history for modern nations.[35] Use of the medieval as a model in the South was determined not just by anti-modern nostalgia, as has often been claimed, but by a 'many-sided ideological struggle' arising in large part from the peculiarity of the slaveholding social structure; this struggle brought together, in Genovese's words, 'the most conservative and, simultaneously, the most revolutionary spirits.'[36] In *The Leopard's Spots*, Dixon concludes with a speech by the novel's Southern protagonist and hero, Charlie Gaston. Here, a Southern Radical viewpoint that insists on the maintenance of white racial superiority – which it negotiates in relation to history, continuity and modernity – is vividly foregrounded. In Gaston's words the 'New South' has achieved a 'manhood' that is equated with technological innovation, progress, nationalism and imperialism; the 'Old South' – which merges seamlessly into an undefined past ('generations') – is characterised by localism, as well as '[t]heories, creeds, and institutions hallowed by age.'[37] Yet Dixon does not jettison continuity; for him *racial* continuity (the 'all-conquering Saxon') is what allows both radical change and an unruptured connection to the past.

This 'new era', the product of the irresistible 'flood' of time, as well as of the evolution of the 'Anglo-Saxon', has also, however, brought about the annihilation of time and space, which undermines his racial argument.[38] The logic of Dixon's racial politics relies on what Johannes Fabian has termed 'spatialized Time', a concept developed by evolutionist anthropology, which 'envisioned social progress not as linear but divergent.'[39] This paradigm, according to which each culture occupied its own 'temporal coordinate', was (and still is) used to justify imperialistic projects. In *The Birth of a Nation*, as well as in Dixon's novels, the racial element of 'spatialized Time' is foregrounded, while space remains important in so far as the geographical origin of each race determines absolutely its respective temporality. The origins of these categories are understood to lie in the past (for the 'Anglo-Saxon' in the early Middle Ages; for the 'African' at some indeterminate point), and it is assumed that these origins are also in themselves racially homogeneous.

The treatment of time in the film echoes the tensions and contradictions evident in the passage from *The Leopard's Spots*. The second intertitle of the film goes to the heart of what is presented as the origin of national strife and fragmentation: '¶ The bringing of the African to America planted the first seed of disunion.' In the second part a scene depicting the State House of Representatives in South Carolina juxtaposes blacks and whites in a manner that further develops the idea that 'the African' disrupts 'American' (which is made synonymous with 'Aryan' or 'Anglo-Saxon') time. Here elected black representatives are shown eating, drinking and resting their naked feet on tables while attending to matters of government, ignorant of its rituals and proprieties. As an earlier intertitle states: 'The negroes were the office holders, men who knew none of the uses of authority, except its insolences.' Like children they are not 'adult' enough to be entrusted with political responsibility.

In *An Old Master: And Other Political Essays* (1893) Woodrow Wilson draws heavily on the notion of 'adulthood' to explain the essence of American democracy, which he compares unfavourably to the political turbulence that for him marks most European democracy movements. For Wilson the consistency, stability and strength of American democracy lie in its 'traditions': 'Its basis [lies in] old wont, its meaning national organic oneness.' These, in turn, are the inheritance of the white, adult Anglo-Saxon male, who is characterised by 'adult self-reliance, self-knowledge, and self-control, adult soberness ... adult sagacity in self-government, adult vigilance of thought and quickness of insight'.[40] Wilson circumvents the potential problem of an absent American Middle Ages by subscribing to a version of the 'improved' American medieval: only the most Anglo-Saxon of the Anglo-Saxons came to America, bearing within the refined memory of democracy, just as proponents of organic memory believed that cells carried within them the traces of their 'parent cells'.[41] These Anglo-Saxon pioneers are in some sense both more progressive and more original than those left behind in Europe. The legacy of Aryan racial childhood (early medieval) phase is marked by a particular essential purity, which is carried, unchanged, to the New World. There it develops – but in ways which allow it to remain most true to itself.[42] Wilson concludes that the 'adulthood' particular to American democracy is 'the heritage of races purged alike of hasty barbaric passions and of patient servility to rulers ... It is an institution of political noonday, not of the half-light of political dawn ... It is poison to the infant, but tonic to the man.'[43] This idea is taken up both in Dixon's novels and in Griffith's film. The scene from the South Carolina State House of Representatives clearly contrasts a race ready for American democracy and another, shown throughout the film as being ruled by either 'hasty barbaric passions' or 'patient servility'.[44]

The trope of childhood is central to this narrative. When Ben Cameron, desperate to help his homeland, gazes out over a majestic Southern landscape, he catches sight of two young white children. He watches them hide under a white sheet, using it to frighten off four black children. When these run off, terrified, Ben is inspired to found the Ku Klux Klan (or a local branch), which will likewise cover up in sheets to terrify black people. The following scenes show members of the Klan in their white costumes, scaring 'a negro disturber and barn burner' by waving their arms and drinking from a bucket of water. In a clear repetition of the earlier scene of the children, white children and adults use advanced techniques, and Ben is shown to have learned, while African-Americans of any age are stuck in primal fear. The temporal disjunction between black and white is reaffirmed and shown to be immutable.

Within this logic, the 'Anglo-Saxon' has a childhood, which is always a stage in a development that leads inexorably to proper adulthood. For the African-American, however, there is no temporal and developmental change. This 'time-lag' between the races serves as an explanation for why national unity cannot be achieved through racial equality. Enforced equality would lead to a situation in which nation-time was out of sync with itself. The only other option, which in the logic of the film is virtually unthinkable, is miscegenation. For what Dixon refers to in his novels as a 'mulatto' nation signifies change as regression: the future would become a turning back, a *devolution*. The novel suggests that this regression would ultimately result in a complete stoppage of time when Gaston likens government founded on the principles of racial equality to a 'decaying corpse', which causes America to 'lag behind the age'. Drawing on a metaphor with medieval overtones, he concludes his speech with the ominous prophecy: 'If we attempt to move forward we are literally chained to the body of a festering Black Death!'[45] The black body becomes a body of death – of the 'black death' – a medievalised, apocalyptic body that hinders the natural, teleological progress of the Aryan. Implicit in this temporal logic is the recognition that the white race *has* a Middle Ages, which, while originary, is crucially also enabling (a childhood capable of learning), while the black race is confined to a 'medieval' stasis that is equated with absence of change and death. Thus, two kinds of 'medieval' are set against one another and are differentiated by their respective relationship to race.

The significations of the medieval in these literary, political and cinematic discourses are so ambiguous because the medieval is made to serve both negatively and positively in the articulation of modern nationhood, and because of the ways medievalism intersects with the temporalities of race. The medieval signifies, at various points: the temporal origin for whiteness; the temporality of black barbarism; the promise of a triumphant future for the nation; the threat of an abject future for the nation. Furthermore, there is still another temporal disjuncture, this time within the 'Aryan' race itself.

Southern time

In *The Birth of a Nation*, the South is repeatedly aligned with tradition and timeless values. This is especially noticeable in the first part, which is otherwise so concerned with historical time, as outlined above. When viewers are first introduced to the Cameron family, the intertitle preceding the sequence introduces the South as a lost Eden: '¶ In the Southland. ¶ Piedmont, South Carolina, the home of the Camerons, where life runs in a quaintly way that is to be no more.' Here, the South is a specific geographical location, but one that exists in an unspecified timeframe. The phrase 'life runs' suggests a present tense, which the viewer is about to witness, while the phrase 'that is to be no more' leaves it unclear whether this way of life has indeed disappeared or not. There is also a tension between the time within which the narrative itself unfolds and the viewer's time: is the viewer being told that in the here-and-now of the film time the 'quaintly way' still exists, while in the viewer's time it 'is no more'? Or is the phrasing rather more open-ended, suggesting an uncertain future time in which this 'quaintly way' is, in fact, still under threat?

The shots that follow, of the Cameron family sitting on their front porch, confirm the prelapsarian nature of the South. Gathered together as a harmonious microcosm, the Camerons represent the ideal of an organic social order in which everyone knows their place and is therefore content.[46] Southern time, in its association with what are presented as time*less* values, is persistently coded as 'true' white time throughout the film. After all, it is in the context of mechanical, linear, historical time that Lincoln's assassination occurs. When historical time, associated with destructive rupture, accelerated and irresponsible change (and the North), is allowed to rule unchecked, the 'quaint old way' of the South, and all that it represents (order, stability, peace) is threatened, with, the film asserts, disastrous consequences for the nation. The South, on the other hand, with its concern for religion, chivalry, honour and hierarchy, should serve as the foundation upon which the future rests.

In its uniqueness the South is presented in Griffith's film – as in Dixon's novels – to some extent as a separate nation. It is not 'America' that is being held up as an ideal paradigm in most of the film (and the novels); instead the audience is being shown that southern values can stand synecdochally for 'true' American values.[47] In this sense, then, the South functions as a geographical and ideological originary Middle Ages for America. This is indicated in the opening intertitle of the second part, where the 'agony' that the South is said to have endured so 'that a nation might be born' is reminiscent of a mother's birth-pangs. The successful reinstatement of this status quo is, in this narrative, due to the actions of the Ku Klux Klan. When the film first opened in Los Angeles, in 1915, horsemen dressed in Klan costumes were hired to advertise the film, revealing the Klan's centrality to the film's ideological project. As well as arguably representing the film's most obvious evocation of medievalism, the scenes focusing on Klan action form its structural, ideological and, in some ways, its formal climax. Robed in white garments embroidered with crosses, the Ku Klux Klan defined itself as a Christian chivalric brotherhood; in the film, it is shown to be the last hope for disenfranchised and abused whites in the South. As Allen Frantzen argues in relation to German First World War propaganda, what is being presented here draws on the medieval Christian trope of 'transformation through abjection'.[48] It is the South's 'agony' that causes the Klan to (re)form and reinstall the order upon which the nation must be founded.

When the Klan gathers together its members, the signal that is sent out to rally them is the 'fiery cross'. In these sequences, which follow the murder of the ex-slave, Gus, for the attempted rape of Flora Cameron, Ben begins the ritual of the fiery cross by taking the bloodied Confederate flag that Flora had wrapped around her when she lay dying, dips it into water and raises it up for all the other members to see. The ensuing intertitle reads: ' "Brethren, this flag bears the red stain of the life of a Southern woman, a priceless sacrifice on the altar of an outraged civilization." ' Taking a burning wooden cross from another follower, Ben raises this up as well. The intertitle reads: ' "Here I raise the ancient symbol of an unconquered race of men, the fiery cross of old Scotland's hills ... I quench its flames in the sweetest blood that ever stained the sands of Time!" '

It is thought that the fiery cross was made popular through literary medievalism, mainly by Sir Walter Scott's poem *The Lady of the Lake* (1810), which takes inspiration for its title from medieval Arthurian romance tradition, but is itself set during the reign of James V of Scotland in the sixteenth century. In the film, as in the poem, the fiery cross functions as a link between the present and a medievalised mythical past: it is 'ancient', and its origins lie in 'old Scotland's hills'. Yet it is also a very modern sign, in that it is shown to serve current needs and political circumstances. The modern turns out to be, in the end, a version of the medieval, and the fiery cross is a symbol that maintains its potency because of what is shown to be a cyclical temporality. Genovese has argued that 'the significance of medieval ritual for modern Southerners' lay in their perception that the emergence of a Christianised chivalry was due to a new respect for 'the rights of womanhood' and in order to counteract the '"downward progress of civilization"'.[49] These are the two things that are presented by *The Birth of a Nation* as forming the core of the Klan's ideology, and both are joined in the film in the scene of the fiery cross.

How Ben Cameron knows about the fiery cross, and how the Klan members know of its meaning and purpose, remains unsaid. This implies that there is a shared knowledge, based on custom and heritage: the ancient spirit of old Scotland's hills lives on in the South as part of its white genetic or 'organic' memory. The Klan is a New World version of the Old World clans; Griffith uses medievalism to suggest that the Ku Klux Klan is a 'repository of cultural memory' presented as synonymous with racial memory.[50] Anne McClintock has shown (in relation to the film *Tweede Trek* (1938), an epic narrative that promoted the idea of a mythic Afrikaner history of racial unity and purity) how cinema could be used to 'inven[t] white nationalist traditions and celebrat[e] unity where none had existed before, creating the illusion of a collective identity through the political staging of vicarious *spectacle*'.[51] The ride of the Klan, accompanied at one stage by the music of Richard Wagner's 'The Ride of the Valkyries' and, later, by the Southern 'national' anthem, 'Dixie', displays the 'visible, ritual organization of fetish objects' that McClintock identifies as being central to such spectacle, such as 'the spectacular regalia of flags, flaming torches … patriotic songs … incendiary speeches, archaic costumes and the choreographing of crowd spectacle'.[52] In these scenes *The Birth of a Nation* offers its audiences a 'potent symbolic amalgam of disjointed times' which makes it, in Walter Benjamin's terms, 'an exemplary act of modernity'.[53] McClintock explains this 'disjointed' temporality as a confluence of linear time (national and imperial progress) and non-linear time (cyclical). In *The Birth of a Nation* the Klan represents *both* linear and non-linear time, the latter through its intimate association with medievalism and 'timeless' values. This connection is reconfirmed through what the film presents as one of the Klan's (and the South's) most urgent missions: vengeance for the virgin who sacrifices her life for the sake of her people.

Virgin time

The virginal heroine was a popular staple in medieval hagiography and romance as well as in subsequent Arthurian literary and artistic revivals and Gothic fiction. In these genres the maiden's virginity and its loss (either consented to or resisted, often to the death) provided numerous plotlines and motivated male heroes to chivalric action. In *The Birth of a Nation* it is the virgin Flora's death that finally triggers the climactic action of the film's second part: the threat to her purity enables the medievalised chivalric masculinity of the Klan to emerge. It is therefore, in conjunction with the children's game, what enables the restoration of white supremacy that marks the 'birthing' of the nation. The blood that stains the 'sands of Time' belongs not primarily to an American woman, but to a Southern child-woman.

Flora's intermediary status as innocent-yet-nubile virgin is signalled in the first part of the film, where we have seen her as the playful (the film refers to her as the 'pet') sister of Ben Cameron. She is repeatedly shown holding or wrapping herself in a Confederate flag which, as one intertitle tells us, represents 'The spirit of the South'. She displays proper 'Southern' outrage at Elsie Stoneman's friendliness towards Silas Lynch, and is closely involved in the making and hiding of Klan outfits. Nationalist discourse frequently posits women as the guardians or repositories of national identity and memory.[54] As Nira Yuval-Davis among others has shown, this is connected to what is perceived as their biological and cultural reproductive functions.[55] But this is not primarily Flora's role – after all, she is the one woman who is *not* involved romantically. At the same time she must die in order to prevent a breach of her virginal body – she must deny the access to it demanded by the ex-slave, Gus. Flora's death represents a denial of miscegenation and the pollution it would bring to the white Southern nation. Flora's role in the film ultimately fulfils a dual purpose: she is the locus both of memory and of national (Southern) purity. Flora's death, in defence of her virginity and, by extension, Southern purity, marks her (and the South) as resistant to change. Virginity is profoundly atemporal and anti-historical in its preservation of the status quo.[56] Flora, as white sacrificial virgin, functions to prevent forgetting; Flora must die in order for change to occur, yet she must also die in order to prevent change: to facilitate and reify memory. Her role as sacrifical virgin participates in the logic of what René Girard claims is the function of sacrifice: the attempt to achieve an 'equilibrium' in 'societies that lack a firm judicial system'.[57]

In the film it is Gus's death that provides a structural parallel to Flora's. His illicit desire for the white virgin is punished, and the spectre of his ambition (to have a white wife) is rooted out, both through the death of his object of desire, Flora, and through his own death. The two deaths inadvertently highlight the similarities between Gus and Flora's respective roles in the film's narrative. This ties in with Frantzen's important point about the scapegoat – that rejected, abjected 'other' that is 'eliminated' so that 'some kind of cultural homogeneity can be reclaimed'. What underlies this is not, in fact, the 'otherness' of that which is scapegoated but its similarity; the 'scapegoat is merely a function of the need for reconciliation between warring factions more powerful than it'.[58] Such a reading is supported by the intertitle in *The Birth of a Nation* that triumphantly announces the co-operation of whites against black soldiers: 'The former enemies of North and South are united again in common defence of their Aryan birthright.' Both Flora and Gus are adrift in a changed world that proves fatal for them. Both – one because of his race, the other because of her age but also her gender – are childlike, which, in the temporal logic of the film, links them to the past. Gus, as a black man, is always temporally delayed; Flora, as 'pure' Southern virgin, symbolises an indeterminate originary, prelapsarian past. Even as their deaths function as a warning against change, both must be sacrificed in the logic of the film if the new nation is to be achieved. Without them, and without their deaths, the ensuing fray and climactic triumph of the Klan would not be possible.

The ambiguous temporality of the Klan itself means that finally all three narrative positions – the virgin, the black man, the Klan member – are ultimately reliant on similar discourses and also reliant on each other. The medievalisation of each cannot, ultimately, be relinquished, for its logic guarantees the coherence of the film's national narrative. What Frantzen argues in relation to German medievalism of the same period is also applicable here; *The Birth of a Nation* 'does not simply invite a medieval gloss but yields its full theological and political meanings only in the context of medieval [and medievalism's] ideas and the images it invokes'.[59]

The end: providential time

What prevented Southerners from dismissing the Middle Ages was, as Genovese notes, 'not their appreciation of Gothic cathedrals or, in contrast, their revulsion of dirt and ignorance, but their concern with God's will as revealed through history'.[60] The centrality of Christianity as a uniting and civilising force (both in the Middle Ages and in the forging of the modern American nation) is evident in *The Birth of a Nation*'s eschatological timeframe. The film closes with two possible options for the (current? future?) nation, which is represented by the two white newly wed couples: the first is a scene of carnage and destruction, presided over by what seems to be a god of war; the latter is a harmonious and peaceful scene in which men and women, dressed in costumes that look vaguely classical and medieval, wander around a beautiful plaza.[61] In the background a Christ-figure spreads out his arms to embrace the scene. After this the film cuts back to a shot of Ben and Elsie sitting, staring out to sea. This is a split-screen shot, in which they are juxtaposed with the image of a beautiful (again, vaguely medieval-looking) city, presumably the 'City of Peace'. The swelling notes of the 'Star-Spangled Banner', which has now replaced 'Dixie', accompany this prophetic vision.

Arguably, *The Birth of a Nation* functions in a manner comparable to Erich Auerbach's definition of what Davis calls 'providential time' – which he saw as representative of a medieval, Christian mentality – both within its narrative logic and because of the medium itself.[62] Presenting both past (immediate and distant) as well as future in the cinematic syntax of the 'continuous present', the film ends without making it at all clear at what point – if indeed at all – the nation is meant to have been born. This clearly provides a large part of the film's ideological power: each audience that sees it is reminded of historical events which, set outside purely historical time owing to their significance for the national epic, are also always equally relevant. In addition the values that are shown to be rooted in a medievalised (and therefore historically past) originary moment are also presented as timeless. In both of these temporal guises they are necessary for the modern nation.

Yet the temporal disjunctures that enable the film's success once more threaten to reveal and demystify its ideological foundations. While it appeals to linear, historical time in its narrative format as well as in some of its ideological premises, the syntax of the 'instantaneous present' – again, both formally and ideologically, in the film's medievalism – repeatedly interrupts and, through the pleasure of spectacle, displaces linearity. Thus, the temporalities that jostle with each other in the film are resolved by an appeal to providential time at the film's end, which, however, merely defers the nation's birth with its reference to a simultaneously uncertain and predetermined (or circumscribed) future tense. This, in turn, is shown to be dependent on present choices, which are themselves determined by origins that lie in the past. Future, past and present are ultimately inextricable, but not necessarily in a teleological sense – thereby constituting as well as denying the linearity of national narrative. In the logic of *The Birth of a Nation*, as well as in the logic of its contemporary racial and political contexts, the modern nation never quite manages to be born. The effect of the film's multiple medievalisms, which it shares with other contemporary discourses, is to unravel the oppositions and unmake the categories on which the rhetoric of nationhood is founded. Here national narrative, racialism and cinematic form all participate in the powerful and mutable tropes of medievalism.

Notes

1 For example, Joel Williamson, *The Crucible of Race: Black–White Relations in the American South Since Emancipation* (Oxford: Oxford University Press, 1984), pp. 176, 175.
2 Nickieann Fleener-Marzec, *D. W. Griffith's* The Birth of a Nation: *Controversy, Suppression, and the First Amendment as It Applies to Filmic Expression, 1915– 1973* (New York: Arno, 1980), p. 5.
3 Clyde Taylor, 'The re-birth of the aesthetic in cinema', *Wide Angle*, 13:3–4 (1991), 12–30 (13, 14). See also James Agee, 'David Wark Griffith', *The Nation* (4 September 1948), in Carl Bromley (ed.), *Cinema Nation: The Best Writing on Film from* The Nation, *1913–2000* (New York: Thunder's Mouth/Nation, 2000), pp. 35–40 (p. 35). For more on the film's context and reception see Robert Lang (ed.), *The Birth of a Nation: D. W. Griffith, Director* (New Brunswick, NJ: Rutgers University Press, 1994).
4 On the close interconnections and mutual influence between politics, academia and popular culture in this period, with specific reference to Dixon, Griffith, Wilson and the historians of the 'Dunning School', see Jack Temple Kirby, 'Griffith, Dunning, and "the Great Fact of Race"', in Kirby, *Media-Made Dixie: The South in the American Imagination* (Georgia: The University of Georgia Press, 1986 [1978]), pp. 1–22.
5 Oswald Garrison Villard, 'The regulation of films', *The Nation* (6 May 1915), in Bromley (ed.), *Cinema Nation*, pp. 19–22 (p. 21).
6 See, for instance, Patrick J. Geary, *The Myth of Nations: The Medieval Origins of*

Europe (Princeton, NJ: Princeton University Press, 2002), and Allen J. Frantzen, *Desire for Origins: New Language, Old English, and Teaching the Tradition* (New Brunswick, NJ: Rutgers University Press, 1990).

7 Frantzen, *Desire*, p. 204.

8 See Henry W. Bragdon, 'The historical seminary at Johns Hopkins', in Bragdon, *Woodrow Wilson: The Academic Years* (Cambridge, MA: Belknap Press of Harvard University Press, 1967), pp. 101–23.

9 *Ibid.*, p. 106.

10 Laura Kendrick, 'The American Middle Ages: eighteenth-century Saxonist mythmaking', in Marie-Françoise Alamichel and Derek Brewer (eds), *The Middle Ages after the Middle Ages in the English-Speaking World* (Cambridge: Brewer, 1997), pp. 121–36 (p. 122).

11 Stephen G. Nichols, 'Modernism and the politics of medieval studies', in R. Howard Bloch and Stephen G. Nichols (eds), *Medievalism and the Modernist Temper* (Baltimore, MD: Johns Hopkins University Press, 1996), pp. 25–56 (p. 28).

12 Stephen Kern, *The Culture of Time and Space, 1880–1918* (Cambridge, MA: Harvard University Press, 2003 [1983]), p. 81.

13 *Ibid.*, p. 70.

14 Richard Maltby, *Hollywood Cinema* (Oxford: Blackwell, 2003), p. 289.

15 Maltby, *Hollywood Cinema*, p. 288.

16 For more on this see Sandra Gorgievski, 'The Arthurian legend in cinema: myth or history?', in Alamichel and Brewer (eds), *Middle Ages*, pp. 153–66 (p. 155); Robin Blaetz, 'Cecil B. DeMille's *Joan the Woman*', in Kathleen Verduin (ed.), *Medievalism in North America*, Studies in Medievalism VI (Cambridge: Brewer, 1994), pp. 109–22 (pp. 110, 111).

17 Simon Bradley, *St Pancras Station* (London: Profile, 2007), p. 28.

18 Bradley, *St Pancras*, p. 39. See also Jeff Rider, 'Roger Sherman Loomis: medievalism as antimodernism', in Verduin (ed.), *Medievalism*, pp. 143–62.

19 See Maltby, *Hollywood Cinema*, p. 313.

20 See Blaetz, '*Joan the Woman*', p. 111.

21 John Ganim, *Medievalism and Orientalism* (New York: Palgrave Macmillan, 2005), pp. 83–129.

22 See Blaetz, '*Joan the Woman*', p. 111.

23 Kathleen Davis, 'Time behind the veil: the media, the middle ages, and orientalism now', in Jeffrey Jerome Cohen (ed.) *The Postcolonial Middle Ages* (Basingstoke: Palgrave, 2001), pp. 105–22 (p. 107).

24 There were also other models, in which the medieval was figured as the parental precursor to a now-decadent and 'childish' modernity, but these were less prevalent.

25 Kern, *Culture*, pp. 40, 42.

26 On the 'continuous present' of film, see Maltby, *Hollywood Cinema*, pp. 304–18.

27 Bettina Bildhauer, Chapter 2 above.

28 28 Cary D. Wintz, 'Introduction', in Wintz (ed.), *The Clansman: An Historical Romance of the Ku Klux Klan by Thomas Dixon, Jr.* (Armonk, NY: Sharpe, 2001), pp. vii–xxviii (p. xv); see also Kirby, 'Griffith, Dunning', p. 3.

29 For this phenomenon in period films generally see Maltby, *Hollywood*, p. 311.

30 Homi K. Bhabha, 'DissemiNation: time, narrative and the margins of the modern nation', in Bhabha, *The Location of Culture* (London: Routledge, 1994), pp. 139–70.

31 Elizabeth Fox-Genovese and Eugene D. Genovese, *The Mind of the Master Class: History and Faith in the Southern Slaveholders' Worldview* (Cambridge: Cambridge University Press, 2005), p. 314.

32 Thomas Dixon, *The Clansman: An Historical Romance of the Ku Klux Klan* (New York: Doubleday, Page, 1905), p. 316. On the medievalised origins of the name of the Ku Klux Klan, see James Chandler, 'The historical novel goes to Hollywood: Scott, Griffith, and film epic today', in Lang (ed.), *The Birth of a Nation*, pp. 225–49 (p. 246). On the interconnection between medievalism, the Ku Klux Klan and Dixon's novels see also James Taft Hatfield, 'Goethe and the Ku Klux Klan', *PMLA*, 37:4 (December 1922), 735–9. On medievalism in Dixon's work, see Peter Schmidt, 'Walter Scott, postcolonial theory, and New South literature', *The Mississippi Quarterly*, 56:4 (Fall 2003), 545–54 (548).

33 Mark Twain, *Life on the Mississippi*, The Oxford Mark Twain, ed. by Shelley Fisher Fishkin (Oxford: Oxford University Press, 1996), pp. 468–9; also cited in Hatfield, 'Goethe', 736–7.

34 See Carolyn Dinshaw, 'Getting medieval: *Pulp Fiction*, Foucault, and the use of the past', in Dinshaw, *Getting Medieval: Sexualities and Communities, Pre- and Postmodern* (Durham, NC: Duke University Press, 1999), pp. 183–206.

35 See Fox-Genovese and Genovese, *Mind of the Master Class*.

36 Eugene D. Genovese, 'The Southern slaveholders' view of the Middle Ages', in Bernard Rosenthal and Paul E. Szarmach (eds), *Medievalism in American Culture: Papers of the Eighteenth Annual Conference of the Center for Medieval and Early Renaissance Studies*, Medieval and Renaissance Texts and Studies, 55 (Binghamton, NY: Medieval and Renaissance Texts and Studies, 1989), pp. 31–52 (p. 33). See also Schmidt, 'Walter Scott', esp. p. 549, and David Stricklin, ' "Ours is a century of light": Dixon's strange consistency', in Michele K. Gillespie and Randal L. Hall (eds), *Thomas Dixon Jr. and the Birth of Modern America* (Baton Rouge, LA: Louisiana State University Press, 2006), pp. 105–23.

37 Thomas Dixon, Jr, *The Leopard's Spots: A Romance of the White Man's Burden – 1865–1900* (New York: Doubleday, Page, 1902; repr. Gretna, LA: Firebird Press, 2001), pp. 434–5. See also Scott Romine, 'Thomas Dixon and the literary production of whiteness', in Gillespie and Hall (eds), *Thomas Dixon Jr*, pp. 124–50.

38 On the connection between imperialist modes of thought that were articulated in relation to both spatial and temporal categories see Kern, *Culture*, esp. p. 92; and Anne McClintock, *Imperial Leather: Race, Gender and Sexuality in the Colonial Contest* (New York: Routledge, 1995), esp. p. 359.

39 Davis, 'Time', p. 108; she is citing and discussing Johannes Fabian, *Time and the Other: How Anthropology Makes Its Object* (New York: Columbia University Press, 1983), p. 15.

40 Woodrow Wilson, *An Old Master: And Other Political Essays* (New York: Scribner's, 1893), pp. 116–17.

41 On America's search for a Middle Ages, which some scholars characterised as 'its quest for one as for a mother', see Morton W. Bloomfield, 'Reflections of a medievalist: America, medievalism, and the Middle Ages', in Rosenthal and Szarmach (eds), *Medievalism in American Culture*, pp. 14–19.

42 Dixon echoes this view in *The Leopard's Spots*, p. 438.

43 Wilson, *An Old Master*, p. 118.

44 Taylor notes that 'Griffith subscribed to a traditional Southern view of African Americans as "pre-moral children" of whom moral understanding was not to be expected'; Taylor, 'Re-birth', p. 24.

45 Dixon, *The Leopard's Spots*, p. 436.

46 See Fox-Genovese and Genovese, *Mind*, p. 308.

47 See Taylor, 'Re-birth', p. 17.

48 Allen J. Frantzen, *Bloody Good: Chivalry, Sacrifice, and the Great War* (London: University of Chicago Press, 2004), p. 30.

49 Genovese, 'Southern slaveholders' view', p. 36, citing Perceval Renier.

50 For the phrase 'repository of cultural memory', which Davis argues is usually the role attributed to women in orientalist and nationalist discourses, see Davis, 'Time', p. 117.

51 McClintock, *Imperial Leather*, p. 373.

52 *Ibid.*, pp. 374, 375.

53 *Ibid.*, pp. 376, 377.

54 Women are also often presented as founders or as originary figures in narratives of nation; see Patrick J. Geary, *Women at the Beginning: Origin Myths from the Amazons to the Virgin Mary* (Princeton: Princeton University Press, 2006).

55 Nira Yuval-Davis, *Gender and Nation* (London: Sage, 1997; repr. 2007), esp. pp. 26–67. On more of this specifically in relation to a Southern context see Anne S. Rubin, *A Shattered Nation: The Rise and Fall of the Confederacy, 1861–1868* (Chapel Hill, NC: University of North Carolina Press, 2005), p. 247.

56 See Anke Bernau, ' "Saint, witch, man, maid, or whore?" Joan of Arc and writing history', in Bernau, Ruth Evans and Sarah Salih (eds), *Medieval Virginities* (Cardiff: University of Wales Press, 2003), pp. 214–33.

57 See René Girard, 'Sacrifice as sacral violence and substitution', in James G. Williams (ed.), *The Girard Reader* (New York: Crossroad Publishing Company, 1996), pp. 69–93 (p. 87).

58 Frantzen, *Bloody Good*, p. 46.

59 *Ibid.*, p. 30.

60 Genovese, 'Southern slaveholders' view', p. 32.

61 While the medieval and the classical are thought to have been posited as antithetical referents, their relationship was in fact more complex and varied. While certain elements of 'the medieval' were certainly reviled (its Catholicism in particular), the early Middle Ages became, from the seventeenth century onwards, central to a narrative of English national (and religious) continuity, a worthy precursor to the 'Renaissance'. This 'Saxonism' was then, as shown earlier in this chapter, taken up in American political thought. For more on this see Raphael Samuels, *Island Stories: Unravelling Britain: Theatres of Memory, vol. II*, ed. by Alison Light, with Sally Alexander and Gareth Stedman Jones

(London: Verso, 1999).

62 Kathleen Davis, 'National writing in the ninth century: a reminder for postco-
   lonial thinking about the nation', *The Journal of Medieval and Early Modern
   Studies*, 23:3 (1998), 611–37 (613); she is referring to Erich Auerbach, *Mimesis:
   The Representation of Reality in Western Literature* (Princeton, NJ.: Princeton
   University Press, 2003 [1953]), esp. pp. 73–4.

5

The medieval imaginary in Italian films

Marcia Landy

Introduction: whose Middle Ages?

The cinema has long ransacked historical and literary texts for their spectacular appeal to popular audiences. Medievalism in film is no exception. From the era of silent film to the present, the Italian cinema, long inclined toward historical topics, has created versions of the medieval imaginary as popular entertainment and also as social critique. This chapter focuses on a select group of films set in Middle Ages, produced in Italy at two moments of dramatic transformation in Italian culture and politics – the Fascist era during the 1930s and early 1940s and the epoch of the 'Economic Miracle' in the 1960s. Luis Trenker's *Condottieri* (1936), a biographical or adventure film, was made during the peak of power for the Italian Fascist regime, and Alessandro Blasetti's *La corona di ferro* (The Iron Crown, 1941), a fictional film set in a medieval fantasy world, was produced in the last unsettling days of Fascism. Over a quarter of a century later, Mario Monicelli directed two extremely popular and innovative historical films set in the Middle Ages: *L'armata Brancaleone* (Brancaleone's Army, 1966) and *Brancaleone alle crociate* (Brancaleone at the Crusades, 1969). I have chosen these films for a variety of reasons that will become clear, but particularly because they have been neglected undeservedly.

In sheer numbers of films the medieval period was less popular in Italian cinema than classical Rome and the Renaissance. Indeed Gianfranco Miro Gori suggests that only eighteen 'medieval' films were realised, the majority of which are no longer extant.[1] In the silent era the films on the Middle Ages were associated with such directors as Augusto Genina (*Il corsaro* / The Corsair, 1923) and Enrico Guazzoni (*Gerusalemme Liberata* / Jerusalem Delivered, 1910). During the era of sound Alessandro Blasetti's historical films set new standards of narration and created new film stars such as Gino Cervi, Elisa Cegani,

Luisa Ferida and Massimo Girotti, who all appeared in Blasetti's fable of the Middle Ages, *La corona di ferro*. The various sources from which the producers and directors derived the scenarios were drawn loosely from biographies, novels and Hollywood costume dramas. Modifications in the style of historical subjects were introduced with the coming of sound technology and tied to changes in the cultural and political climate.

The early critical literature on films produced during the Fascist era regarded them pejoratively as frivolous 'white telephone films', devoted to the foibles of the upper classes in elegant surroundings, or as political propaganda, using history as a pretext to inculcate the values of nationalism and imperialism.[2] More recent critical work has been attentive to the pitfalls of labelling and judging the films as 'Fascist' as if this designation can account for how the cinema served in complex fashion to create consensus.[3] Rather than being monolithic, cinema produced during the Fascist years reproduced diverse, often contradictory, new and traditional images.[4] Films shaped their material to stress the visual appeal of spectacle and adventure, and, in James Hay's words, concealed their political message and 'their rhetorical nature through myths about historical events and figures'.[5]

The cinema of the postwar era did not abandon its historical preoccupations. While neo-realism was in reaction against the artificial and stylised historical spectacles of the Fascist era, neo-realism was, none the less, 'historical in the end', according to Guido Fink.[6] Whether set in a contemporary milieu or in a remote past, the films of Luchino Visconti, Roberto Rossellini, Bernardo Bertolucci and the Taviani brothers, among numerous others, were testimony to an abiding concern with Italian history, its continuities and ruptures.[7] In the late 1950s, when the Italy of the Economic Miracle was in the throes of transformation from the politics and social structures of Fascism to economic and social modernising, the cinema was a source of experimentation in subject matter and styles, and, as Angelo Restivo claims, 'it is no surprise that history itself is a subject obsessively revisited'.[8] The *Brancaleone* films are often relegated to the world of popular comedy and, therefore, often dismissed as peripheral in the critical literature, while the art cinema is given serious attention. Yet in many ways Monicelli's films set in a medieval context address historical and cultural issues also treated in the films of Pier Paolo Pasolini and Michelangelo Antonioni concerning what Restivo calls 'the camera's ability to register reality' and 'the body as guarantor of authenticity'.[9] Monicelli's films, too, through their uses of allegory and folklore in comic and satiric fashion, shed light on how the texts bind the medieval past to a contemporary present and illuminate connections among cinematic forms, spectatorship, social history and the national imaginary.

In thinking about history on film, I am aware of Philip Rosen's observation that

> no modern historicity – not even the most careful and scholarly – ever quite rids itself of at least some residue of the fantastic, the desire for temporal transcendence, the mummification of change. But this leaves open the question of whether imaginary and fantastic components always must necessarily be excluded from claims to knowledge.[10]

These comments are particularly relevant for an understanding of inventions of the Middle Ages where fantasy has been a central feature in the re-imagining of medievalism and where historicising cannot be separated from such 'desire, persuasion, and belief'.[11] Invention of fantasy is not a sign of mendacity: rather it exposes how the imaginary confrontation between past and present is inevitably subject to subsequent revision, review and critical reconsideration.

Since the films' uses of history were a prominent feature of their representational strategies, my object in this chapter is to examine how cinema appropriates the past so as to recognise 'the power it holds from its shameful kinship with the makers of history and the tellers of stories', in Jacques Rancière's words.[12] Therefore in the films that I have chosen to discuss I probe their kinship with modes of history making, to understand better how these different cinematic inventions shed light on conceptions of medievalism and, further, on the contemporary cultural and political moments of their creators.

Imagining the Middle Ages as history

Medievalism on film is not unitary and stable: it inevitably changes during different moments in the social history of the twentieth century and in the corresponding history of narrative styles, language and modes of interpretation. Based on oral, written and visual traditions, cinematic conceptions of the Middle Ages are formed from an assemblage of intertexts that have accreted and been reworked over a long period of time and, as such, are inevitably dependent on a temporal and conceptual framework that is derived from contemporary discursive as well as aesthetic positions. Too often historians regard the presence of anachronism as a violation of the text's claims to historicity. Yet anachronism as a poetic approach is at the heart of these historic inventions, an inescapable dimension of the art of cinema. Anachronism involves characters, journeys into the past or into the future. Another expression of this journey is the migration of earlier or later texts into the enunciation. Acknowledgement of the anachronistic character of cinematic history can serve to render visible a text's political and cultural investments, as we shall see in the discussion below of the films produced during the Fascist era.

On a material level the presence of a camera, the uses of costume, architecture, furniture, armour, weapons, art works and set design are often a further sign of how different orders of time collide.[13] Anachronism can function transparently, unrecognised as such, or it can become a recognisable mark of intervention in interpreting historical events. Further, film genres and their reliance on popular or mass discourses rarely adhere to the strict chronology of historiography. The juxtaposition of texts from elite and mass culture plays a critical role in understanding contemporary inventions (and revisions) of a medieval past, bringing past and present, humour and erudition, emergent and residual forms into dialogue.[14] The presence of parody and pastiche is a further expression of intertextuality, whereby language usage and genre forms are re-imagined for the modern viewer but with reference to earlier models.[15] As we shall see, the functioning of intertextuality also involves the adoption of visual motifs from such sources as drama, lyric opera, popular romances, historical novels (particularly from the nineteenth century), historical paintings and folk culture.[16]

Two fables of power: cinematic history and Fascism

Condottieri

Condottieri focuses on the late medieval period and on the heroic exploits of Giovanni de' Medici, played by the German film-maker Luis Trenker. While *Condottieri* identifies itself in the titles as being situated in the Renaissance, it adopts images and motifs identified with medievalism through its uses of statuary, landscape, iconography and religiosity. This is not surprising, since historical cinema under Fascism tended in a populist direction, and the cinema of medievalism was less appealing than the Renaissance. The years of Fascism became increasingly committed to a cinema that could reach broad segments of the cinemagoing population, but such a position necessitated an accommodation to flexible (and less scholarly) conceptions of periodicity. Furthermore, given the fluctuating identifications between the medieval and the early modern, the film is significant for its particular identification of the Middle Ages in terms of the Renaissance. In its themes and style the film bears the imprints of Trenker's mystical mountain films of the 1930s, and especially of *Der verlorene Sohn* (The Prodigal Son, 1934) and the western *Der Kaiser von Kalifornien* (The Emperor of California, 1936), also starring Trenker. Like all Trenker films, *Condottieri* develops a contrast between wild nature and a corrupt material civilisation. The style of *Condottieri* is clearly monumental, focusing on how the central character struggles heroically against the corruptions of the mundane world. Trenker's films fulfil Friedrich Nietzsche's description of 'monumental history' as the 'masquerade costume' of the great and powerful in which 'empires are destroyed, princes murdered, eras and revolutions launched'.[17]

Indeed Trenker's earlier films are a prologue to *Condottieri* that, to use Jacques Le Goff's terminology, is an instance of 'the Wilderness in the Medieval West'.[18] The tradition that Trenker's films inhabit is that of the struggling individual in a wild, natural, often magical and dreamlike setting, a site of initiation for the hero and regeneration for the land. Thus heroic figures of these dramas of trial, suffering and redemption, it is suggested, belong to nature rather than to town and castle. The heroic figure disdains material gain, and is identified with the spiritual and martial rewards that accrue to the warrior who sacrifices himself for God and realm. In *Condottieri*, for example, Trenker portrays the life and trials of the courageous Giovanni delle Bande Nere, alias Giovanni de' Medici, in his fight against corrupt aristocrats, mercenaries and brigands to found an Italian nation. A 'metaphoric landscape for exaggerating the hero's own lofty ideals and aura', as Hay puts it, adds to the film's monumentality.[19] The use of an untamed and magical natural world is a feature common to the romance tradition (e.g. Tasso's *Gerusalemme Liberata*), German epic (*The Nibelungenlied* and its operatic expression by Richard Wagner) and also the popular mountain films of the 1930s. In his mission to revitalise a 'moribund' society Giovanni de' Medici is portrayed as wandering beyond cultural boundaries, his world being one of mountains, sky, water and open vistas. The imagery belongs, as Christopher Frayling observed, to 'a distinctly Teutonic brand of agrarian mysticism'.[20]

Condottieri was filmed in both a German and an Italian version. The film might be classified as a biopic, in its focus on the life of Giovanni de' Medici, but it is also a costume or adventure drama. The film evokes comparison with Fritz Lang's *Die Nibelungen* (*Siegfried* and *Kriemhilds Rache* / Kriemhild's Revenge, 1924) as a mythological epic. However, *Condottieri* uses myth and allegory differently from Lang's spiritualised treatment of the hero's life and death. What has been generally considered worthy of comment about the film is its partisan, if not propagandistic, appropriation of Italian medieval history and, as many critics and viewers have commented, its evocation of the figure of Benito Mussolini through the figure of Giovanni delle Bande Nere.[21] *Condottieri* invoked the wrath of Joseph Goebbels and Adolf Hitler, who demanded cuts in the film pertaining to the scene where 'the SS men dressed as Italian knights, kneel before the Pope (Hadrian IV)'.[22]

The tradition upon which Trenker drew in his portrait of Giovanni is hagiographic, akin to medieval lives of saints, but his use of medieval legends is more likely derived from their contemporary oral, literary and cinematic versions to conform to present politics. The film's medievalism relies less on Christian doctrine and rituals, but weds religion to nation formation in a fashion inherent in Fascism and Nazism. As a text designed for mass consumption, the film shifts its politics to the terrain of myth through its romance scenario, its portrait of an ideal hero, metaphoric and spectacular treatment of statuary, landscape, dramatic lighting, and choreography of crowd and battle scenes.

The film begins by foreshadowing the turmoil that will confront the hero in his quest to redeem the land. After a series of shots of massed troops and of banners set against a dramatic background of clouds, the film inserts a prologue that announces: 'This film is a free evocation of the time and spirit of the Italian condottieri who against the passionate background of the Renaissance [*sic*] led the civil militia who rose against the mercenary troops and halfway brought about the unity of the people.' The shots of clouds will become an integral image of the film. A fade to clouds, and an image of a statue of a man on horseback (which will become a coda), dissolves to rapid editing of a fierce battle during which the young Giovanni and his mother are forced to leave their ancestral home and take refuge in the mountains. Moving forward in time to his adulthood, he is photographed in statuesque fashion sitting astride his horse. A lengthy montage sequence associates the rider with an eagle, sky and craggy mountains. A distinction is made between Malatesta, a mercenary and adventurer for worldly gain, and Giovanni, destined to become the mythic saviour of the people. The image of the 'man on horseback' resonates with

The Decline of the West (1918–22), in which Oswald Spengler regards modernity as the ambiguous new barbarism ('Caesarism').[23] Spengler finds parallels between the premodern era, identified with medievalism, and his time. The 'man on horseback' is sometimes construed to allude to the figure of Benito Mussolini, Il Duce, and the coming of the Nazi Führer.

Giovanni is portrayed not as a usurper of power but as a popular charismatic leader. Music plays a central role as a sign of the unity of the leader with his followers. Throughout the film their solidarity is punctuated by choral moments, balanced against a tenor aria, distinguishing the stages of Giovanni's romance with Maria. His identification with the legendary and Wagnerian Siegfried is also alluded to by Giovanni's forging the sword that he carries into battle and which is placed on his body in the final death scene.

In this hagiographic narrative Giovanni is represented as being immersed in situations that are, in Le Goff's words, 'profoundly hostile to the system of the warrior nobility, whose ruin the city wants and appears to be capable of bringing about.'[24] Accordingly the Florentine council, threatened by Giovanni's growing power, warns him to abjure his revolutionary objectives. Undeterred by their threats, he is arrested and tortured, but is liberated by his men. He once again returns to the mountains where he encounters his future wife, Maria Salviati. In contrast to the raven-haired and worldly consort of Malatesta, Tullia, whom Giovanni rejects, blonde Maria is a shepherdess, associated with rustic wholesomeness. Recapitulating the early scenes of Giovanni with his mother, the lovers are filmed against an expanse of sky as if to visualise their spiritual rather than carnal unity. In terms of allegory Tullia is an image of Italy as courtesan, while Maria, as her name suggests, is a pure ideal of woman, identified with his mother. This opposition between the contrasting archetypes of the courtesan and the virginal woman can be traced to Virgil's Dido and Lavinia, and reappears in German and Italian romance literature. The marriage of Giovanni and Maria is celebrated in church with Giovanni's band as witnesses to the ceremony, followed by a series of tableaux that include an image of an angel against a background of sky, shots of grain fields and the recurring image of the statue of a warrior on horseback. These images reinforce the film's allegory, signifying the union of bountiful nature, divine sanction and heroic greatness.

Giovanni's eventual death is visualised through a dissolving of his image into the real heroic statue of Giovanni de' Medici, thus fusing the fictional with the real, and seeking to dramatise, in Hay's words, how the 'movie fiction becomes an authentic legend'.[25] As befits a legendary narrative, the film is indeterminate in its historical invention. In the opening intertitle the action is designated as taking place in the Renaissance, though the events portrayed and the characters, it could be argued, belong to the 'waning' or 'extended' Middle Ages. The historical Giovanni delle Bande Nere was one of the last of the *condottieri*, mercenary captains who were in the service of governments or specific lords acting as hired military combatants. But the film's style and selection of situations are invested in myth and legend rather than strict adherence to a specific moment in time, anachronistically combining Germanic as well as Italian legends, allusion to the western hero on a horse and to Mussolini, if not Hitler.

The film displays, according to Hay, 'a capacity to displace current ideological conflict to a mythical setting, and in turn to reduce history to a diegetical world where the present suddenly becomes charged with value'.[26] The film's mythologising works by its monumental treatment of nature, which transforms the historical landscape of Florence and Rome and serves further to accord legendary status to its historical figure. In its recourse to the past, the film employs affective strategies, analogies and emphases on nature and architecture that situate it in the context of what Gilles Deleuze has described as the movement-image, the conventional filmic storytelling that glosses over its manipulation of time and tends to become ahistorical.[27]

Yet the film is ultimately contradictory. What is striking about *Condottieri* is its reliance on organic images of nature that are, ultimately, overridden by its monumental character through fusing images of statuary with those of the protagonist. Giovanni's image dissolves into sculptures identified with pagan warriors (e.g. Perseus with the head of Andromeda and classical reliefs from Giovanni de' Medici's tomb), rendering him an aesthetic object rather than a specific historical figure. Ironically for the attentive viewer, the film betrays its form of historicising. This form of monumentalising serves to identify the image of Giovanni with an ideal of the Italian nation. It fuses past time with the present, invoking and conjoining two conceptions of time, the linear time in which imperative (and imperial) conflict unfolds and a mythic, eternal time that envisions the hero as reincarnation of past grandeur and glory. His preservation in stone paradoxically also reveals how the film forecloses on historicising. Thus the film corroborates Nietzsche's view of monumental history as having 'no use for absolute veracity ... making what is dissimilar look similar,' diminishing 'difference of motives and instigations,' and culminating in the motto: '"let the dead bury the living"'.[28]

La corona di ferro

Blasetti's *La corona di ferro* appeared in 1941, a critical year for Italy. The coming of war and its attendant privations contributed to the loss of confidence in Mussolini and the Fascist regime. The film is set in a mythical Middle Ages, and its allegory has been interpreted as alluding obliquely to Fascism's abuses of power through dramatising, in Blasetti's words, an 'aversion to violence, conquest, and sterile power'.[29] In contrast to *Condottieri*'s monumentalism, *La corona di ferro* adopts the form of a fairy tale to create an allegory of the illegitimate uses of authority, offering a different perspective on historicising.

Blasetti was an innovative director, editor and scenarist, who in the 1930s and early 1940s was identified with spectacular historical films set in the Middle Ages and the Renaissance, such as *Ettore Fieramosca* (1938) and *La cena delle beffe* (The Fools' Feast, 1942). *La corona di ferro* exemplifies Blasetti's uses of folklore and myth to create a fantastic setting designed to evoke medieval romances. Aimed at a mass audience, the film is populated with legendary Amazonian women, imprisoned princesses, chivalric tournaments, marvellous animal guides and a 'natural' strong man.[30] Indeed, the film's uses of architecture, costuming, landscape and stylisation of characters to create a mythic Middle Ages does not aim for realism. In its eclecticism and use of spectacle, François de la Bretèque comments, 'the entire material of the film constitutes folkloric bric-a-brac simulating a return to the cultural origins of Europe and imprinting on the text a secularisation of themes inherited from the medieval and post-medieval period'.[31]

The film is representative of how the appropriation of medieval images, clothed as fantasy, becomes a vehicle to serve anachronistically the interests of modern history, a treatment repeated later in Monicelli's films. The film text's uses of history become a political allegory in Blasetti's film, with Fascism displaced by medievalism. But *La corona di ferro* is also a spectacle, and one of the first films of the sound era to vie with the visual and technical splendour of silent films, combining allegory, romance and action. The film's predilection for medievalism as fantasy enables the film to address political concerns in oblique fashion, since fantasy, like comedy, is congenial to indirect forms of discourse. Further, the film appears to be an unacknowledged compendium of various literary works, most especially the romances of Tasso and Ariosto as well as of Arthurian legend. A look at Blasetti's sketches for the costumes and sets also suggests parallels between the medieval setting and the film's contemporary historical situation, particularly between the portrait of the king and Mussolini, and between the style of this film and Hollywood costume dramas of the era.

La corona di ferro uses intertitles, as if this were a silent film. The intertitles have the look of medieval illuminated manuscripts and serve as a visual and verbal commentary on antiquity. The print is Gothic and the letters are ornately designed. The film will utilise these intertitles from a 'book' to simulate oral legend as well as historical documents. In addition the film's conventional use of the image of an actual book serves not only to designate passing time in its fluttering pages but to visualise a form of chronicle that metamorphoses from words to visual images. The book lends an aura of authenticity to the fictional narrative, the legend of the Iron Crown, claimed to have taken place in 1240. The film's opening scenes introduce the motifs of war, violence and usurpation of power that will ultimately destroy the court of King Sedemondo, the perpetrator of familial and civil unrest, who had banished his male heir to the throne, Arminio.

Among the folkloric motifs loosely drawn on by Blasetti are the decline and destruction of a kingdom common to Arthurian legend, the switching of babies for their protection ubiquitous in fairy tales, and telltale marks on the body, particularly scars that serve to identify nobility, a device that travelled from the *Odyssey* into medieval romances. The Iron Crown's association with legitimacy, identity and justice mimics the allegory of Excalibur in Arthurian legend. The crown, too heavy for Sedemondo's hands (a sign of illegitimacy), sinks into the earth only to arise after his defeat.

Blasetti exercises restraint in his use of supernatural elements. But when present at the end of the film as wondrous natural transformations, they reveal the impotence of the king, the triumph of Arminio and the reconciliation of warring factions. The narrative recapitulates the myth of the changeling of royal birth who is raised in natural surroundings and then, after a series of trials, is restored to his rightful status as heir to the kingdom.[32] The exiled Arminio's name is possibly an allusion to Tacitus' heroic rebel chieftain Arminius, who defeated the Romans and brought peace to the land. The fully grown and physically powerful Arminio, dressed in animal skins, escapes from the gorge with the aid of a giant who kills the guard, a lion and later a stag.

Athletic, he swings from trees and swims to firm ground. Arminio is a hybrid creation, an amalgam of several heroic figures: Rinaldo; Orlando; Robin Hood; Tarzan; the Italian popular tradition of the 'uomo forte' (strong man) who is finally tamed and assumes his proper aristocratic position; and the 'wild man' (*un selvaggio*), a familiar figure in Arthurian legend and in romance literature (e.g. Edmund Spenser's *Faerie Queene*).

The film's tournament scene becomes the opportunity not only to introduce the spectacle of pageantry and physical trials but also to reintroduce Arminio into the world of the court, where he will be a contender for the hand of Elsa, Sedemondo's daughter. Elsa is modelled on many heroines of romance, Angelica or Alcina in *Orlando Furioso* and in folk tales. Played by blonde and delicate-looking Elisa Cegani, she contrasts sharply with dark-haired and athletic Tundra. Elsa is the fairy-tale princess of Sleeping Beauty. She has been imprisoned in the splendid court at Kindaor that resembles the architecture of an oriental palace, since the orient is often equated with exoticism. Elsa is barely visible through numerous veils that surround her chamber as she languidly reclines on a luxurious bed (Figure 9). A tournament will be her first opportunity to see the world. The king comes to awaken Elsa, covers her in jewels and praises her beauty. The element of incest is suggested here and will play a role later in confounding Elsa's romantic attachment to Arminio. The other prominent female figure in the narrative, Tundra, who dresses and acts like a warrior and attempts to rescue Arminio twice, is derived from a host of romance narratives: Spenser's Amazonian Britomart, the Wagnerian Brünhilde, Ariosto's Bradamante and Tasso's Clorinda.

The tournament is a vision of antiquarianism in which the book, costumes, jewellery, goblets, tapestries, banners and weapons animate the historical mise-en-scène. As might be expected from popular, particularly cinematic, renditions of medievalism, the tournament is announced by long-stemmed trumpets, carefully choreographed images of the assembled royalty and bystanders, the arena of combat and the richly ornate costumes of the participants from different regions, including the Prince of Tartars who offers another familiar vision of oriental splendour in his garb and in the gifts he brings to the king. Elsa and Arminio fall in love at this point, but the film ends with Elsa's death and the miraculous reconciliation of father and son.

This eclectic film proffers a catalogue of the medieval imaginary derived from earlier heroic poems and fairy tales. The style demon-

9 The fairy-tale princess Elsa in *La corona di ferro* (1941),
Superfilm Dist. Corp/ Photofest, copyright Superfilm Dist. Corp,
Courtesy of Photofest, by permission

strates, as Adriano Aprà and Patrizia Pistagnesi have it, the director's
'visual and narrative madness' that bespeaks a commitment to 'film
spectacle in which his ambitions as a moralist could find a metaphoric
outlet'.³³ Blasetti's 'madness' pertains to the film's highly stylised acting,
lavish and ornate sets, costuming, camera position, lighting and
montage editing. Special effects produce the spectacular milieu of
combat and tournament scenes, and the design of the fabulous landscape and architecture to invent the aura of a marvellous, remote and
magical mise-en-scène that evokes parallels between the mythical and
the contemporary world. The stereotypical costumes by Gino Sensani
also enhance the dreamlike and mythic characters of the narrative:
Arminio's Tarzan-like outfit, the king's rich furs and jewels, Elsa's light
colours and gossamer fabrics and Tundra's male clothes.

La corona di ferro is an example of the spectacular dimensions
of mass cinema, using literary allusion and cinematic techniques to
provoke associations between an invented past and an elusive present.
The film is also illustrative of how the medieval imaginary, even when

it seeks to address national identity, exceeds geographic boundaries. Further, the film participates in the recognisable and shared international language of fantasy and of the cinematic medium, making it accessible certainly to Western European audiences. The film's folkloric treatment does not produce a view of the past as it really was, but relies on analogies to make connections to the present. Umberto Eco has identified parallels between that time and the present as more numerous than those of the succeeding eras. This neo-medievalism involves illegitimate usurpation and abuse of power, nomadism, cultic practices, apocalyptic thinking, the disasters of war and a utopian desire for new leadership and peace.[34] However, a study of cinematic uses of the past reveals that the penchant for historical films is not confined to medievalism but also includes other epochs like the Risorgimento and Fascism, and other ideological, political and aesthetic concerns. What the films share is a tendency toward allegorising to re-imagine the past and present, if not future.

The eclectic and spectacular use of folklore, legend and myth used in Blasetti's film is related to forms of allegorising history in a manner proposed by Walter Benjamin: 'Allegories are, in the realm of thoughts, what ruins are in the realm of things ... The quintessence of these decaying objects is the polar opposite to the idea of transfigured nature ... But it is as something incomplete and imperfect that objects stare out from the allegorical structure.'[35]

Significantly, the imagery of decay and ruin belongs to a later, baroque mode of allegorising that, as Benjamin was at pains to elaborate in his *Origin of German Tragic Drama*, is strikingly different from classical conceptions of history and aesthetics: 'The allegorical physiognomy of the nature-history is present in reality in the form of the ruin ... in this guise history does not assume the form of the process of an eternal life so much as that of irresistible decay.'[36] Modern allegory belongs to a world of time, to a vision of history whose importance 'resides in the stations of its decline ... [and] gives rise not only to the enigmatic nature of human existence' but also to 'the biographical historicity of the individual.'[37] In the case of Monicelli's films we are given a world that emphasises the inevitability of failure, of death and perpetual dissolution. The film's preoccupation with mortality, decline and violence couched in terms of a dark medievalism is a reflection on 'man's suffering and cruelty, made bearable through stately, even absurd form: A play of sorrow.'[38] Hence the comedic vision of the film, reliant on irony and parody and on fragmentary episodes and parabolic form, introduces a view of history that satirises heroism and a belief in material progress.

The fragmentary and imperfect character of history is a correlative for modernity. Cinema, too, in its editing and framing process, is an instance of yoking discrete images and bringing them into association or conflict with each other, a process similar to high modernism and its 'open work', which, in Eco's terms, describes James Joyce's writing (and his own): 'If you take away the transcendent God from the world of the Middle Ages, you have the world of Joyce [or of cinema]'.[39] You also have the historical world of Monicelli's *Brancaleone* films.

Antonio Gramsci's conception of folklore is also germane to an understanding of the eclectic nature of folklore, if ultimately directed toward rational, revolutionary and politically unifying goals. For Gramsci folklore was a heterogeneous mode of thinking. In identifying its historical and cultural significance, he wrote:

> This conception of the world is ... many-sided – not only because it includes different and juxtaposed elements, but also because it is stratified, from the more crude to the less crude – if, indeed, one should not speak of a confused agglomerate of fragments of all the conceptions of the world and of life that have succeeded one another in history. In fact, it is only in folklore that one finds surviving evidence, adulterated and mutilated, of the majority of these conceptions.[40]

The 'conceptions' to which Gramsci alludes are 'sediments' of the past, involving language, literature, popular history and technologies. Gramsci's comments, like those of Benjamin, suggest that folklore expresses the stratified, elusive character of history and memory. Cinematic fables of power, such as *Condottieri* and *La corona di ferro*, are allegories containing the shards of residual elements and emergent cultural memories of medievalism as legend and folklore.

'The crystals of time': decomposing the past

Angelo Restivo has characterised Italian cinema and society as in a state of 'vital crisis ... connected, first, to the process of political and economic organisation that reconstructed the nation into the Italy we know today; and, secondly, to the larger and more "invisible" processes that have marked the transformation of global capitalism in the postwar period'.[41] This 'crisis' witnessed a radical historical rupture and the emergence of a new 'aesthetic of reality', in which the cinema played a commanding role in altering representation, especially evident in its address of narratives of history and nation.[42]

Critical attention in the postwar years focused on the art cinema of Michelangelo Antonioni and Pier Paolo Pasolini, while largely ignoring the contributions of such popular film-makers as Mario Monicelli. Each of these three film-makers works within the paradigm Gilles Deleuze has termed the 'time-image' characteristic of the tendency to examine 'the social antagonisms that existed at the level of the Real of history'.[43] In the cinema of the time-image the boundaries between the imaginary and the real, the physical and the mental become indiscernible, whereas in the traditional realist cinema these boundaries are distinct. In the time-image disconnected spaces and aberrant movement privilege temporality, opening on to new modes for thinking history through images. Cinema of the time-image is no longer a cinema of chronology and action: it is a cinema where different layers of present and past co-exist and character is 'prey to a vision, pursued by it or pursuing it, rather than engaged in an action'.[44]

Monicelli's comic vision of how belief in agency has fallen into crisis was eminently suited to the cinema of the time-image. Working in the generic mode of *commedia all' italiana*, in films set in earlier historical moments, such as *La grande guerra* (The Great War, 1958) and *I compagni* (The Organiser, 1959), Monicelli creates anti-heroes, who are 'inept, self-centred, shallow, yet often lovable'.[45] He places them in absurd situations that often end in failure, portraying, as Peter Bondanella believes, a 'darker, more ironic, and cynical vision of Italian life'.[46] Consonant with the time-image, the characters are no longer truthful; they are forgers, thieves, impostors and confidence men; and truth becomes a matter not of judging their goodness or badness but of the truthfulness of the storyteller and the act of storytelling. Monicelli's *L'armata Brancaleone* and *Brancaleone alle crociate*, starring the versatile actor Vittorio Gassman, are parodies of historical epics and romances.

Unlike the Trenker and Blasetti films, Monicelli's films serve as a critical gloss on the narrative strategies that have animated 'the medieval imagination' by modifying folklore and, hence, introducing a different, but not necessarily nostalgic or antagonistic conception of that past in relation to modernity. Monicelli's films are satiric, utilising parody and farce to explore affinities between medievalism and contemporary cultural and political life that belong to a modernist or postmodernist perspective in their comic uses of irony, pastiche, animation and metacinema.

The films present a protagonist who overturns heroic patterns to render serio-comic a lofty vision of knight errantry. The influence of the *commedia dell'arte* is most obvious in Gassman's portrayal of Brancaleone, who is reminiscent of the figure of the braggart, the *miles gloriosus*. Brancaleone ('the lion's talon') is also a descendant of picaresque literature, in particular of Don Quixote and his squire Sancho Panza. Adhering to the quest narrative, the films employ an episodic form that permits an encyclopaedic treatment of a range of characters and situations.

In the first film, *L'armata Brancaleone*, Brancaleone's squires are thieves, a Jew, a wayward prospective bride, a mad monk leading a group of crusaders and a disinherited nobleman. In the second film, *Brancaleone alle crociate*, Brancaleone's followers are a German mercenary, a sorceress, a deranged religious fanatic, a dwarf and a princess disguised as a leper. The films take Brancaleone through a landscape fraught with obstacles that will inevitably entail his having to join crusaders (but the spectacle of the crusades is not the primary focus in these films). The stages of the journey of the knight involve him (and the spectator) in encounters designed to invoke a medieval social milieu, including social, gendered and religious differences.

L'armata Brancaleone

In *L'armata Brancaleone* the viewer is invited to witness the effects of disease, war, anti-Semitism, religious intolerance, and self-seeking and corrupt economic institutions that are as much indebted to medieval literature as to modern films. The film's portraits of medievalism and parody of quest narratives draw on character types and events characteristic of novels by such writers as Sir Walter Scott (*Ivanhoe*, 1819, and *The Talisman*, 1825) and also by such Hollywood films as *The Adventures of Robin Hood* (1938) and *Ivanhoe* (1952). However, to assume that *L'armata Brancaleone* is a negative picture of medievalism in contrast to enlightened modernity would be to misconstrue the film's indebtedness to the *commedia dell'arte*, Dante, Boccaccio, Chaucer and to their comic vision. The film returns to a deceptively realistic past to demolish nostalgic portraits of medievalism. Instead of setting the past in opposition to the present, the film ironically finds parallels; and Brancaleone, for all of his vaingloriousness, emerges as a sympathetic character, as do his ragged outcast followers.

The images convey the physical hardships of this world; but, instead of offering a sentimental portrait of its inhabitants, present them as mercenary, superstitious and devious. The journey is set in motion by the (assumed) brutal killing of a knight. Two peasants, Mangoldo and Taccone, plunder the knight's belongings and sell them to an anti-Semitically portrayed Jewish merchant, Abacuc. Abacuc, Mangoldo and Taccone chance on Brancaleone, an impoverished knight who becomes their leader. Gassman, as the picaresque Brancaleone, with wild hair, tattered garments, rusty armour and a recalcitrant yellow-painted nag Aquilante (reminiscent of Quixote's Rosinante), undertakes the journey to claim the dead knight's kingdom of Aurocastro (Figure 10). In a mock-epic scene Brancaleone proclaims himself the men's 'Duce', a term reverberating with its Fascist associations, and commands them to swear fealty.

As a means of distancing, the ragged men's journey is accompanied by persistent refrains of a lyric ('Branca, Branca, Branca, leone, leone, leone') and by inserted animated segments. Further, similar to the cartoons, the characters resemble marionettes in their stilted and highly choreographed movement. Through these techniques the film deflects viewers' attention away from affective identification with the characters on to an absurd world where expectations are constantly thwarted. For example, their journey for booty takes them to a castle where Brancaleone finds a beautiful woman who offers him sexual delights. His anticipation is abruptly curtailed when he discovers that the inhabitants of the castle have died from the plague. In the men's terror and haste to escape this pestilential place, the film portrays the anxiety occasioned by the fear of contagion and of sexual contact with 'otherness' that is identified with the infirm body and death.[47] This episode not only introduces the preoccupation with mortality that will play an even more prominent role in *Brancaleone alle crociate* but also serves to draw attention to the element of chance that governs their movement. The comedy arises from a disparity between their confidence in success and its predictable frustration. The film's incremental, reiterative concern with the inevitability of failure is its most cogent challenge to the consolations of religion as well as the belief in modern conceptions of material progress and individual agency.

The men's encounter with crusaders on their way to the Holy Land underscores the theme of religious intolerance in the form of anti-Semitism as well as of false piety. Zenone, a fanatical Christian, inveighs against the presence of the impure Jew in Brancaleone's army, and demands that Abacuc be cleansed. The Jew is 'baptised' by being dropped from a bridge and plunged in the rocky waters below. Zenone insists further that an unwieldy large group of men is able to traverse an unstable bridge only to see some fall to their death. Zenone, the man of faith, piously ascribes this misfortune to God's will; the dead

10 The picaresque impoverished knight Brancaleone in *L'armata Brancaleone* (1966), Superfilm Dist. Corp/ Photofest, copyright Superfilm Dist. Corp, Courtesy of Photofest, by permission

will be redeemed in the afterlife. Thus the film addresses the expend-
ability of life. When Abacuc dies, the Jew is buried by Brancaleone
with the reassurance that he will go to a better life than that on earth,
whether it be Christian paradise or not, thus invoking the long history
of excluding Jews from social and ethical consideration as human.

The film concludes with failure. Brancaleone and his followers have
not succeeded in any of their enterprises, though they have managed
to escape from imprisonment and death. The film has resisted any
opportunity to offer either material or spiritual resolution to the hardships encountered on this allegorical journey, though it has offered
the spectator an opportunity to question values and beliefs in a
benevolent and just world. The film's invention of the Middle Ages
pits threadbare, well-meaning rogues against well-equipped, ruthless
forces: Brancaleone's torture and imprisonment by the vengeful Duke
in the Matelda episode, the cruel customs that force a young woman
to marry a nobleman for status, the vain attempts of a son to regain his
patrimony and the crusaders' cruel treatment of Abacuc.

Through comedy, the film has appropriated narratives of chivalry
and romance epics to expose their often idealist representation in the
cinema, focusing on the vulnerable physical body and on the likeli-
hood of failure rather than success. Instead of emphasising spiritual
rewards for the subjugated, the film suggests how cinematic history,
especially the popular history of medievalism on film, often forgets or
works against subalterns. While appearing to be a parody of knight
errantry, the more serious dimension of the history portrayed through
Brancaleone's army is a history of survival through wits and collective endeavour, a history that connects it to a desired critique of the
present of the film's production. There are no economic miracles, nor,
for that matter, miracles at all. In Monicelli's comic world, as T. G. A.
Nelson writes of comedy, 'all goodness is weakness or hypocrisy and
the supreme virtue is quickness of wit'.[48] Monicelli's conception of the
Middle Ages is informed by the heritage of neo-realism with its resistance to idealised character portraits and situations. His medievalism
bespeaks his contemporaneity, preferring to focus on the dispossessed
and lower classes in their struggle to survive in a hostile world.

The characters in this film embody this view in their attempts to
stay alive by their cleverness. By making them picaresque rogues, they
become examples of what Nelson terms 'knight-errantry minus the
illusions'.[49] The film has followed the route of comedy that debunks the
mighty and powerful through parodying traditional values and offi-

cial perceptions of behaviour. In its visualisation of an unsuccessful quest, the film has consistently portrayed a world turned upside-down to reflect on contemporary social values and political injustice. This comic reversal is not far removed from earlier satiric forms of medievalism expressed in Cervantes, Boccaccio and Chaucer, as well as in Pasolini's cinematic versions in *La trilogia di vita* (The Trilogy of Life): *Il Decameron* (The Decameron, 1971), *I Racconti di Canterbury* (Canterbury Tales, 1972) and *Il Fiore delle mille e una notte* (Arabian Nights, 1974) to probe the travesties of bourgeois culture.

Brancaleone alle crociate

Brancaleone alle crociate focuses more specifically on the crusades compared to *L'armata Brancaleone*. The crusades have been particularly popular in films with medieval content. The crusades most commonly represented in film are the First Crusade (1095–99) with its focus on the conquest of Jerusalem, and the Third Crusade (1189–92), the Crusade of the Kings, involving the English King Richard I, the German Emperor Frederick Barbarossa, Philip II of France and the Sultan Salah al-Dīn (Saladin).[50] Monicelli's film eclectically calls on select aspects of these crusades as well as elements of the 'Children's Crusade' (1212), reputed to have been composed not of actual children but more likely of serfs and dispossessed young men. *Brancaleone alle crociate* delves more deeply than the earlier *Brancaleone* film into a medieval landscape, focusing on madness, witchcraft, leprosy, dwarfism, papal legitimacy, fanaticism and death. This film also incorporates animated cartoons, drawn in childlike fashion under the credits and interspersed throughout the film. The animation serves to minimise the epic dimensions of the action, to reduce its monumentality through deliberate understatement, meiosis and familiar satiric devices. The familiar characters and situations identified with many popular films on medievalism and the crusades are systematically altered or demolished by the film's comic tone.[51]

In this sequel to *L'armata Brancaleone*, the dubious knight and a group of chanting Christian pilgrims set out on their journey to the Holy Land. Unfortunately, the pilgrims land in Sicily and are massacred by supporters of Pope Clement. Brancaleone confronts Death, reminiscent of the knight in Ingmar Bergman's *The Seventh Seal* (1975), and bargains with him for his life. Brancaleone chooses a short and glorious life consonant with legends of chivalry; and Death allows him a momentary reprieve, vowing to return for him at the end of seven months.

Brancaleone's adventures begin with the rescue of a baby, whom he will undertake to restore to its father, the King of Sicily. This lofty mission becomes the pretext for subsequent adventures, providing him with the motivation to assume the role of a knight rescuer, with the assistance of new followers drawn from the ranks of desperate, stunted and outlawed humans whom he encounters. One of his first recruits rams his head repeatedly against a tree trunk while raving that he has committed an unpardonable sin that cannot be revealed. The satiric dimension of this episode focuses (as do all the other episodes) on ignorance and superstition largely attributed to Catholicism. The various characters who are enlisted in this crusade are perpetrators and victims in what de la Bretèque calls a 'catalogue of representatives of medieval social institutions'.[52]

Another outcast, Tiburzia, is a woman encountered while about to be burned at the stake for witchcraft. She must pass bizarre and nonsensical 'proofs' of witchcraft similar to those portrayed in another, later, television comedy set in the Middle Ages, *Monty Python and the Holy Grail* (1975). Tiburzia is 'rescued' by Brancaleone, and witchcraft and magic become central to the events that follow. This film is more attentive than *L'armata Brancaleone* to the outcast and diseased creatures of God and to physical, status and social difference. According to Monicelli, who not only directed the film but also wrote the story and script together with the brilliant duo of Agenore Incrocci and Furio Scarpelli (identified together under the name of Age), 'we wanted to show an epoch of barbarism ... ignorance, fear, famine that characterised this time ... A Europe peopled with illiterates and ravaged by wars and epidemics'.[53]

Brancaleone alle crociate may seem didactic, addressing the Middle Ages conventionally in accord with the clichés characteristic of popular representations of the period.[54] But this film is an invented history built on a medieval imaginary in harmony with the film's political and philosophic critique of barbarism in the present, a critique that through its portraits of the brutal treatment of women, the diseased and the physically deformed; senseless massacre of populations; and quest for economic gain invites parallels with the present. The film epitomises through satiric allegory and parody, excess, exaggeration and inversion Walter Benjamin's thesis on history that 'there is no document of civilization which is not at the same time a document of barbarism'.[55] The stylised treatment alerts the spectator to incongruities – names, body parts and actions – that strip away the surface to reveal incongruities, disorder and violence masquerading as civility. The film's comedy becomes a form of 'effective history' in its puncturing of inherited conceptions of the past not from superior heights but, in Michel Foucault's terms, from a shortening of 'vision to those things nearest it … [and] if it chances on lofty epochs, it is with the suspicion – not vindictive but joyous – of finding a barbarous and shameful confusion.'[56]

The papacy also does not escape satirising. The legitimacy of the crusade (and of papal power) is called into question; and Brancaleone, at the instigation of a holy man, the stylite Columbino, volunteers to walk on hot coals to distinguish the 'real' pope from the anti-pope. Brancaleone's physical trial to determine proper authority to the papal throne parallels and satirises legendary trials of torture as a theatre to coerce and legitimise 'truth'. In this episode, one familiar to romance narratives and similar as well as to the episode of Tiburzia's nearburning at the stake, the film exposes the senselessness of violence done to the body in the name of conformity.

The film also plays with other images of the body, especially those that do not conform to common standards of beauty, to highlight its irreverent outlook. Another familiar character in medieval narratives, the leper, associated with the 'repulsive Middle Ages', becomes, in the film, a pretext for a meditation on death.[57] Comedy relies on the materiality and integrity of the human body and its connection to the body politic, and the film is relentless in its insistence on corporeality as an index to social health or disease. Thus leprosy becomes a significant element of the film's medievalism. The outcast leper is presented through the terrified responses of others fearing contagion and the sight of disfigurement. At first the group, reacting in horror and disgust, order the leper to leave. After reconsideration, they allow the leper as a creature of God to join them, but command him to remain at a respectable distance. Later the leper is revealed to be a princess in disguise. Seeking to regain her kingdom after the death of her husband, she adopted the garb of a leper to protect herself from being assaulted by men. However, the introduction of leprosy is a clue to the film's designs on the body, a form of what Carlo Ginzburg identifies as 'aphoristic … an attempt to formulate evaluations of man and society on the basis of symptoms and clues.'[58] The clues to these parallels also involve a dwarf who joins the group and is then mortally wounded. Before he dies, the dwarf asks if he will go to Paradise and is reassured by Brancaleone that he will go to a special Paradise where all men are dwarfs. The dwarf's dissatisfaction with his body has served to highlight the film's exploration of the nature and effects of physical monstrosity. Ultimately, his monstrosity is an example of the film's challenge to reigning aesthetic and cultural norms, both past and present.

These norms are tied to the motif of visibility that are integral to cinematic (and cultural) perception. This motif is further developed when Brancaleone returns the royal baby. The king rejects his son, claiming he cannot see the child's birthmark. However, Tiburzia claims to have caused it to disappear, and, to prove her sorcery, she causes herself to disappear. In a work that is reflexive about its role as cinema, vision serves a dual function. Firstly, vision functions through the magic of cinema that can make images appear and disappear with enormous consequences for recollection and memory. Secondly, vision functions through the film's uses of medievalism that, through allegory and parable, make visible to the spectator the consequences of blindness to physical, hence mental and ethical life.

The final episodes of the film involve a paradoxical sense of success through failure. As Death is about to end Brancaleone's life after seven months, Tiburzia intervenes. The episode is reminiscent of the final canto of *Gerusalemme Liberata*, where the dying sorceress, Armida, is reconciled with Rinaldo. Tiburzia is mortally wounded, but Death disappears. Asked by Brancaleone why she intervened, Tiburzia confesses that her sacrifice was out of love for him. Thus Brancaleone's worldly defeats are mitigated by a magical gesture: *amor vincit omnia*.

At the heart of Monicelli's comedy is a cinematic historian at work, self-consciously drawing on an ensemble of numerous sources for his medieval imagination: Cervantes, folklore, heroic epic (like *Gerusalemme Liberata*) and also films (like *The Seventh Seal*). The images are eclectic: cartoons, ceremonial tableaux (of combat, wedding feasts, funeral rituals), and a cornucopia of caricatures of young females, moribund elderly males, diseased and malformed figures derived from these sources. The verbal language is also eclectic, a mixture of various regional (often Sicilian) dialects, Latinate and pseudo-Latinate constructions and foreign phrases.[59] The second *Brancaleone* film injects poetry into the dialogue: the characters begin to speak in rhymed couplets (another instance of the film's evocation of earlier heroic poems), but the elevated poetry is joined to prosaic, colloquial, even obscene language reminiscent of goliardic literature with its crude satiric characterisations. The eclectic language highlights the film's juxtaposing high and low culture and of advancing the film's mixing of genres (epic, romance and satiric comedy), of physicality and spirituality, and of medievalism and modernity.

Epilogue

Italian cinema from its earliest years has been the heir of literary texts that have drawn on the historical past, including Virgilian epic, writings on Roman history, heroic romances and Dante's *Commedia*. Indeed one of the dominant characteristics of Italian cinematic production has been its obsession with historical representation. The mass media have played a role in the creation and dissemination of the medieval imaginary. From silent versions of Dante's *Inferno* (1909) to *Condottieri* and *La corona di ferro*, the postwar epoch of Rossellini's *Francesco giullare di dio* (Francis, God's Jester, 1950), and *Giovanna d'Arco al rogo* (Joan of Arc at the Stake, 1954), Pasolini's *Uccellacci e Uccellini* (Hawks and Sparrows, 1966), his *Trilogia di vita* and Monicelli's *Brancaleone* films, film-makers have gravitated toward medievalism to explore philosophical, political and aesthetic concerns, albeit in different styles and with differing effects. History may be represented monumentally as in *Condottieri*, as fantasy and folklore in Blasetti's *La corona di ferro*, and as satire in Monicelli's works.

The Trenker film belongs to Deleuze's regime of the movement-image that relies on a form of monumentality, on an epic vision that valorises heroic action on behalf of ensuring the continuity of the 'nation-civilisation'.[60] The medievalism of the Blasetti film also relies via allegory on implied parallels between the imaginary medieval world and the implied present of the film's production. It also involves warring factions and duels, but its antiquarianism emphasises material opulence (architecture, costuming, jewels, armour) that visualises the stakes in the contest between decadent and healthy civilisations. But both films meet in their tendency to construct a form of universal history by way of utopia.

By contrast, the *Brancaleone* films adhere more closely to the regime of the time-image. While situating their action within the medieval imaginary, the films disturb binary analogies between the great moments of the past and the present. They tend in the direction of Benjamin's conceptions of modern allegory, whereby 'the false appearance of totality is extinguished'.[61] As exemplary of the cinema of the time-image, Monicelli's films unsettle conceptions of totality and consensus. In their fractured and elliptical narratives; disconnected spaces and aberrant movement; and inept, dysfunctional characters, they introduce, as Deleuze says of modern cinema, 'a break in the link between man and the world', forcing the viewer to confront 'something intolerable in the world and ... unthinkable in thought'.[62] Their form of medievalism opens on to new modes for rethinking history through cinematic images.

These four films on medievalism, irrespective of their genres, reveal their transnational character through their reliance on intertextuality and anachronism; their uses of literary and cinematic texts that transgress national boundaries; their union of elite and popular texts; and their reliance on an allegorical mode that refashions the past. As illustrated by the writings of Jacques Le Goff and François Amy de la Bretèque, an important access to the medieval imaginary is not only through academic histories and canonical literature but also through popular literature and cinema of the kind described here. These critics' analyses of the forms and reception of medievalism address the role of popular beliefs and transmitted folklore as an inevitable component, for better or worse, of making and remaking history. Their critical works illuminate how medievalism engages with contemporary cultural and political issues to assess the role of the past in the twentieth and twenty-first centuries.

Notes

1 Gianfranco Miro Gori, *Patria Diva: la storia d'Italia nei film del Ventennio* (Florence: Usher, 1988), p. 12.

2 Marcia Landy, *The Folklore of Consensus: Theatricality in the Italian Cinema 1930–1943* (Albany: State University of New York Press, 1998), p. 45.

3 James Hay, *Popular Film Culture in Fascist Italy: The Passing of the Rex* (Bloomington: University of Indiana Press, 1986); Ruth Ben-Ghiat, *Fascist Modernities: Italy, 1922–1945* (Berkeley: University of California Press, 2001); Marcia Landy, *Fascism in Film: The Italian Commercial Cinema, 1931-1943* (Princeton: University of Princeton Press, 1986).

4 Edward R. Tannenbaum, *Fascism in Italy: Society and Culture, 1922-1945* (London: Allen Lane, 1973), p. 12.

5 Hay, *Popular Film Culture*, p. 155.

6 Guido Fink, 'Italian cinema, to be or to have been: time and history', *Cultures: Flashback: Films and History*, 2:1 (1964), 115–39 (121).

7 Angela Dalle Vacche, *The Body in the Mirror: Shapes of History in Italian Cinema* (Princeton: Princeton University Press, 1992), pp. 218–51.

8 Angelo Restivo, *The Cinema of Economic Miracles: Visuality and Moderniza-

tion in the Italian Art Film (Durham, NC: Duke University Press, 2002), p. 10.

9 Restivo, *Cinema of Economic Miracles*, p. 153.

10 Philip Rosen, *Change Mummified: Cinema, Historicity, Theory* (Minneapolis: University of Minnesota Press, 2001), p. 87.

11 *Ibid.*, p. 87.

12 Jacques Rancière, *The Names of History: On the Poetics of Knowledge*, trans. Hassan Melehy (Minneapolis: University of Minnesota Press, 1994), p. 103.

13 See Sue Harper, 'Historical pleasures: Gainsborough and the costume melodrama,' in Christine Gledhill (ed.), *Home Is Where the Heart Is: Studies in Melodrama and the Woman's Film* (London: BFI, 1978), pp. 167–97.

14 Peter Bondanella, *Umberto Eco and the Open Text: Semiotics, Fiction and Popular Culture* (Cambridge: Cambridge University Press, 1997), esp. p. 33; Umberto Eco, *Travels in Hyperreality: Essays*, trans. William Weaver (San Diego: Harcourt Brace Jovanovich, 1988 [1973]), esp. p. 83.

15 Bondanella, *Umberto Eco*, pp. 18, 39–40.

16 See François Amy de la Bretèque, *L'Imaginaire médiéval dans le cinéma occidental* (Paris: Champion, 2004), esp. pp. 111, 117.

17 Friedrich Nietzsche, 'The uses and disadvantages of history for life,' in Nietzsche, *Untimely Meditations*, trans. R. J. Hollingdale (Cambridge: Cambridge University Press, 1991 [1874]), pp. 57–125 (pp. 71, 72).

18 Jacques Le Goff, *The Medieval Imagination*, trans. Arthur Goldhammer (Chicago: University of Chicago Press, 1988 [1985]), p. 47.

19 Hay, *Popular Film Culture*, p. 162.

20 Christopher Frayling, *Cowboys and Westerns from Karl May to Sergio Leone* (London: Tauris, 2000), p. 19.

21 See, for example, Gian Piero Brunetta, *Storia del cinema italiano*, 4 vols (Rome: Riuniti, 2001 [1979–82]), Vol. 2: *Il cinema del regime 1929–1945*, p. 134.

22 Franz A. Birgel, 'Luis Trenker: a rebel in the Third Reich? *Der Rebell*, *Der verlorene Sohn*, and *Der Kaiser von Kalifornien*, *Condottieri*, and *Der Feuerteufel*,' in Robert C. Reimer (ed.), *Cultural History through a National Socialist Lens: Essays on the Cinema of the Third Reich* (Rochester, NY: Camden House, 2000), pp. 37–64 (p. 49).

23 Oswald Spengler, *The Decline of the West*, trans. Charles Francis Atkinson, 2 vols (London: Allen & Unwin, 1926–28 [1918–22]).

24 Le Goff, *The Medieval Imagination*, p. 175.

25 Hay, *Popular Film Culture*, p. 164.

26 *Ibid.*, p. 186.

27 Gilles Deleuze, *Cinema 1: The Movement-Image*, trans. Hugh Tomlinson and Barbara Habberjam (Minneapolis: University of Minnesota Press, 2001 [1983]), pp. 148, 149, 150.

28 Nietzsche, 'The uses and disadvantages of history for life,' pp. 70, 72.

29 Brunetta, *Storia del cinema Italiano*, vol. 2, p. 287.

30 Claver Salizzato and Vito Zagarrio (eds), *La corona di ferro: un modo di produzione italiano* (Rome: Di Giacomo, 1985), p. 3.

31 De la Bretèque, *L'Imaginaire médiéval*, p. 962, my translation. See also Mario Savio, *Ma l'amore no: realismo, formalismo, propaganda e telefoni bianchi nel*

cinema italiano di regime (1930–1943) (Milan: Sonzogno, 1975), p. 93.

32 Hay, *Popular Film Culture*, p. 163.

33 Adriano Aprà and Patrizia Pistagnesi, *The Fabulous Thirties: Italian Cinema 1929–1944* (Milan: Electa, 1979), pp. 76–7.

34 Eco, *Travels in Hyperreality*, pp. 59–87.

35 Benjamin, *The Origin of German Tragic Drama*, trans. John Osborne (London: Verso, 1998), pp. 178, 179, 186.

36 *Ibid.*, pp. 177–8.

37 *Ibid.*, p. 166.

38 *Ibid.*, p. 24.

39 Bondanella, *Umberto Eco*, p. 32.

40 Antonio Gramsci, *Selections from the Cultural Writings*, ed. David Forgacs and Geoffrey Nowell-Smith, trans. William Boelhower (Cambridge, MA: Harvard University Press, 1985), p. 189.

41 Restivo, *Cinema of Economic Miracles*, p. 4.

42 *Ibid.*, p. 5.

43 Deleuze, *Cinema 2: The Time-Image*, trans. Hugh Tomlinson and Robert Galeta (Minneapolis: University of Minnesota Press, 2001 [1985]), p. 10.

44 Deleuze, *Cinema 2*, p. 3.

45 Restivo, *Cinema of Economic Miracles*, p. 89.

46 Peter Bondanella, *Italian Cinema: From Neorealism to the Present* (New York: Continuum, 2003), p. 145.

47 John Aberth, *A Knight at the Movies: Medieval History on Film* (New York: Routledge, 2003), pp. 197–257.

48 T. G. A. Nelson, *Comedy: An Introduction to Literature, Drama, and Cinema* (Oxford: Oxford University Press, 1990), p. 101.

49 *Ibid.*, p. 93.

50 De la Bretèque, *L'Imaginaire médiéval*, pp. 23, 514.

51 *Ibid.*, p. 533.

52 *Ibid.*, p. 533.

53 *Ibid.*, p. 533.

54 See also Eco, *Travels in Hyperreality*, p. 69.

55 Walter Benjamin, *Illuminations* (New York: Schocken, 1976 [1955]), p. 256.

56 Michel Foucault, *Language, Counter-Memory, Practice: Selected Essays and Interviews*, trans. Daniel F. Bouchard and Sherry Simon (Ithaca: Cornell University Press, 1980 [1977], p. 155.

57 De la Bretèque, *L'Imaginaire médiéval*, pp. 699–706.

58 Carlo Ginzburg, *Clues, Myths, and the Historical Method*, trans. John and Anne Tedeschi (Baltimore: Johns Hopkins University Press, 1989 [1986]), p. 124.

59 Brunetta, *Storia del cinema italiano*, vol. 4: *Dal miracolo economico agli anni novanta, 1960-1993*, p. 97.

60 Deleuze, *Cinema 1*, p. 151.

61 Benjamin, *Origin of German Tragic Drama*, p. 176.

62 Deleuze, *Cinema 2*, p. 169.

6

Towards a theory of medieval film music

Alison Tara Walker

Even though studies of medieval films include articles, books and entire conferences, critics tend to be silent on the subject of music in films about the medieval period, even though music is a conventional part of narrative cinema. Films use their soundtracks to engage audiences' emotional responses, to sell CDs and to provide a musical counterpoint to the images on screen. This chapter highlights the music of four medieval films: the folk-inspired melodies of *Brother Sun Sister Moon* (1972), the synthesised keyboards of *Ladyhawke* (1985), the sweeping orchestration of *Robin Hood: Prince of Thieves* (1991) and the rock-and-roll soundtrack of *A Knight's Tale* (2001). The films I analyse use music to bridge a gap between the postmodern and medieval and to add new narrative information that is not present in the films' visual story. These films question the subservient position of the soundtrack within most films, which traditionally relegates film music to the background in favour of the onscreen images.[1] Music is integral to the filmic process, and does not simply accompany onscreen images. So, too, can the study of film music serve as a powerful analytic tool for critics studying medievalism.

Image and sound in medieval cinema: medievalism and disphasure

Our notion of what constructs the medieval period cannot be separated from the many different versions of the medieval that scholars, authors and directors have presented to us. Films that are set within the medieval era are examples of medievalisms – post-medieval refashionings of the medieval age, posing as the real thing. 'We are looking at a version of the Middle Ages', comments Arthur Lindley on medieval films, 'that has been carefully lifted out of historical sequence in order to serve as a mirror and an alienating device for viewing the ... present.[2] While many descriptions of medievalism in film exist, they primarily define the ways in which the visual aspects of film present the medieval period and do not take into account the ways in which film music plays a part in the ongoing conversation between the past and the present.

A number of film scholars who have analysed soundtracks in their criticism explore the way that time functions when one takes film music into account. Many of these theorists base their understanding of time on Julia Kristeva's essay 'Women's time', which claims women experience time differently than men – that time is essentially gendered. Kristeva argues that masculine time is historical and linear while women's time is linked to 'anterior temporal modalities', usually tied to gestation or characterised as having a cyclical nature.[3] Feminist film theorists such as Tania Modleski and Mary-Ann Doane have applied Kristeva's notion of gendered time to melodramas of the 1940s. In these films men are able to affect change – to participate in the world – while women can never fully enter the man's linear timeline. Instead, when these films show a woman participating in any sort of timeline, it is usually when she has flashbacks to her youth, resulting in what Modleski calls a 'hysterical notion of time and place'.[4] Doane claims that in these films women are always waiting, excluded from full subjectivity and from the main narrative of the film. They are essentially 'tied to a form of mistiming, of bad time, or a disphasure'.[5] Most important for a discussion of film music is perhaps Caryl Flinn's book *Strains of Utopia: Gender, Nostalgia and Hollywood Film Music*, in which disphasure is linked to films' musical scores.[6] Like Doane, Flinn also examines women's role in Hollywood cinema and finds that women are connected to music, but that women and music are often linked to an idealised and nostalgic version of the past. Flinn also points out that disphasure, usually a term associated in a negative sense with female characters' out-of-sync-ness with a masculine linear time, can in fact be linked with 'nascent form[s] of utopian alternatives'; women's association with nostalgia gives them a world apart from a masculine timeline.[7] While I do not wish to argue that film music in medieval films is always nostalgic to take away disphasure from its context within feminist film theory, examining disphasure within medieval film music provides a way to bring aural sensibilities to the fore. Disphasure also enables alternative readings of medieval films that musical elements can provide. Disphasure, then, can be a useful term to describe the ways in which film music plays a unique role in films that endeavour to represent the medieval period. Instead of creating dissonant moments between two time periods, music can serve to sever a film's ties to a specific timeline as well as introduce new multiple timelines into a film.

Introit: a brief history of film music in historical cinema

Music and film have been tied together since the cinema's early days. Silent films used existing nineteenth-century theatrical models for musical guidelines, which paired early cinema with live or recorded orchestral music from the late Romantic era and also borrowed from popular music. On the topic of music as a complement to silent cinema, Claudia Gorbman states:

> Music for silent films developed as an outgrowth of nineteenth-century dramatic traditions. Further, in the silent film, music communicated narrative information that has since been restored to the province of dialogue and sound effects. It also had the decidedly practical task of drowning out the unromantic noise of the movie-house projectors.[8]

At the beginning of cinema, music's position within the moviegoing experience was to give early audiences a familiar performative context within a new medium, to help the onscreen image by providing emotional and narrative cues, as well as to cover any unwanted sound of early film machinery.

Historical films of the silent era also used orchestral arrangements for their soundtracks. Edison and Vitagraph created cue sheets for those who screened silent films, which listed the proper orchestral pieces to include for each emotion.[9] Hannu Salmi comments:

> A cue sheet catalogue from 1927 offered 165 pieces with different character, including keywords such as lonely, serious, fanatic, happy, graceful, joyful humorous, mystical, poetic, oriental, pastoral, anger, sorrow, abandoned, tragic, doubtful. One of the keywords is 'historical', and the cue sheets under this character include only romantic music, either programmatic music or opera.[10]

This cue sheet marks one of the first distinctions of historical films requiring a certain type of music. The Romantic music that became popular in early cinema continued to be paired with historical films in the 1930s and 1940s.

By the advent of the classic Hollywood film in the 1930s, music – and especially the orchestral score – was considered a natural part of the moviegoing process.[11] As Kathryn Kalinak points out, 'composers in the crucial decade of the thirties, themselves trained in the late Romantic style, reinforced the connection' between films and romantic music; whether using pre-existing orchestral arrangements or relying on composers of the day to write new symphonic pieces for films, classical Hollywood cinema 'adapted the late-romantic orchestra of ninety-plus players for the recording studio.'[12] Not only did romantic music rely on a large orchestra, its emotional qualities and theatricality paired well with the drama unfolding on screen.

The trend of symphonic and Romantic-inspired film scores continued as composers like Miklós Rózsa built entire careers creating soundtracks. Rózsa's career as a Hollywood composer spanned six decades and more than one hundred films, and he became known as a composer of historical, premodern epics such as *Ivanhoe* (1952), *Julius Caesar* (1953), *Knights of the Round Table* (1954), *Ben-Hur* (1959), *El Cid* (1961) and *The Golden Voyage of Sinbad* (1974). Rózsa, who continued to compose film scores until 1982, became known for his well-researched musical compositions that helped to retell epic, premodern histories by using musical tropes from period music and reinterpreting them in an orchestral context. His orchestration is theatrical and lush, providing a musical complement to the large casts and intricate sets upon which movies like *El Cid* relied. It was Rózsa who cemented the connection between the premodern, epic film with a lavish orchestral score. Rózsa's films are only now being properly studied, with Ralph Erkelenz's assessment of *Ben-Hur*'s score being the most complete. Erkelenz notes:

> Interestingly enough, ... in *Anno Domini* (no. 2 in [*Ben-Hur's*] score) Rózsa uses nothing but perfect fifths for the opening chords of the movie – the first chord consists of eight notes, but only two different ones: C and G, which are a fifth apart ... thereby giving maximum impact to the subject matter of this movie: the full orchestration ('*tutti* strings, woodwind, trumpets, gong, trombones, low woodwinds, violoncelli, [double] basses, tubas') represents Roman power, the open fifths suggest 'Antiquity' ... as has been said by Dr. Rózsa himself.[13]

Open fifths and octaves are most common in medieval organum singing, and for many contemporary ears have the telltale sound of Gregorian chant. Rózsa employs this chord in the beginning of *Ben-Hur* to announce the film's premodern subject matter, but uses open fifths to signify antiquity, even though using such a chord is historically a medieval phenomenon. Disphasure functions on multiple levels within the medieval Hollywood cinema that Rózsa helps to develop. From early films' reliance on romantic tropes to composers like Rózsa, who re-imagine romantic music with 'antique' sensibilities, medieval film music cannot help but introduce a volatile notion of time. Rózsa's choices in films like *Ben-Hur* reach towards historical accuracy, but only in so far as putting premodern aural cues into his orchestral scores. A large proportion of contemporary historical films continue to use Rózsa's blend of realistic sounds with Romantic, orchestral arrangements.

Symphonic music continues to be a popular option for historical films' scores, but today a film's soundtrack is a critical component in the marketing schemes, DVDs and music videos for the film. Most films, and especially historical ones, use symphonic music for most of their scores simply so that vocals do not compete with the onscreen dialogue. A contemporary director's choice of an orchestral soundtrack also hearkens back to the complex history of orchestral music within films, especially those that portray the past. In the film analysed below Franco Zeffirelli forgoes traditional film scores and relies on a folk musician to compose the soundtrack for his film *Brother Sun Sister Moon*.

Let me be an instrument of peace: the counter-culture and *Brother Sun Sister Moon*

Franco Zeffirelli released *Brother Sun Sister Moon* in 1972 as his first film since 1968's *Romeo and Juliet*. *Brother Sun Sister Moon* depicts the life of St Francis of Assisi and follows his spiritual awakening and the early years of the Franciscan order. Through the film's soundtrack Zeffirelli links a medieval saint's struggles with Church hierarchy to the counter-cultural revolution of the 1960s. In the following quotation from Zeffirelli's autobiography he describes St Francis's experience with music and links it to contemporary culture:

> Francis was one of the first to reject the fearful medieval world with its dark view of God, the first to go out into the countryside and to see the work of the Almighty in the natural world – flowers and God's humble creatures. As part of that new openness and lightness Francis composed new hymns, not in Latin but in Italian, which was an unheard of provocation, and set them not as chants and hymns but to the popular tunes

his mother had taught him. This was, of course, shocking to the tradi-
tionalists, the merchants and the Church of his day. But young people
were entranced and followed him in the thousands. He was able to
transform an entire way of thinking to the point where the Pope himself
was obliged to acknowledge the rightness of the Franciscan mission.

How close this all seemed to what we felt in the 1960's – that the
young would create a new world order based on love and gentleness
after those fearful Cold War years. And how similar it seemed musically,
with rock music being played in churches and the Jesus people singing
on the streets. That was what I wanted to bring together: something that
would unite the love-songs of Provence with the music of our day.[14]

Zeffirelli mentions Francis's relationship with the natural world as a
main factor in Francis's spirituality, and links Francis's love of peace
and harmony to the Flower Children of the 1960s. Just as Francis challenges Church authorities with the tenets of the Franciscans, so does
the hippie movement clash with governmental institutions. Zeffirelli
brings the past into the present by introducing a new generation to St
Francis's revolutionary ideas by way of music, and specifically through
Brother Sun Sister Moon's soundtrack, which combines contemporary
and medieval compositions. Zeffirelli sees the music in his film as integral to understanding his film and Francis.

The soundtrack to *Brother Sun Sister Moon* contains prayers of St
Francis set to music, choral renditions of mass-settings, Gregorian
chants and original songs sung by Donovan, the Scottish folk singer.
According to Mario Aste, Zeffirelli originally picked John Lennon
to compose and sing songs for the film, but, after problems with the
script, Donovan was chosen instead.[15] Both Lennon and Donovan
were known for their connections with the 1960s counter-culture. By
this time Lennon had begun his solo career; and his album *Imagine*
was released in 1971, its title song heralded as an anti-war anthem.
As John Covach argues, Donovan's music was associated with similar
sentiments: 'Donovan's gentle melodic sense, eclectic stylistic range,
and often mystical lyrics made him a leading figure for hippie pacifism.'[16] Zeffirelli's choice of the work of these two musicians for his film
underscores his interpretation of St Francis as a revolutionary figure.

In the film Donovan's voice and lyrics do more than simply provide
background music for Francis's story. The film encourages the audience to identify St Francis with Donovan, as many of Francis's most
introspective moments are set to the latter's lyrics; and the few times
that St Francis sings, it is Donovan's voice that the audience hears. This

creates a synergistic relationship between counter-culture singer and revolutionary saint. Zeffirelli portrays St Francis as an ethereal young man who experiences wonder in the world around him; and Zeffirelli's casting of the twenty-five-year-old Graham Faulkner connotes Francis's innocence. Donovan's quavering vibrato and tenor range perfectly fit Faulkner's soft speaking voice, further encouraging the audience to connect Donovan's lyrics with St Francis's wide-eyed optimism. Anton Karl Kozlovic comments: 'Indeed [Donovan] was an excellent choice because of his youthfulness, alternative life style, anti-establishment beliefs and pop music hits like *Sunshine Superman* and *Mellow Yellow,* which augment [the film's] flower power feel'.[17] As much as Zeffirelli tries to turn Francis into a flower child, he also turns Donovan into a modern-day saint, as he links contemporary music to revolutionary powers. Donovan himself comments on the position of the musician as one who writes about universal themes. In a recent interview with the BBC, Donovan, commenting on his music's lasting popularity, remarked that: 'like troubadours, ... I can write about any facet of the human condition'.[18] The themes touched upon in the film tentatively connect the universalism of the hippie movement with St Francis, but having a modern musical icon provide the film's soundtrack suggests overt connections between the two periods. The addition of Donovan's score allows audiences to view Francis's change from a spoiled young man to one who abandons all his worldly possessions, and to make the connection with hippie ideals, thereby creating a shared space of spiritual passion and social virtue that reaches across two very disparate time periods. This results in a representation of the character of St Francis as a person who is not constrained by temporality.

In one scene, crying and obviously spiritually overcome, Francis makes the sign of the cross, as strings introduce Donovan's melody. When Donovan begins to sing, the scene cuts abruptly to a dramatic Italian landscape of green hills against a field of golden flowers; the audience soon sees Francis running and skipping amongst the flowers. As the film cuts to another bucolic landscape, the audience's eyes are drawn again to Francis running in another field, his face lit with spiritual bliss. Donovan's simple but heartfelt lyrics combine with Francis's divine awakening: 'Brother Sun and Sister Moon, / I seldom see you, seldom hear your tune / Preoccupied with selfish misery. / / Brother Wind and Sister Air, / Open my eyes to visions pure and fair. / That I may see the glory around me. / / I am God's creature, of God I am a part / I feel your love awaking in my heart. / / Brother Sun and Sister

Moon / I now do see you, I can hear your tune / So much in love
with all that I survey.' Donovan takes Francis's prayers and re-imagines
them in a contemporary context so that the audience can make further
connections between Francis's experiences and present-day ones. For
example, in *Brother Sun Sister Moon*, St Francis's experience of war
leads to his disillusionment with Church leaders and the 'selfish misery'
of which they are a part. As well as relating specifically to St Francis's
experiences of war, Donovan's lyrics also link the saint's pacifism with
his own stance against the Vietnam War, which can be seen in albums
such as *Universal Soldier* (1965).

The soundtrack to *Brother Sun Sister Moon* highlights the complexity
that film-makers face when they wish to introduce contemporary
elements in a film about the medieval period. Zeffirelli manages to
connect two periods through his soundtrack alone, creating a space of
disphasure when Zeffirelli's representation of medieval Italy collides
with Donovan's vocals. By involving a contemporary singer known for
his pacifism in his film about St Francis, Zeffirelli makes clear his position regarding the peaceful counter-culture and its possible influence
on mainstream society. Not only does Zeffirelli make a film about St
Francis, he also comments on the connections between the medieval
and the contemporary through the film's soundtrack.

Synthesising fantasy and the Middle Ages in *Ladyhawke*

Filmed in 1985, Richard Donner's *Ladyhawke* is a blend of Dungeons
and Dragons high fantasy and Marie de France's *lais*, particularly
Bisclavret and *Yonec*. The film follows two cursed lovers, Etienne
Navarre (Rutger Hauer) and Lady Isabeau (Michelle Pfeiffer). They
meet up with a thief, Philipe Gaston (Matthew Broderick), and together
the three must vanquish an evil bishop. The bishop has cursed Etienne
and Isabeau: during the day Isabeau turns into a hawk and in the night,
Etienne changes into a wolf, so the two lovers can never meet when
they are both in human form. The crux of the film (and the subject of
many intriguing scenes) centres on dusk, when the sky is both light
and dark and when the characters are both human and animal. *Ladyhawke*'s soundtrack relies on a blend of two disparate musical entities:
typical orchestral scoring, but also heavily synthesised music, making
the soundtrack rock and symphonic at the same time. Essentially, the
movie itself is about disphasure, since timing and a mixture of periods
govern the film's plot, its genre (fantasy or medieval) and its music.[19]

Eric Woolfson and Andrew Powell composed most of the original score for *Ladyhawke*. Both work with Alan Parsons or are in The Alan Parsons Project, a band known for its progressive-rock sounds and concept albums.[20] As a genre progressive rock grew popular in the 1970s and, according to Covach, focused on 'avoid[ing] lyrics dealing with romance or sexual prowess, opting instead to address big philosophical issues such as religion and spirituality, politics and power, the forward march of technology, and existential angst ... and in some cases even an attempt to raise rock music to the level of classical music.'[21] For example Alan Parsons based his band's first album, *Tales of Mystery and Imagination* (1977), on the poems of Edgar Allan Poe, creating a rock album that used nineteenth-century poetry as lyrics. With the combination of conceptual music and classical scoring in mind, one can analyse *Ladyhawke*'s synthesised-yet-orchestral soundtrack with a better sense of the conversation between visual and aural media within the film. Even though the film's score explores new sounds by adding synthesised elements, the foundation of the soundtrack rests on a symphonic sensibility. Using the synthesiser, Royal S. Brown argues, has completely changed the way that film music is made as well as the style of music that the audience hears, since many pieces that sound orchestral actually use synthesisers to save money.[22] In 1985 synthesised music had just gained mainstream popularity, especially through bands like The Alan Parsons Project, and the aim of these groups was not to emulate the exact sound of a violin or orchestra, but instead to play with the new aural possibilities that the synthesiser and synthesised sound had to offer. It is this kind of synthesised sound that the audience encounters in *Ladyhawke*; a sound that announces its electronic foundations against a background of traditional instruments, just as the fantastical elements in the film challenge the medieval world of the film.

From its very beginning *Ladyhawke* plays between moments of light and dark and synthesised and orchestral music. The film's opening shot is of a sun, on the cusp of rising above a line of clouds. Violins play a minor chord in slow quarter notes, while basses saw back-and-forth in a *tremolando*, leading to a mood of anticipation as the clouds on screen shift to reveal more of the sun. A dark, vertical stripe slowly moves across the screen from right to left, turning the sky into night. When the stripe passes through the sun, it changes into the moon. Soon the sunrise has turned into a moonrise. When the image changes from the sun to the moon, a synthesised piano, playing in a high register, takes over the melody from the traditional strings. Just as the synthesised piano begins to play, a stripe of daylight replaces the moon with the sun again; in the next moments the audience realises that the dark stripes of colour are actually the letters of the film's title, *Ladyhawke*, travelling across the screen. The synthesiser leads the action of this scene: it is not until the soundtrack is both orchestral and synthesised that the onscreen image begins to blend night with day. At the end of the opening credits, the title freezes on the screen in the orange colour of the sun, while the moon remains onscreen. At this moment synthesised trumpets (which almost sound like actual trumpets) play a final, triumphant chord, as neither light nor darkness prevails, but a mixture of the sun (the title's letters) and the moon suggest the mix of both contemporary and medieval themes.

Classical meets commerce: film music in *Robin Hood: Prince of Thieves*

In contrast, during the course of Kevin Reynolds's *Robin Hood: Prince of Thieves* the audience hears a symphonic soundtrack. Michael Kamen, one of the most noted composers of film scores, wrote the original score for *Robin Hood*. He had already garnered fame for his orchestrations in, for instance, the *Die Hard* (1988–) and *Lethal Weapon* (1997–) films. *Robin Hood* became one of the few 'period' films in Kamen's oeuvre.[23] Pairing Kamen's expertise with a medieval film suggests that, on a musical level, Reynold's wanted to market *Robin Hood* as a film that would appeal to those familiar with the music in action films. Given that each composer has a unique style he or she brings to a film, and that Kamen's musical dossier includes some of the most popular films of the 1980s and 1990s, *Robin Hood's* soundtrack aurally conjures up contemporary action-adventure films for its audiences. Even though the music in *Robin Hood* may be secondary to image during the making of the film, the addition of Kamen's score broadens the film's audience base because of its shared aural cues with action films. In one of the film's trailers Kamen's musical score draws attention to the more action-filled moments of the film. He uses the horn fanfare, which commonly functions as the musical introduction for the entrance of a king or knight, and uses it as one of the main orchestral themes throughout the film. Kamen changes the role of the fanfare from that of an introductory theme to that of main aural signifier of action, as loud horns accompany most of Robin Hood's sword fights and chase scenes. The horn fanfare provides an overarching aural theme for the frenetic action of the trailer, which moves from one fight sequence to another; persuading action-lovers that this film is filled with what they most enjoy.

Robin Hood's soundtrack has a complex history and reception that bears mentioning in a discussion of medieval films' soundtracks. The soundtrack itself is made up of eight of Kamen's orchestral compositions (tracks 1–8) and two rock songs that played during the film's credits (tracks 9–10). Each orchestral piece on the soundtrack gets its name from its corresponding scene in the film: for example, 'Marian at the Waterfall' and 'The Abduction and the Final Battle at the Gallows'. The song titles rely on the film's medieval images for context and meaning, situating the orchestral arrangements as subservient to the film's actions. When one listens to one of the orchestral songs from the soundtrack without its visual counterpart, the large range of tempos and dynamics startles the ear; without the onscreen image to contextualise the music, the song seems overly dramatic. Indeed, without the added emotive impact of the orchestration, the images on screen lose some of their passion and striking timing, even though the music fades into the background of the film in favour of the images on screen. Thus, without the images of Robin Hood and the Sheriff of Nottingham fighting, the fanfare that forms the centre of the film's soundtracks seems hollow. Kalinak asserts that film scores like Kamen's use 'music to sustain unity; a high degree of correspondence between narrative content and musical accompaniment; the use of music in the creation of mood, emotion and character'.[24] For example, in one scene a carriage careers down a wooded path as Robin Hood's men set up a trap underneath it. Without the music the audience simply sees a carriage rattling along a path. With the soundtrack's addition, however, the triumphant horn-blasts indicate to the audience whose carriage it is that is passing by, while the timpani lend the rather rickety carriage a more majestic air. In this sense the horn's fanfare not only introduces characters passing by but also alludes to Robin Hood's homecoming, the aim of which is to regain his father's lands and to triumph over the Sheriff.

Robin Hood is one of the first films to market successfully a soundtrack that features mainly orchestral music while also including popular songs, giving an audience who would not normally buy an orchestral soundtrack a reason to purchase the album. Warner released the soundtrack in July 1991, and its immediate success surprised the entertainment industry, as can be seen from *Entertainment Weekly's*

recap of the week's music events, punningly titled 'Hits N the "Hood" '
because of the film's success: 'And look out for the soundtrack from
Robin Hood: Prince of Thieves, which makes a quivering debut at No.
7.'[25] Part of the popularity of *Robin Hood*'s soundtrack stems from
Bryan Adams's song '(Everything I Do) I Do it For You', which is not
played during the film at all, but accompanies the film's closing credits.
Adams's song received an Oscar nomination in the category of Best
Original Song; his own CD, released three months after the soundtrack to *Robin Hood* arrived in record stores, also featured this track.
'In order to use a song effectively in a score,' Fred Karlin argues, 'there
must be a space for that song on the soundtrack and a reason for its
use.'[26] Most people walk away from a film as soon as the credits start
rolling, which would argue against the relevance of Adams's song for
the action of the film itself; but Karlin's point – that there needs to
be a reason for each song in a soundtrack – rings true in light of the
film soundtrack as a money-making tool. The last thing that most
people hear when they leave *Robin Hood* is the catchy strains of Bryan
Adams's song. In the UK Adams's song was number one for sixteen
weeks. As it gained in popularity, it propelled CD sales of *Robin Hood*'s
soundtrack as well as giving Adams's own CD publicity.

Visually, the music video for '(Everything I Do) I Do it For You'
continued to promote Adams's song as part of *Robin Hood*. It features
Adams singing in a forest that looks suspiciously like the film's Sherwood Forest. His band members (including one playing a grand piano)
are interspersed around a clearing in the woods next to a waterfall.
The video cuts from close-up shots of Adams singing to long shots
of Robin Hood, merging them into the category of 'medieval' hero
who will do anything for chivalry and his lady. The video continues in
this manner, with snippets of the film's plot juxtaposed with shots of
Adams's band. The video uses the song's lyrics to highlight important
moments in the film; for example, when Adams sings the words 'I'll
fight for you', the shot cuts to Robin Hood and the Sheriff fighting in
time with the drum beat. It is not until the music video that the film
and, arguably, the most popular song from its soundtrack, share any
kind of visual moment together. In technical terms the music video
is very basic but it establishes metaphorically a connection between
Adams and the film, both in relation to music and plot and by aligning
Adams with Robin Hood. In *Robin Hood* the blend of 1990s rock music
and a medieval hero creates an amalgamation of periods that makes a
medieval film marketable to a larger audience.

Disphasure and medievalism in *A Knight's Tale*

Like *Robin Hood*, *A Knight's Tale* uses contemporary music to accompany a plot set in a medieval context, providing its audience with a complex blend of temporalities. *A Knight's Tale* uses disphasure by incorporating 1970s rock music as diegetic sound in the visual landscape of a medieval film. With only a brief back-plot established, the first major action scene in *A Knight's Tale* is set in the jousting arena. The camera hovers above the field, focusing on different members of the sporting audience as they wave pennants and sing along with the song (Queen's 'We Will Rock You'). One particular scene conjures up a familiar occurrence at American and European football games: four overweight men without shirts wave their mugs of ale, roaring at the sport that is about to take place. Director Brian Helgeland equates modern sporting events, complete with grandstands, to medieval jousting. 'We Will Rock You', originally sung by the glam-rock band Queen and quite popular at contemporary American football games, calls attention to the film's blend of modern and medieval. The synchresis between the soundtrack and characters in the film emphasises that 'We Will Rock You' is not simply a song played for both of the audiences' benefit, but also as an action within the film itself.[27] The movie plays on the audience's knowledge of contemporary sports by adding scenes that conjure up familiar images in the audience's mind, even though the sport in question here is medieval jousting.

In this scene it is not so much the commonality between medieval and modern sports, but rather the song which succeeds in bringing the two periods together in the narrative and aesthetic logic of the film. It is therefore unsurprising that the song takes a prominent place in the film's marketing campaign: 'He Will Rock You' is the movie's tagline, and most previews contain part of the song. While Queen's song has associations with male sports culture, it is also linked to the gay and glam-rock subculture of the 1970s. The second most prominently featured song in the film, 'Golden Years' by David Bowie, was also central to that subculture. Choosing songs that possess such strong subcultural undertones appears to contradict the film's obvious attention to a mainstream sporting audience (which is usually perceived as heteronormative); attention that many critics were quick to note, calling the film, among other things, 'a Middle Ages *Rocky*'.[28] The sparse instrumentals in 'We Will Rock You' were partially a response to the increasingly male-centred punk culture emerging in the 1970s, as well

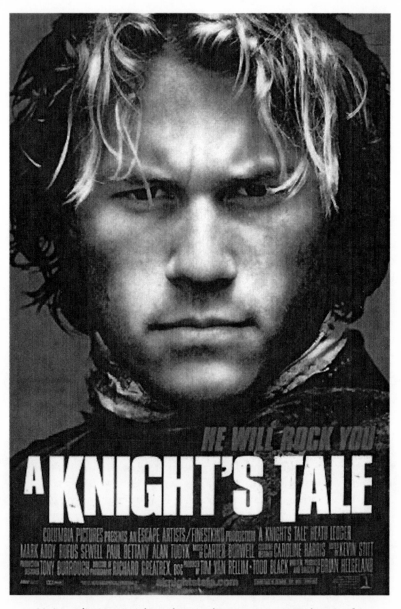

11 Appealing to straight and gay audiences: promotional poster for
A Knight's Tale (2001), by Egon Edrenyi, copyright Columbia Pictures Inc.,
by permission

as a move to encourage audience participation at concerts. Queen's guitarist, Brian May, recalls that this song

> was a response to a particular phase in Queen's career, when the audience was becoming a bigger part of the show than we were. They would sing all the songs. And in a place like Birmingham, they'd be so vociferous that we'd have to stop the show and let them sing to us. So both Freddie [Mercury] and I thought it would be an interesting experiment to write a song with audience participation specifically in mind. My feeling was that everyone can stamp and clap and sing a simple motif, so 'We Will Rock You' was based on that.[29]

Participation between those on stage and the audience reflects Helgeland's use of the song perfectly. He weaves the soundtrack into the tapestry of the film as the audience at the jousting tournament sings along, reminding cinema audiences of their own participation at similar mass events.

The film's poster (Figure 11) also suggests that the film's target audience is more diverse than the jousting sequences in *A Knight's Tale* imply. Here the actor Heath Ledger (who plays the protagonist, Will Thatcher) is presented in a close-up shot with the line 'He Will Rock You' running along underneath it. Clearly referencing Queen's song, the poster ignores what the trailers suggest is the film's most important aspect: combative sport. Here the reference to Queen's song shifts away from its ubiquitous association with sports culture, catering to the desires of straight female as well as queer audiences instead. 'We Will Rock You' returns here to its ties with glam-rock and 1970s gay culture. Now the words 'He Will Rock You' take on a more overtly sexualised meaning. No longer does Heath Ledger appear charging towards the audience on horseback, lance raised towards the camera; instead, he is framed in a classic Hollywood glamour shot. Ledger is arguably both feminised and sexualised in this poster, a stark contrast to the images of him that appear in the trailer. In the poster it is Heath Ledger that will rock you, offering both heterosexual females and gay males a site of pleasure, while elsewhere the film appears to focus on a straight male audience. The poster makes the film's medievalism less straightforward in its use of a close-up shot that dislocates it from both its contemporary and medieval associations. In it Ledger appears almost out of time and place, especially with the red background mirroring the red letter of the tag-line. As a result it is impossible to situate him temporally.

Another instance of temporal disphasure in the film tied to the film's musical score occurs when Jocelyn, the female lead in *A Knight's Tale*, appears for the first time. When the audience first sees Jocelyn it is in a high-angle shot from the perspective of Will, who is riding a horse. Jocelyn, completely framed in a medium close-up shot, turns in profile and pauses, inviting the audience, along with Will, to examine her. This shot also encourages the audience to view Jocelyn as the object of Will's desire. At this moment the sounds of a guitar and lute introduce Jocelyn with a flamenco-inspired riff, suggesting an exotic aspect to her, especially in its contrast to the rock music that has permeated the soundtrack up to this point. As Jocelyn walks, the guitar riff from a moment ago expands into a medieval-inspired tune, adding a flute to the minor-keyed melody.

As Will begins to follow Jocelyn (at this point it is unclear whether she notices him or not), the camera cuts to a medium close-up shot of Jocelyn from Will's perspective (still on his horse). As he begins to pursue her in earnest, the sound changes from that of an acoustic guitar and lute to that of an electric guitar and snare drum, revising and modernising the original theme. The music continues to morph from medieval to a distinctly rock-inspired melody, complete with a weak beat, blending with the original melody so that it is impossible to tell if the song is a medieval melody with contemporary accompaniment, or vice versa. Jocelyn's melody, in contrast, is played without any percussive instruments; only wind and string instruments create a counterpoint. When Will follows her, his melody, played by an electric guitar, overtakes Jocelyn's theme as the primary instrument, hers now serving as accompaniment instead of maintaining her dominant position. It is a bar after the electric guitar takes over that the snare drum begins demarcating the beat, in cadence with Jocelyn's steps away from Will's horse, thus giving the dominant beat back to her. The weak beat established here, combined with the electric guitar, mirrors the onscreen chase between Will and Jocelyn, but the very specific and gendered instrumentation contributes to an audience's perception of the communication between them, even though the two characters have yet to speak to one another. Susan McClary points out that specific musical cadences are used to signify gendered positions, suggesting strength and weakness; specifically, a backbeat is considered masculine and a weak beat – like the one used at this moment in *A Knight's Tale* – is defined as feminine:

The two are differentiated on the basis of relative strength, with the binary opposition masculine/feminine mapped onto strong/weak. Moreover, this particular definition betrays other important mappings: if the masculine version is ... normal, then the implication is that the female version is abnormal.[30]

McClary then goes on to note that feminine beats are associated with more romantic music while masculine beats are linked to linear (an important word to use in light of a discussion on disphasure) cadences, which fall directly on the beat and are what one comes to expect in most rock music.

These distinctions play out musically in the conversation between Will and Jocelyn, especially as it becomes obvious to the audience that Jocelyn knows Will is following her. Initially it appears as though Jocelyn's acoustic theme is pushed into the background by Will's more aggressive and masculine melody, but as the power shifts from Will following Jocelyn to Jocelyn leading an oblivious Will, still on horseback, into a church, the changing cadences of the music show the tables turning. Jocelyn and Will's back-and-forth movement, coupled with the score's juxtaposition of their musical themes, adds to the scene's complexity and mirrors the visual interplay between the two characters. Will's theme does not simply reflect a dominant masculinity that the electric guitar would seem to imply – his theme is presented with a weak beat – one that, according to McClary, signifies a more feminised position for Will than is initially suggested by the action. It is Will who becomes the marker of a beat that is not quite in sync with a more masculine time signature, again highlighting the temporal disphasure within the musical structure of the scene as well as suggesting that disphasure's original connotations with gendered time. However, in this case, the driving beat of drums matches Jocelyn's steps, which are propelling the film's action forward, leading Will to follow her into the church. When the score is taken into account in an analysis of this scene, power relations shift to reveal alternative or more nuanced ways of reading the onscreen narrative.

David Bowie's song 'Golden Years' offers another instance of musical and temporal complexity in the film, as medieval characters are shown to dance to music from 1976. The dance sequence begins rather typically in a filmic sense, with an overhead long shot, as Will teaches the partygoers an alleged dance from his homeland. As Will begins to muddle his way through the first step of his dance lesson one thing is evident: there is no music. Will's lack of rhythm is amplified by the absence of instrumental accompaniment. Jocelyn, seeing that people are beginning to snigger at Will, whispers percussive noises, creating musical sound for herself and Will, and takes over Will's dance by clapping for music to begin. The music that begins to play, medieval-inspired lute and flute, starts at an andante tempo as the couples in the hall stage a partner dance. The movement of the dance is regimented at this point: the men and women stand at least five feet away from each other and begin by bowing to their partners. Here medieval referents abound, from the formal dancing to the lute melody played by an unseen band. The music then begins to quicken subtly and become louder as finger cymbals announce a back-beat that was previously unmarked. The partners are still dancing with each other, but their choreography has become slightly less strictly controlled than before as the movements of the dancers grow more fluid. At the same time an electronicised lute begins to play and David Bowie begins to sing as the music accelerates over two bars. Bowie then sings a downward glissando, marking a distinct change in the music, which has moved from referencing the medieval to a mélange of medieval and contemporary.

David Bowie seems to be a perfect choice for such a discursive musical shift, as he has long been heralded for his ability to reinvent himself in different musical genres and styles. It is Bowie's falsetto vocal that sings over the previously established melody; as the flute and guitar pause in a fermata his voice inflects more contemporary elements to emerge in the song. At the point when Bowie's voice slides down a musical scale and the instruments pause, the camera focuses on Jocelyn in a medium close-up shot as her movements become less rigid; her wrist breaks the straight line of her silhouette, ushering in contemporary dance steps. The timbre of Bowie's vocals, along with the camera's focus on Jocelyn's more contemporary moves, gives the effect that the entire dance is pausing to draw breath until the music returns and the couples leave the scripted movements of a medieval courtly dance in favour of a more free-style choreography. Yet while everyone's dancing becomes less regimented, the partners do continue to follow a recognisable pattern, mirroring each other as they move. As Helgeland introduces visual and aural elements into the scene from a range of different times, it is increasingly difficult to fix the scene within a specific temporal framework.

As the music completely changes into the song 'Golden Years', Jocelyn and Will's dancing only loosely mirrors those around them.

While the rest of the dancers air-punch to the beat of the music, they alternate between discoing across the floor and dancing close together. At this point, in contrast to the moment the song began, all the dancers have smiles on their faces; and it is obvious that they are enjoying themselves. Will and Jocelyn dance close together as the rest of the dancers form lines around them. Yet even the others are not all performing identical moves – some have their hands raised, others appear to be moving forward, and one person is even dancing behind them. Although this dance probably took days to choreograph, at this point in the film it seems as if the actors were moving spontaneously. Dancing to music, which is usually governed by a time signature, begins to transform into free-formed movement. The disphasure in this scene occurs together with movement, bright costumes and music, creating a moment on screen that is not bound by any single period.

In conclusion

Much work has been done on the ways in which visual aspects of medieval films correspond to their source texts and participate in medievalism. Music, too, plays a large part in this and should not be ignored as more scholars take up medieval film as a research area. Examining disphasure within medieval film can become a powerful analytical tool for exploring the ways that film scores interact with and contribute to films that represent the past. Film music not only provides background noise for onscreen images but soundtracks add to the images on screen. Film music can provide critics with a framework within which to examine issues such as record rights, popular song and film marketing. Its study can also help critics understand more fully the business involved in producing and marketing a medieval film that is a commercial success. Medieval films are not just created for a niche market; their soundtracks and scores make films about the Middle Ages attractive to a wider audience.

Medievalism is the standard term that critics use to define the reappropriation of the medieval period by other eras; thus far medievalism has focused almost exclusively on the visual aspects of media and not the ways in which music – in this case film music – shapes the way audiences perceive the Middle Ages. Using a term like disphasure to describe aural medievalism draws attention to the multiple temporalities involved in medievalism, while also taking into account the ways in which music can create meaning in conjunction with images in medieval films. Film music shapes the way an audience views and experiences a medieval film, often inviting new viewers into the filmic space of the motion picture. Music can challenge and disrupt audiences' and critics' expectations of what can be considered a medieval film, as well as their expectations of what is enjoyable. Most importantly, however, medieval film music has the ability to expand significantly the ways in which medieval film can be thought about.

Notes

1 For a detailed account of the history of music and film see Claudia Gorbman, *Unheard Melodies: Narrative Film Music* (Bloomington: University of Indiana Press, 1987).

2 Arthur Lindley, 'The ahistoricism of medieval film' (1998), p. 3, at www.latrobe. edu.au/www/screeningthepast/firstrelease/fir598/ALfr3a.htm, accessed 16 October 2007.

3 Julia Kristeva, 'Women's time', trans. Alice Jardine and Harry Blake, *Signs: Journal of Women in Culture and Society*, 7 (Autumn 1981 [1979]), 13–35 (16).

4 Tania Modleski, 'Time and desire in the woman's film', *Cinema Journal*, 23 (Spring 1984), 19–30 (23).

5 Mary Ann Doane, 'The moving image: pathos and the maternal', in Marcia Landy (ed.), *Imitations of Life: A Reader on Film and Television Melodrama* (Detroit, MI: Wayne State University Press, 1991), pp. 283–306 (p. 300).

6 Caryl Flinn, *Strains of Utopia: Gender, Nostalgia and Hollywood Film Music* (Princeton, NJ: Princeton University Press, 1992).

7 *Ibid.*, p. 148.

8 Gorbman, *Unheard Melodies*, pp. 185–6.

9 David Robinson, *Music of the Shadows: The Use of Musical Accompaniment with Silent Films, 1896–1936* (Pordenone: Giornate del cinema muto, 1990), p. 12.

10 Hannu Salmi, 'Composing the past: music and the sense of history in Hollywood spectacles of the 1950s and early 1960s', *Screening the Past*, 5 (1998), 1–10 (5). Also available at www.latrobe.edu.au/screeningthepast/firstrelease/fir1298/HSfr5d.html, accessed 26 October 2007.

11 I use the term 'classical Hollywood cinema' much in the same way Kalinak does when she uses this term to mean films produced within the Hollywood studio system and to 'designate a narrative practice' and 'a label which implies not only a historical designation but a nexus of style, ideology, technology, and economics which coalesced during a particular time and in a particular place' (Kathryn Kalinak, *Settling the Score: Music and the Classical Hollywood Film* (Madison: University of Wisconsin Press, 1992), p. xiv).

12 Kalinak, *Settling the Score*, pp. 100, 101.

13 Ralph Erkelenz, '*Ben-Hur*: a tale of the score', *Pro Musica Sana*, series 2, 5:1 (2005), 1–40 (6).

14 Franco Zeffirelli, *Franco Zeffirelli: The Autobiography* (London: Arena, 1987), p. 253.

15 Mario Aste, 'Zeffirelli's personal encounter with St Francis: *Brother Sun Sister Moon*', *RLA-Archive* (1991), 1–17 (2).

16 John Covach, *What's That Sound? An Introduction to Rock and Its History* (New York: Norton, 2006), p. 289.

17 Anton Karl Kozlovic, 'Saint cinema: the construction of St Francis of Assisi in Franco Zeffirelli's *Brother Sun Sister Moon*', *Journal of Religion and Popular Culture*, 2 (2002), 1–15 (15).

18 Donovan, 'Donovan remembers Dylan' (23 May 2001), http://news.bbc.co.uk/2/hi/entertainment/1347199.stm, accessed 26 October 2007.

19 Doane, 'The moving image', p. 300.

20 Alan Parsons first became known for his sound engineering work on the Beatles' *Abbey Road* and Pink Floyd's *Dark Side of the Moon* albums; see Covach, *What's That Sound?*, p. 408.

21 *Ibid.*, p. 323.

22 Royal S. Brown, *Overtones and Undertones: Reading Film Music* (Berkeley: University of California Press, 1994), p. 265.

23 The other most notable historical film Kamen scored is *The Three Musketeers* (1993).

24 Kalinak, *Settling the Score*, p. 190.

25 'Hits N the "Hood" ', *Entertainment Weekly*, 75 (19 July 1991); also available at: www.ew.com/ew/article/0,,314840,00.html, accessed 26 October 2007.

26 Fred Karlin, *On the Track: A Guide to Contemporary Film Scoring* (New York: Routledge, 2003 [1900]), p. 525.

27 Michel Chion defines synchresis as: 'a word [Chion] has forged by combining *synchronism* and *synthesis* [that] is the spontaneous and irresistible weld produced between a particular auditory phenomenon and visual phenomenon when they occur at the same time'; Chion, *Audio-Vision: Sound on Screen* (New York: Columbia University Press, 1994), p. 63.

28 Rene Rodriguez, film review of *A Knight's Tale*, at www.rottentomatoes.com/m/AknightsTale-1107871/, accessed 26 October 2007.

29 Alan di Perna, 'Brian's Song', *Guitar World*, January 1993; also available at www.queen-rocks.com/~unicorn/bri_gw93.txt, accessed 6 November 2007.

30 Susan McClary, *Feminine Endings: Music, Gender and Sexuality* (Minneapolis: University of Minnesota Press, 1991), pp. 9, 10.

7

Border skirmishes: weaving around the Bayeux Tapestry and cinema in *Robin Hood: Prince of Thieves* and *El Cid*

Richard Burt

The Bayeux Tapestry as cinematic textilography

The Bayeux Tapestry appears most often in historical fiction cinema as a prologue integrated into an opening title sequence, and, less frequently, in scenes of it being embroidered and assembled by women: Chimene (Sophia Loren) in *El Cid* (1961); Ophelia (Helena Bonham Carter) and other women in *Hamlet* (1990); and Marian Dubois (Mary Elizabeth Mastrantonio) in *Robin Hood: Prince of Thieves* (1991; see Figures 12 and 15).[1] As much as these historical fiction films link women and sexuality to the Bayeux Tapestry, they do not (en)gender the latter in a straightforward way, reducible either to a narrative of women's subordination, silencing, exclusion or marginalisation with regard to history or to some counter-narrative of that history as subversively stitched by women.[2] Contrasting its citation in *Robin Hood: Prince of Thieves* with its citation in *El Cid*, I maintain that the Bayeux Tapestry figures cinema, most explicitly not when the entire screen image mimetically reproduces a Tapestry panel but when we see the apparatus of the Tapestry's production with Tapestry panels strapped in wooden frames before they are to be assembled into a continuous strip. The Bayeux Tapestry in cinema is a para-mimetic *text*-tile, a form of cinematic writing or inscription that includes both mimetic alphabetic letters (the Latin inscriptions on the Tapestry itself) and an extra-mimetic, non-alphabetic cinematic 'writing'. By para-mimetic writing I mean the making of meaning not only through mimetic representation but through the formal composition of the shot and the mise-en-scène. Put in terms of recent film theory of cinematic writing and representation, the Tapestry's cinematic textilography sews together what Tom Conley terms 'film hieroglyphs' (cinematic icons and graphic elements such as credits in title sequences that remain within mimesis but 'betray and also subvert any continuity of edited images') and what Tom Cohen calls cinematic 'cryptonymies.'[3] Cryptonymies refer to signifying agents that precede a hieroglyphic, mimetic logic and may take phenomenal forms such as a series of marks or bars in a film not reducible to alphabetic writing (letters, a signature of the auteur), and which constitute a (pre)figural series of 'cross-relays and trace chains' that repeat but fall short of 'analogy or metaphor' and that lack 'any possible mimetic value.'[4]

A cross between the film hieroglyph and film cryptonymy, the Bayeux Tapestry in cinema calls attention to para-mimetic cinematic writing in historical films generally: recurring elements in shots that match and recall one another by analogy or metaphor but that do not involve continuity editing to unify the narrative. Indeed, to be made intelligible as such, para-mimetic writing must be read anamorphic-ally: marks must be singled out in the frame and read from a distorted perspective that makes the rest of the screen image unviewable as a mimetic representation. In the conclusion I will briefly discuss the ways in which the Bayeux Tapestry in cinema clarifies the limits of the dominant ways in which literary and film historicism has been thought in terms of mimetic matching between film and history or in terms of a framing effect.

Unpricking the Tapestry

Both *Robin Hood: Prince of Thieves* and *El Cid* transform the Bayeux Tapestry's secular narrative into a religious one, involving a conflict between Christianity and Islam.[5] The two films differ, however, in imagining the possibility of an ending to such a conflict. *Robin Hood: Prince of Thieves* has been chided both for its anachronistic political correctness and for its neo-colonialism; and two critics have linked it to the Gulf War.[6] Production of the film began a month after Iraq's invasion of Kuwait in 1990, and it was released a few months after the US declared victory. A close reading of *Robin Hood: Prince of Thieves*'s opening title sequence, which condenses and recuts panels of the Tapestry as a montage, helps explain how the film fails to deliver both on its ostensibly liberal politics of multicultural tolerance and as a narrative film of any consequence. Focused on a post-authentic, anachronistic medieval imaginary separating both the good pricks (Robin and his merry men) from the bad pricks (the Sheriff and his men), and the good pricker (Marian Dubois) from the bad pricker (the witch Martianna), Reynolds's film reaches for cinematic pyrotechnics and prostheses that fizzle in cinematic detumescence: a flattened, two-dimensional screen image and foreshortened vision return the film to the racism and xenophobia of the America West which the film claims to have overcome.

Equally close attention to the Bayeux Tapestry in *El Cid* helps explain its far more complicated narrative structure and Cold War politics. Whereas *Robin Hood: Prince of Thieves* makes the Bayeux Tapestry analogous to film by transforming it into a film montage, equating mimetic representation with the extension of vision and the non-mimetic with blindness, *El Cid*'s Bayeux Tapestry sequence enables us to see obliquely how the film's apparently conventional editing techniques stretch narrative repetition as mimetic matching to breaking point, generating a recursive and uncanny cinematic historicism.[7]

Marian, unmaid

Just after the Sheriff of Nottingham tells his allies that he is about to marry Marian Dubois, a sequence of Marian's abduction follows, beginning with a cut to a low angle shot of the back of a panel of the Tapestry lit from the reverse side by candlelight (Figure 12, top left). This scene invites an analogy between woman embroiderer and film editor. The analogy between the Bayeux Tapestry and cinema may be easier to see if we recall that the links between sewing and film, especially film projection and film editing, are extensive and multiple. Walter Murch notes that women were hired for film editing in the early days of cinema, and compares their splicing the 'fabric of film' to sewing and fitting a suit.[8] Unlike the Tapestry panels shown in the film's opening title sequence, of which more later, Marian's panel is a composite, combining elements of two Tapestry panels: the two men in her panel are derived from William and an adviser to his left in panel 37 of the Tapestry, in which William meets Harold; and the architectural frame of William's palace in that panel is replaced in Marian's panel with a smaller building taken from panel 75, with Harold sitting on a throne, Halley's comet in the upper border and ghost ships in the lower border. In addition, the name 'Willelm' (misspelled by Marian as 'Wilgelm') has been moved from the left of the Tapestry panel where William meets Harold (panel 37) and into the building in Marian's panel, integrating text and image much the same way as occurs in panel 113 of the Tapestry, where William's name is written directly

12 Weaving the Bayeux Tapesty in *Robin Hood: Prince of Thieves* (1991, top)
and in *Hamlet* (1990, below)

next to his head: 'Wil' on his upper left, 'lelm' (now spelled 'gelm' by
Marian) on his upper right, as he sits on a throne inside a building,
flanked by a man on each side.

Though we see Marian's panel only in one shot of the film, it provides
a furtive, if significant, opening for a reading of the film, linking women
as shadow film editors and Marian as embroiderer in the dark. As a
composite replica, Marian's panel resembles the dissolves in the film's
opening title sequence that momentarily superimpose one image of the
Tapestry fading out as another image fades in. Furthermore, Marian's
Tapestry panel is almost projected like a screen image, illuminated from
behind by candles. Sitting behind the panel, Marian appears almost
entirely in shadow: silhouettes of her right forearm and her head are
visible through the panel she is embroidering at night; and her left
forearm is seen in front as she reaches behind the panel to get the needle
she is threading through the panel. The shot marks female labour as
strictly 'behind the scenes'. The camera pulls up to show Marian sitting
on the other side, but stops just as the lower bar of the Tapestry panel
appears at the bottom of the film frame (Figure 12, top right). By not
showing us the panel from the front side, the scene broadly suggests
an analogy between Marian as embroiderer and women as film editors.
Both the work of continuity editing and the women who perform it are
supposed to remain invisible, in the shadows.

Far from suggesting that women are marginal in the film narrative, however, the Tapestry sets up Marian's abduction as an issue of visibility, in relation to both what she can see and what can be seen of her. Hearing a strange sound, Marian puts down her needle and picks up her dagger and candle. She cannot see very far ahead by candlelight, and is assaulted by a Norman knight obscured from her view. He says, after pinning her on a table: 'I've never seen a lady's breasts.' At this point, Marian manages to free her left arm and grabs some spice from a bowl on the table, blinding the knight as she throws it in his eyes. Pushing him away, she then goes to the fireplace, grabs a roasting spit, turns and, brandishing it, runs towards him screaming. Other knights enter and kidnap her.

The behind-the-scene shot of Marian's Bayeux Tapestry panel in progress, a shot that gets on top of Marian but does not reveal anything of her ordinarily hidden from our view, highlights the visual dynamic of the film. Just as we do not see the front of the panel, so too we do not cut to a reverse angle shot of Marian looking for the source of the sound. Instead we see her again in medium long shot from another room as she enters with her candlestick. The assault is filmed with both Marian and the knight shot in profile, and we do not see where she sticks the knight with the spit. The shot ends with her holding the spit so close to the camera that it becomes a blur as we hear it penetrate the knight, making a squishy sound. The knight holds his hands directly over his eyes and bends over the table crying out in agony, suggesting she has either wounded him in the genitalia or blinded him.

The relation between *Robin Hood: Prince of Thieves*'s interest in extending the gaze to men and women through visual prosthetics and the film's overextended, straight-arrow narrative that falls short of being liberal and multicultural may be elucidated by attending closely to the film's opening title sequence (Figure 13, top row and bottom left). The opening title sequence lays claim to unprecedented visual and narrative mastery over the Robin Hood legend as it gives us an idealised, fully restored, even colourised replica of the Tapestry. Taking the narrative form of a montage prologue, the opening title cites fourteen panels from the Tapestry: first, two knights on horseback charging as they lower their lances (panels 125–6), then a war council with a king and two advisers (panel 1), then aristocrats on horseback riding to the sea (panels 2–3), then horses and sailors in ships (panels 93–9), then knights about to begin a cavalry charge (panels 123–4).

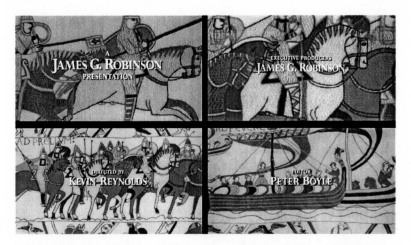

13 Opening title sequence of *Robin Hood: Prince of Thieves* (1991) begins again at the end (top row and bottom left) and ship with papal banner cropped (bottom right)

The opening title sequence consists of sixteen very similar shots, each around eight to ten seconds in length, all of which begin close up and then track right as the camera pulls back (with the exception of the title credit '*Robin Hood: Prince of Thieves*'), to show more of each Tapestry panel. Each shot ends with a dissolve lasting two seconds as the next shot comes into focus. As is typical of such montage sequences, the extra-diegetic symphonic music further sutures the panels together into a continuous whole. The film credits also stitch together, so to speak, shots of Bayeux Tapestry panels: 'A James G. Robinson Presentation' and 'A Morgan Creek Production' appear one after the other over the first dissolve; 'A Kevin Reynolds Film' over the second dissolve, and so on until the end of the sequence.

The sequence makes only one small change to the restored Tapestry in the final shot: the words 'ad prelium' ('for battle') appear in the upper left of the film frame (Figure 13, bottom left). These words have been moved from their location in the actual Bayeux Tapestry (panel 125), which had been shown at the beginning of the title sequence, where William urges his troops 'ut preparent se viriliter et sapienter ad prelium' ('to prepare themselves manfully and wisely for battle'). They here replace the words 'et venerunt' ('and they came'), which appear in panel 45 above Harold rescuing French soldiers from quicksand.

In the title sequence 'ad prelium' is a signature effect that recursively puts the beginning at the end, not just by repeating the title sequence's beginning, but by fading to black and then beginning the film with two intertitles that set the story in Jerusalem in 1194, thereby inviting a retrospective reading of the opening title sequence as a montage prologue that provides the back-story for the film. Thus the Tapestry's narrative of a Norman invasion has been re-edited – knights' charge, war council, ride to sea, shipping, charge – as a narrative of Richard I leaving England for the Third Crusade, from which Robin Hood is now shown to return. The title sequence retells the story of Robin Hood so that the prologue ends by marking the beginning of a new story. Moreover, the prologue establishes a claim for virtuoso cinematic mastery in retrospectively matching the title sequence to the film. Moving forward as a continuous, regular series of tracking shots that proceed at the same pace from extreme close-up to medium long shot, they establish closure while inaugurating the phallic plenitude of the film to follow. The swelling sail, swelling music and medieval textile – seen from extreme close-up to establishing long shot – all anticipate the camera's extended reach in the film proper. *Robin Hood: Prince of Thieves* can both see the medieval past in unprecedented ways and tell it anew, moving beyond the putatively authentic medieval imaginary of earlier films like Michael Curtiz's *The Adventures of Robin Hood* (1938) into openly anachronistic medievalism not defined by authenticity (hence the use of a coloured replica of the Tapestry rather than the genuine Tapestry now on display in Bayeux).

Yet the film undercuts its opening claims to cinematic and narrative mastery in several ways: through how it shows the Tapestry (ranging from extreme close-up to medium long shot); through how much of a given Tapestry panel it shows; and through the recursive narrative structure of the title sequence. The shots of the Tapestry in extreme close-up show the texture of the replica, letting us see it as if through a microscope, in a density of detail that has an almost three-dimensional surface, as if the stitches cast shadows. The medium long shots, however, lose much of this detail and look like two-dimensional drawings. The slow zoom out, in other words, has the effect of flattening out the image. Similarly, we never see the full Tapestry panel when the camera zooms out. In the second shot, some of the upper border appears, but it is only in the final shot (panels 123–4) that both upper and lower borders become visible. Nevertheless, even this shot crops both borders, leaving each only half-visible. The sequence stops short of making the Tapestry fully visible, showing us retrospectively that what we saw close-up involved a cropping instead.

Less obviously, but arguably more importantly, the prologue's claim for narrative mastery is undercut by its recursive structure, revealing that the film cannot move back to the very beginning or forward into the future. The final shot of the sequence, showing the first cavalry charge of the Battle of Hastings in the Tapestry (panels 123–4), returns us to the same cavalry charge seen in immediately following panels of the Tapestry (panels 125–6), which we saw in the first shot of the sequence of the charging knights with spears lowered. The final shot is not only a beginning but a rewriting of the film's own beginning as a cut-and-paste. The change in the placement of the words 'ad prelium' is significant because they match the prologue to the film only by cropping them: the first shot of the film dissolves just before the words 'ad prelium' become visible above the Norman knight charging on horseback. In the opening shot, in place of the Tapestry's writing, 'A Morgan Creek Production' fades in as the shot dissolves into the second shot of the sequence (panel 2). The opening sequence thus matches the Tapestry narrative to the film narrative not as an extension of vision, rewriting the Tapestry as a back-story, but as cutting; that is, the opening title sequence provides a match only by dissolving the Tapestry's writing and making it disappear, replacing the Latin letters of its beginning with the film credit.

Three series of recursive loops within the title sequence that similarly undercut its ostensible narrative mastery may be detected if we put the opening title sequence more explicitly in dialogue with the Bayeux Tapestry panels cited by the film prologue. The last three shots of the title sequence all end with a green horse, the final two ending in the same place, just before the face of the green horse becomes fully visible. The shots of ships in the invading fleet (panels 4–10) are similarly recursive. These six shots go backwards and forwards in the Tapestry, first showing the third invading ship (panels 93–9), then moving to the fifth, the forth, the fifth, the sixth and, again, the fifth ship.

Viewed in dialogue with the Tapestry, then, we see more clearly that the opening title sequence falls short of inaugurating a narrative break with past versions of the story, unwittingly revealing the film's lack of narrative and cinematic mastery in the awkward ways in which it conceals sex and violence, especially religious violence. *Robin Hood: Prince of Thieves* begins with the crusades in order to leave them behind. The prologue stops short of violence – especially violence inspired by religion. Significantly, the papal cross at the top of the mast in the fifth ship of the invading fleet (panel 96) is only very briefly visible in the shot just as the shot begins to dissolve; similarly, the charging knight with the papal cross on his lance (panel 126) seen in the opening shot does not reappear in the final shot of the film (Figure 13, bottom right). The sequence also stops short of sexual explicitness. The legs of the naked couple in the upper border (panel 123) are seen in the upper left of the shot, and the camera stops tracking left in the final shot just short of the second naked pair in the upper border (we see only the right leg of the first figure).

This close reading of *Robin Hood: Prince of Thieves*'s opening title sequence as a narrative that ends by returning to a moment just short of its beginning enables us to see that the film's politically correct anachronisms – the editing out of interracial violence and sex – actually reinscribe the errors of sexism and racism it wants to correct. For example, the film begins with a marked racial opposition. Robin frees the Moor Azeem (Morgan Freeman) from an Arab prison in Jerusalem and they escape together in an image of cross-racial unity. The film contrasts their intercultural friendship to the racist domination of the Sheriff of Nottingham (Alan Rickman), and the barons, when first seen outside Lord Locksley's (Brian Blessed) castle, appear in white robes that make them look more like members of the Ku Klux Klan than Knights Templar. As the film proceeds, Robin and the Sheriff become similarly opposed as rivals for Marian's hand in marriage. Yet these oppositions between anti-racist, virile hero and racist, detumescent villain quickly fall apart in cinematic, if not narrative terms. This can be seen in relation to the example of Azeem's telescope, a visual prosthesis that both symbolises the superior status of Azeem's culture and is meant to give Robin a technological advantage over his enemies. When Robin and Azeem return and save a poacher, the sequence begins with Robin looking through the telescope and spotting Guy of Gisborne (Michael Wincott) and several knights on horseback. The telescope is explicitly matched to an iris shot with the rounded image shot with a telephoto lens. Here there is a shot-reverse-shot sequence of Robin looking through the telescope and of Guy and his men from Robin's point of view, a shot that matches the telescope to the camera lens (see Figure 14, top row). As Robin comes to understand that what he sees in the telescope is not in front of him but is actually quite far away, the matching of telescope image to the camera image visually flattens out space. A similarly flattening effect occurs in the shots of

14 Telescope as telephoto lens in *Robin Hood: Prince of Thieves* (1991)

Robin as he looks through the telescope while waving his sword in the other hand. Robin holds his sword so close to the camera that it is seen only as a flat blur (Figure 14, bottom row).

Although the telescope and swords are gendered male in the film, since only men are shown using them, a similar virtual prosthesis is afforded Marian in a scene which shows Robin bathing in the nude near a waterfall. The film cross-cuts from close-ups of Marian's face, smiling in appreciation as she looks down from a cliff at Robin's naked backside, to medium shots of Robin, who is unaware of being watched. Marian sees Robin through a virtual telescoping of her eyesight, the camera here functioning like the telescope and extending her vision in ways that are physically impossible.

While the film makes prosthetic extensions of vision open to both genders, it also marks that extension as often Cyclopian – hence lacking in depth: Robin's telescope, which requires that he shut one of his eyes to see through it, appears again when Robin uses it to spot the Celtic mercenaries advancing to attack the band of outlaws. The telescope parallels both the witch Mortianna's (Geraldine McEwen) single seeing eye, shot in extreme close-up from her point of view as she looks through a peephole, and the one eye of the Sheriff peeping through a hole in the castle wall. The single seeing eye figures intelligence-gathering as visual spying, extending vision to one who sees and is not seen at the cost of depth perception.

This loss of depth perception is registered most acutely in the shots that most explicitly align Robin's mastery with the bow and the film's technical mastery, with both understood as an extension of vision. Here Robin's arrows are shot in close-up when in flight, as if a tiny camera were mounted on the arrow. The first time we see this shot, his arrow splits another that has already been shot into the tree trunk. Yet far from surpassing the similar filmic shot of Robin's shot in *The Adventures of Robin Hood* (1938), in which Robin Hood (Errol Flynn) wins the archery contest by splitting his opponent's arrow (already lodged in the bull's eye), this shot keeps the arrow in focus but blurs the rest of the image. In the siege sequence near the end of *Robin Hood: Prince of Thieves*, when Robin and his band save nine of their men from being hanged, the arrows become more pyrotechnical, with the arrow tips literally set on fire and the shafts longer in length. Robin misses the hanging rope with his first arrow; but his second arrow is now filmed as it flies horizontally, its tip rotating in the centre, the arrow almost stretching across the entire middle of the screen, as if its greater extension compensated for the flattening out of the entirely blurred image behind the arrow as it flies to its target.

In making vision uniform across genders and races, thereby making moral difference a matter of extension rather than depth, *Robin Hood: Prince of Thieves* continually reinstates the political differences in gender and race it ostensibly sets out to overcome. The more the film invests in extending the plot so that we may see more and see it more closely (as in the tediously overlong final swordfight sequence between Robin and the Sheriff), the more the film deflates, both becoming increasingly camp and taking its politics less seriously. As a result Robin and the Sheriff actually become increasingly similar. The stitches on the Sheriff's face and also on the statue of himself he keeps in his castle are thus echoed by the cut we see across Robin's forehead just before he shoots his arrows to prevent the hanging of Little John's young son. Marian's volume is also turned down. She becomes a yelper, no longer a 'scream queen', and reverts from a woman who wields a dagger and a fireplace spit to a woman who cries for 'Robin!' when held against her will by the Sheriff and stands idly by while her man fights his enemy to the death. Azeem, in turn, accidentally kills Mortianna as she runs into a spear he is holding, which seems to reference Marian's earlier use of the roasting spit against her assaulter, thereby aligning Arab masculinity with English femininity. Arguably, Mortianna's death needs to seem accidental so that any connotations of interracial violence –

particularly violence coded as rape – are avoided. As if to resolve the tension between the stereotypes of aggressive non-white masculinity and feminised non-white masculinity, the film restages Mortianna's death: when she suddenly comes alive and is about to stab Robin in the back, Azeem hurls his scimitar through the air at her, much like Robin shoots his arrows, killing her a second time. In the second death, however, Azeem's flying scimitar is shot in old-school cinema style, much like the axes that are thrown in *The Vikings* (1958) to prove a wife's sexual fidelity or infidelity. Rather than deconstruct oppositions between moral and immoral characters, *Robin Hood: Prince of Thieves* leaves these oppositions intact, dispersing its critical energies in focusing on minor differences. None of these is big enough to make a political difference; rather, the film replicates traditional patriarchal and US imperialist values.

Stumped speech: the Bayeux Tapestry as bar and breaking faith with history

The Bayeux Tapestry sequence in Anthony Mann's *El Cid* differs notably from *Robin Hood: Prince of Thieves* in concentrating both on the Tapestry itself and on the wooden frame to which it is strapped (see Figure 15).[9] The sequence begins when Chimene, wife of Spanish nobleman Rodrigo (also known as El Cid), has taken refuge in a convent, unwilling to consummate the marriage because she cannot forgive El Cid for having killed her father in a duel over Rodrigo's honour. She is visited by Princess Urraca, interceding on behalf of her brother Alfonso, about to become King after ordering their elder brother Sancho's murder. Rodrigo plans to force Alfonso to swear his innocence in public at his coronation; and Urraca now demands that Chimene dissuade El Cid. The film cites panels 154–5 of the Bayeux Tapestry, a scene from the Battle of Hastings including the inscription: 'Hic ceciderunt simul Angli et Franci in prelio' ('Here English and French fell together in battle'). Cinematically speaking, the Bayeux Tapestry sequence in *El Cid* is rather straightforward, consisting mostly of shot-reverse-shots of the two women standing next to a panel of the tapestry Chimene is embroidering. The sequence falls into two parts, the first part focusing on the tapestry panel, and the second on the wooden bar on to which the embroidered panel is strapped. In the first part of the sequence Chimene's tapestry panel is seen from both sides in a series of shot-reverse-shots. In the first shot we see the front

15 Chimene weaving the Bayeux Tapestry in *El Cid* (1961)

side in close-up from Chimene's point of view as she sits to the right, reaching underneath to grab a needle she has put through the panel (see Figure 15 top left), the camera pulling back to a medium shot as Urraca enters the room from the upper left (Figure 15 top right). Then we see it from behind in medium long shot from Urraca's point of view as Chimene stands and tilts the panel upwards, then slightly bows in deference to Urraca's higher rank (Figure 15 bottom left). Then we see it once more from the front, with Chimene standing to the left side of the tapestry panel.

Though the panels cited from the genuine Bayeux Tapestry are clearly recognisable, Chimene has given the story of El Cid a religious cast by representing the Norman knights as Christians and the Saxons as Moors. The knight on foot holding a battle axe, immediately to the left of the Norman knight on horseback, has been given Moorish dress, and crosses have been added both to the mounted knight's shield and to the right flank of his horse (the horse's colour has been changed from green to yellow). A Norman-looking Christian knight has been added to Chimene's panel, placed just behind the horse's flank. He faces a Moorish knight with a scimitar, who has also been added and placed above and behind the upended, vertically positioned horse, which has been drawn in but not yet embroidered. The upended horse's erection in the genuine Tapestry is missing in Chimene's re-edition.[10] In the second sequence we see only the upper left of the frame, with the women standing on either side. Urraca is shot standing behind the tapestry, its upper wooden bar at the bottom of the shot. Initially agitated as she addresses Chimene, Urraca wraps her right hand in the mourning veil she removed from her head after having entered the convent room (worn in memory of her dead brother Sancho, who was murdered in the previous scene). Increasingly angered by Chimene's courteous defiance, Urraca strikes her veiled right hand down on the right post holding the tapestry panel frame, and then strikes it down again, this time on the centre of the frame (see Figure 15 bottom right). Each time Urraca's hand strikes, the film immediately cuts away to Chimene.

What makes the sequence recognisable and significant as an encrypted allegory of film editing and women as editors is less the resemblance between Chimene's panel and the genuine Tapestry than the tapestry frame itself. The sequence disrupts a mimetic relation between the genuine Tapestry and Chimene's copy not only in terms of the content of the panels but also in the way Mann shoots the drawing that Chimene uses as a template for her tapestry as partially rolled-up scroll, so as to make its contents only partly visible. Though there is clearly a mimetic relation between the drawing and Chimene's copy of it, there is also a subtle yet significant mismatch between them: whereas the tapestry panel is part of a longer piece of fabric that has been rolled up and strapped down at the left and right sides of the panel, the drawing to Chimene's lower left is unbound, leaning against a column, and folded at the ends. Although the edges of the drawing and the folded rolls of the tapestry are comparable, they differ in the way they figure what is exterior to the film image and, hence, to mimesis. The shots of the tapestry panel call attention to this exteriority through Chimene's placement and lighting. We never see Chimene's panel completely because Chimene obscures first the right side (when seated) and then the left side (when standing). The lighting of the shot similarly obscures the edges of the tapestry panel. The upright panel frame posts (which allow Chimene to tilt the panel frame up or down) and the bound parts of the tapestry cast shadows when shot from either side. Furthermore, when shot with Chimene standing behind it, the tapestry's reverse side does not match its front side: the drawn, upended horse that Chimene has yet to embroider is not visible in the shot in which we see the panel from the back.

Significantly, Chimene's version does not change the word 'simul' present in the Bayeux Tapestry, creating a disjunction between the word and the image in the panel that marks and remarks her simulation of the Bayeux Tapestry as a break – or cut – in simulation rather than the product of an act of faithful (copy-)editing.[11] The sequence inscribes this cinematic cut in the second frontal shot of Chimene's tapestry panel, as a castration of the vertical horse's phantom erection. The sequence thus allegorises as a cropping effected by the cinematic frame itself – a cropping that occurs prior to any cutting of a film strip into recorded segments – rather than as a mimetic copying and suturing that extends continuous, panoramic visibility. Like Marian's, Chimene's actions are shown to be analogous to those of a film editor. In Chimene's case, however, editing resembles less Chimene's embroidered stitches in the tapestry panel itself than the rope around the top, used to stretch the cloth on to the wooden panel frame, and the thread, used to strap the wrapped-up cloth down and hold it in place on the left and right sides of the panel frame.

Significantly, the tapestry panel itself drops out of the sequence with Chimene and Urraca. The upper part of the wooden panel frame becomes the prominent focus of the second part of the sequence as the power struggle between the two women intensifies and reaches its climax. When first shot from behind, the tapestry frame alone appears, since the panel is tilted forward. We see the backside only when Chimene tilts it forward as she stands up (Figure 15 bottom right). This is followed by a shot revealing a small continuity error, in which the panel is still (or once again) shown tilted although Chimene has stood up. The break in continuity is crucial, however, for the upper horizontal piece of the tapestry frame becomes a bar which Urraca cannot break or get past (Figure 15 bottom right). The film cuts away from her hand in an act of both mutilation (as if she had no hand) and phobic blindness (as if her hand were already missing, her arm a stump). Figuratively, she is giving a stump speech for Alfonso.[12] Yet Urraca is too late. The historical narrative is already strapped down, held in place in the panel itself, and the thread cannot be cut, nor the frame be broken. The following scene marks Urraca's defeat as Rodrigo forces Alfonso to swear in public that he had no part in his brother Sancho's death. Chimene's position on the opposite side of the panel frame places her in a space beyond Urraca's reach, making Chimene's immobile body into an unbreakable, statuesque monument.

Yet Chimene's position in the shots at the end of the sequence which no longer include the tapestry panel frame also limits her ability to resist Urraca. While Chimene may have gained the upper hand (and the way she tilts the panel frame up when Urraca enters the shot mimes the scene's dissolve from Chimene to the tilt shot of a church

tower with bells ringing, implying that she shares the moral righteous-
ness the call of the bell represents), neither woman finally controls
the narrative frame. For Chimene, as for Urraca, that is, the narrative
frame is out of reach. Her immobility throughout the scene suggests
that she is less an agent than a projected image, a vertical version of the
horizontal panel frame. As the sequence ends, the source of Chimene's
backlit projection becomes visible when a wheel window to her left
comes into the shot, strongly resembling a film reel (see also Figure
15 bottom left). Her wide eyes may resemble the scope of the 70mm
widescreen vision of the film, but her vision is nevertheless limited.

In contrast to *Robin Hood: Prince of Thieves*, *El Cid* makes its allegory of the Bayeux Tapestry as cinema visible not through a mimetic
match but as a literal and figurative stretch, a reach. This allegory
becomes visible and legible as such because of Mann's frequent use of
geometric compositions and recursive para-mimetic graphic elements,
which resemble a bar like that of the top of the wooden frame of the
Tapestry (see Figures 16 and 17). These bars become evident in, for
instance: the shot of Rodrigo holding the priest's arm as he raises him
up in the film's second sequence; the yoke on the back of the loyal Arab
emir, Lord Moutamin, to which his arms are strapped before Rodrigo
cuts him loose, earning him the name 'El Cid' (Figure 16 top right);
the people standing across the bottom of the screen demanding that
Rodrigo's Moorish prisoners be hanged; Count Ordóñez and Count

16 Paramimetic Elements in *El Cid* (1961): a broadsword in Rodrigo's
duel with Count Gormaz; the yoke on Lord Moutamin; the guardrail
in tournament for Calahorra; and the extended arms of Rodrigo and
Chimene in their marriage ceremony

Gormaz, Chimene's father, embracing, their arms in profile as the doors of the room close; Rodrigo, before drawing his sword on Count Gormaz, holding his broadsword still in its scabbard with both hands, so that it forms a bar across the entire lower screen (Figure 16 top left); the guardrails in the fight for the Calahorra sequence, in which two-handed broadswords are planted in the middle of the screen (Figure 16 bottom left); the top of a tent running across the bottom of the frame before the first joust; a scimitar sword drawn moments before the surprise attack to kill Rodrigo and Prince Sancho; Chimene and Rodrigo shot from behind when they marry, their arms joined horizontally across the lower part of the frame (Figure 16 bottom right); Alfonso's arm stretched across the bottom of the frame as Rodrigo holds Alfonso's hand on the Bible and forces Alfonso to swear his innocence of Sancho's murder; a man holding a dagger horizontally in the bottom of the frame before cauterising Alfonso's wounded right arm; and numerous shots of bars on doors and doorframes.

The bearing of *El Cid*'s recursive para-mimetic elements on our understanding of the film's politics becomes clearer if we consider how they differ from the film's mimetic repetitions that take emblematic form. *El Cid*'s geometric formalism and mimetic repetition of shots inscribe a vision of patriarchal and royal power by aligning the King with a vertical position in the centre of the shot. Shots of King Ferdinand at court, for instance, when he is seated there before the fight for Calahorra, reiterate this central placement. Additionally, a number of shots of Ferdinand at the fight for Calahorra show him in a red tent that looks like a theatre curtain, establishing his power as both ideally positioned spectator and ideally positioned screen icon. Vertical posts, identified with Ferdinand, are replaced after he dies with diagonal or horizontal bars, identified with the feuding brothers to signify their loss of power. At his funeral Ferdinand's tomb effigy is also shot in the middle of the cinematic frame, and, in the following shot, Sancho and Alfonso are shown from behind in medium close-up, divided by a suspended statue of Jesus that mirrors Ferdinand's tomb effigy below it.

The phantom father, remembered mimetically as an effigy and statue, no longer keeps order, however. After Sancho enters the crypt, he and Alfonso almost immediately turn on each other in a fight to the death. Even before the first joust begins during the Calahorra sequence, a third shot which positions the vertical, two-handed broadsword in the middle then shows it bending back and forth as the music

17 Horizontal swords and guardrails in Rodrigo's defeat of Don Martin at the tournament in *El Cid* (1961)

goes off-key, signalling the potential loss of Ferdinand's territory. Such emblems of patriarchy are also shot in diagonal positions to register a similar loss of power by the Christian rulers and a corollary gaining of power by the Moors: Sancho holds his sword in a shot diagonally from the upper left down to the lower right when he dies on the ground as Rodrigo holds him. Diagonally shot emblems include Count Gormaz's tomb effigy in the crypt, with Chimene in black sitting upright next to it; Ben Yussef's outstretched arm at the end of the first sequence when he announces his plan to invade Spain; and the scimitar that enters the cinematic frame in close-up before the Moors begin their surprise attack on Rodrigo and Sancho.

The Bayeux Tapestry sequence clarifies that El Cid's position as messianic figure is located both through mimetic repetitions and recursive para-mimetic graphic elements, recalling in particular the frame and veil in the decisive earlier Calahorra sequence in which Rodrigo and Don Martín fight to the death (Figure 17). In this sequence Rodrigo both proves that he is innocent of treason and wins the province of Calahorra for King Ferdinand. In the logic of the sequence a literal cutting through the guardrail, or frame, means death: the fight ends as Don Martín breaks through the guardrail with his broadsword, giving the wounded Rodrigo time to recover and use his broadsword to strike Don Martín fatally in the back. The film links rather than opposes Don Martín's death and Rodrigo's victory to cinematic exteriority. After Don Martín is briefly shot on the ground in medium close-up as Rodrigo drives his sword into him offscreen,

Rodrigo comes back into the shot, holding up his sword above his head with his arms stretched out to create a frame (Figure 17 bottom left). He asks King Ramírez (Gerard Tichy) the rhetorical question: 'To whom does Calahorra belong?' Rodrigo is thus exterior to the frame he creates at the moment of establishing vocal confirmation of victory. Initially positioned by matching shots as two (almost literal) posts in the ground that figure the outcome of the fight, Don Martín and Rodrigo's broadswords end up being only another para-mimetic element (in this case part of a frame) rather than a mimetic emblem of cutting and narrative closure. Taking Chimene's favour, a black veil, from Don Martín's corpse, Rodrigo walks to the other side of the lists and holds his sword up again, now shot from below, with the railing at the bottom of the screen (Figure 17 bottom right). This positions him more explicitly outside a frame, producing a kind of letterbox effect, a frame within the film frame. Rodrigo pierces the bloody veil and then offers it to Chimene on the tip of his sword in the vain hope that she will forgive him for having killed her father. She bluntly refuses his offer. In the scene that follows the Calahorra sequence Chimene is still wearing black, plotting Rodrigo's death at the side of her father's tomb effigy. Anticipating Urraca's pounding of the wooden frame in the Bayeux Tapestry sequence, Rodrigo holds on to the frame but does not manage to box Chimene into it. His position of heroic triumph is also one of abject failure, his bloodied broadsword a supplementary image of male authority that is marked as a lack of authority by Chimene's veil. He may have pierced her veil with his sword, but he has not broken her hymen. This implication is supported by the fact that the film presents no evidence of sexual relations between them until the appearance of their daughter much later on. Indeed, their wedding feast, which features the figures of two jousting knights on the table, repeats the end of Calahorra sequence: here, the joust is a verbal one, in which (to work with the jousting analogy) Chimene manages to unhorse Rodrigo.

Rodrigo's elevation to the legendary figure of El Cid is allegorised from the beginning of the film through a mimetic matching of Rodrigo and Jesus, and a para-mimetic mismatching of Rodrigo and graphic elements involving both a break and a recovery (Figures 17 and 18). El Cid's status as an exceptional man, which elicits variations of the question 'what kind of man are you?' from other characters throughout the film, begins near the opening of the film when Rodrigo breaks off the shafts of arrows that had been shot into a crucifix with a black

Jesus. After taking the cross down from the altar, Rodrigo is figured as a Christ-figure when he carries it, straps it on his horse and then meets up with two Moors who have their arms tied to yokes behind their necks, as if they were the two thieves crucified alongside Jesus. Rodrigo's messianic status as exile and finally (in a twisted form) as resurrected phantom menace at the end of the film is established when Rodrigo breaks the arrow lodged in his chest, repeating his previous action of breaking off the arrows stuck in the Jesus statue. This mimetic repetition of the breaking of arrows makes it emblematic of Rodrigo's martyrdom.

Yet this mimetic repetition also aligns Rodrigo and Christ through a literal break. If *El Cid* avails itself of a cinematic matching enabling a typological reading of history as mimetic repetition, it also shows the need for a sadistic para-mimetic supplement that matches Rodrigo to Jesus by literally strapping them down in a way that begins to transform the crucified Christian hero into his apparent opposite, the crucifying Moorish villain (Ben Yusseff kills Don Ordóñez by driving a knife into his heart after first crucifying and torturing him). The scene in which Rodrigo is tied on to his horse near the end of the film echoes the moment when Rodrigo straps the statue of Jesus on to his horse near the beginning of the film. The first scene matches Rodrigo and Jesus through recourse to one of the film's recurrent para-mimetic elements, namely the outstretched arm. After securing the statue on the horse in the burning village at the end of the film's first sequence, Rodrigo walks out of the shot with his back to the camera. The camera lingers on the priest after Rodrigo has left the frame, showing the priest stretching

18 Rodrigo strapped into the frame of history by the priest in *El Cid* (1961)

his lower right arm across the bottom of the frame while he holds on to the black Jesus statue (Figure 18 top left). Similarly, after Rodrigo frees the two Moorish prisoners, he walks across the frame, past the horse carrying the statue, which is seen in the centre of the shot (Figure 18 top right). The priest stretches out his arm once more, this time to grab Rodrigo as he walks past, in a movement that stretches Rodrigo's arm to match Jesus's horizontally outstretched arms on the crucifix. Moreover, Rodrigo's gesture of covering the broken arrow in his chest with his shield after he is shot during the siege of Valencia suggests that mimetic repetitions also involve a literal recovery, an anti-mimetic and anamorphic obscuring of the repeated, mimetic element much like the veils worn by Urraca, Chimene and even Ben Yusseff (who wears a veils throughout the film except when he murders Don Ordóñez).

This para-mimetic supplement marks El Cid's superhuman exteriority not as a repetition but as a narrative detour away from patriarchy, a detour that marks the initial crisis of the film (Rodrigo was originally on his way to marry Chimene). The first word Rodrigo says in the film is 'father', when he touches the priest to comfort him. Rodrigo then helps the priest up from his kneeling position, so that their right arms form a horizontal line across the bottom of the film frame (Figure 18 bottom right). The two arms double a man who is about to be married and a 'father' who is not literally a father, a celibate priest who, even if by definition a figure of patriarchy representing '*the* father', quickly disappears from the film. This detour away from the shortest path to Rodrigo's wedding opens up progressive possibilities, notably when Rodrigo cuts the Moorish prisoners free in the very next scene rather than turning them over to the King, as Don Ordóñez demands. Yet, as in the Calahorra sequence, this progress stalls with the recurrence of a para-mimetic element, namely, the yoke across Rodrigo's Moorish prisoner's – Lord Moutamin's – shoulders at the bottom of the frame as Rodrigo frees Moutamin. The yoke, placed on the Moor before the film begins, constitutes an impediment, or road block, to Rodrigo's marriage. Rodrigo binds himself to his position outside the King's law by cutting the rope to liberate his former enemy, setting in motion the events that will lead up to the killing of Chimene's father and her refusal to marry Rodrigo.

Reconsidered from the perspective of the film's ambivalent and recursive historicism, *El Cid*'s Bayeux Tapestry sequence may be understood more precisely not only as an allegory of cinematic writing but as an allegory that calls such allegorical readings of cinema, whether messianic or secular, into question by deconstructing their common reliance on matching and paralleling of similar narratives. Through recursive para-mimetic graphic elements that, if looked at awry, resemble a stretched and strapped frame but do not figure it in symbolic terms, *El Cid* breaks with the repetitions of mimetic typology and the historicism and the cinematic logic of superimposition.

Cut and run

As a double-sided, folded textile with two running borders framing the main panels and shot in a wooden frame as it is being assembled, the Bayeux Tapestry in film indirectly raises a broader question of the relation between history and narrative framing taken up by New Historicists. In his essay 'The touch of the Real', Stephen Greenblatt observes that what the historicist takes to be reality effects, or traces of the past, are produced through a narrative frame. As he puts it in discussing the anthropologist Clifford Geertz's seminal essay 'Thick description': 'Thickness is not in the object; it is in the narrative surrounding, the add-ons, the nested frames ... The frame is really crucial, since in this case it helps us to conjure up a "real" as opposed to an "imaginary" world.'[13] The real to which ethnographic and historicist writing refers is an effect of a narrative frame.

   Yet framing remains an intractable problem for Greenblatt's historicism. If in guaranteeing a passage from representation, or traces, to reality outside of representation, the frame also necessarily calls into question the truth value of what is being narrated through the frame. Greenblatt can distinguish the real from the fake as long as he believes the academic doing the framing is telling the truth. 'It was crucial, as part of the pleasure and interest of reading Geertz', Greenblatt comments, 'to believe he had not made up his Mr. Cohen [Geertz's Moroccan native informant] and that Cohen too had not simply made up his story ... If ... it turned out that Geertz had made up Cohen ... his work would have immediately lost much of its value.'[14] Geertz's informant 'may have considerably enhanced the story for rhetorical effect; but Cohen was a real person recounting actual experiences, and his story was his story and not the ethnographer's ... If it is only a matter of rhetoric – then only a reality-effect is conjured and nothing more.'[15] The discussion of the frame here opens up a mise en abîme, since the frame is also a hinge, always having the potential to flip the reality effect over and exposing it as a conjuring trick, or what would be called in cinematic terms a magic trick. In Greenblatt's account the narrative frame provides a touch of the real on the one hand, yet has no guarantee of its own truth value or lack thereof outside itself, especially when the frame takes anecdotal, that is to say, narrative form, typically in autobiographical writing. As a storyteller, the framing historicist, if he or she is adept, will resemble and mime reality. If not, she or he risks being exposed as merely miming a spellbinding magician – perhaps just a vaudevillian, whose traces of the real are nothing more than cheap and cheapening rhetorical effects. The historicist is thus caught within an endless aporetic oscillation between knowing wink and involuntary tic, exposing showmanship as trickery, precisely because the historicist equates history with mimesis, the frame being that which stands outside mimesis and history in making both visible.

The Bayeux Tapestry in cinema offers a more complicated and productive account of the relation between frame and historical narration in being a para-mimetic *text*-tile, both a form of cinematic writing and a figure of editing. Para-mimetic cinematic writing is not outside of historicism or antithetical to it precisely because history exceeds mimesis; in cinematic terms, the continuity editing system which typically seeks to make editing and framing invisible becomes visible in its a-rhythmic tempo. By quietly rupturing narrative and cinematic continuity, the Bayeux Tapestry reveals the violent cutting, binding and blinding that make any narrative or counter-narrative, feminist or otherwise, visible.

Notes

1 For a discussion of the opening title sequences of the historical fiction films see Richard Burt, 'Re-embroidering the Bayeux Tapestry in film and media: the flip side of history in opening and end title sequences', *Exemplaria*, 19:2 (Summer 2007), 327–50. For a broader consideration of the historical film's cinematic paratexts in both celluloid and digital film, see Richard Burt, *Medieval and Early Modern Film and Media* (New York and London: Palgrave, 2008).

2 See Lisa Jardine, 'Unpicking the tapestry: the scholar of women's history as Penelope among her suitors', in Jardine, *Reading Shakespeare Historically* (New York: Routledge, 1991), pp. 132–47; Rozsika Parker, *The Subversive Stitch: Embroidery and the Making of the Feminine* (London: Women's Press, 1984); and Gerald A. Bond, *The Loving Subject: Desire, Eloquence, and Power in Romanesque France* (Philadelphia: University of Pennsylvania Press, 1995), p. 25.

3 Tom Conley, *Film Hieroglyphs: Ruptures in Classical Cinema* (University of Minnesota Press, 2006 [1991]), p. xxxix.

4 Tom Cohen, *Hitchcock's* Cryptonymies, 2 vols (Minneapolis: University of Minnesota Press, 2005), vol. 1: *Secret Agents*, pp. 8, xvii, xvi.
5 For a broader discussion see Richard Burt, 'Re-embroidering the Bayeux Tapestry'.
6 See John Aberth, *A Knight at the Movies* (New York: Routledge, 2003), pp. 187–93; Kathleen Biddick, *The Shock of Medievalism* (Durham, NC: Duke University Press, 1998), pp. 74–5.
7 On *El Cid's* putative 'Fascist vision' and its relation to the Spanish Civil War see Aberth, *A Knight at the Movies*, pp. 142–5.
8 See Walter Murch, *In the Blink of an Eye: A Perspective on Film Editing* (Los Angeles: Silman-James Press, 2001), pp. 75–6.
9 Richard Brilliant offers some connections between El Cid and the Bayeux Tapestry, Brilliant, 'The Bayeux Tapestry: a stripped narrative for their eyes and ears', *Word & Image*, 7:2 (April–June 1991), 98–126 (110–11).
10 See Sarah Larratt Keefer's discussion of 'priapic horses' in Keefer, 'Body language: a graphic commentary by the horses of the Bayeux Tapestry', in Gale R. Owen-Crocker (ed.), *King Harold II and the Bayeux Tapestry* (Woodbridge: Boydell, 2005), pp. 93–108 (pp. 100–5).
11 The letters 'derun simul' in the upper left border of Chimene's panel also rationalise the appearance of 'derunt' in the authentic Bayeux Tapestry, changing the N and T in 'derunt', combined as one letter into an 'n', thereby cropping the mimetic writing of the authentic panel as well.
12 'Stump speech' is a term in the US for political campaign speeches.
13 Stephen Greenblatt, 'The touch of the Real', *Representations*, 59 (Summer 1997), 14–29 (17, 21). For a second version see Stephen Greenblatt and Catherine Gallagher, *Practicing New Historicism* (Chicago: University of Chicago Press, 2000), pp. 20–48.
14 Greenblatt, 'The touch of the real', 21.
15 Greenblatt and Gallagher, *Practicing New Historicism*, pp. 28–9, 29–30.

8

Medieval *noir*: anatomy of a metaphor

John M. Ganim

The argument of this chapter is that certain films with medieval themes and settings, mostly dating from the 1940s to the 1960s, demonstrate a surprising affinity with the themes and techniques associated with film *noir*. The apocalyptic landscapes of these films are often bleak mirrors of the empty streets of film *noir* and sometimes allude to the sense of impending doom that haunted the post-Second World War world and informed *noir*. The arbitrary sense of order and justice in these films parallels the cynical attitude towards authority and due process found in *noir* films. The recurrent concern with religious and moral investigation in these medieval films often results in an existential perspective shared by film *noir*. Certain techniques of *noir* lighting and sets were employed by films set in the Middle Ages. Moreover, this affinity goes both ways. Film *noir* itself is informed by an undercurrent of medievalism. The dark and dangerous streets of the city of *noir* are a modernised version of the haunted castle of the Gothic novel. The hero of *noir* is often explicitly linked with the questing knight of Grail legends. The femme fatale of *noir* gender stereotypes is a descendant of the fatal women of medieval romance, though usually filtered through romanticism's understanding of the Middle Ages. That is, the Middle Ages, or at least images of the Middle Ages as propounded in medievalist discourses, operate as an important metaphor in film *noir*. My shorthand term for this dialectic is 'medieval *noir*', though I am aware that the term has been used to describe recent cultural productions in music and new media where violence and Gothic settings have been combined with occasional historical allusions to a cyberpunk reinvention of the Middle Ages. There may be a connection between the association I am locating in these films and these newer cultural productions, but my aim in this chapter is otherwise. I seek to trouble the theoretical distinction between a film mode, style or genre (scholars disagree as to what film *noir* actually describes) that has been thought of as a model of cinematic purity – film *noir* – and a group of films often regarded as essays on the relation of the past and present, as private auteur expressions of faith or religious crisis or as indulgences in a dated romanticism that film *noir* reacted against in the first place.

Medieval *noir* and the critics

It must be admitted at the outset that an effort to define an equation such as medieval *noir* in film is counterintuitive. On the face of it, no two genres might seem further apart than film *noir* and medieval movies. Given that both have their classic period from the late 1930s to the late 1950s, one might even think of them as polar opposites. The romanticism of medieval films may be regarded as a virtual antidote to the cynicism and nihilism of film *noir*. With the rise of Technicolor, the bright banners and costumes, sunlit battlefields and sweeping natural landscapes of historical epics, such as *El Cid* (1961), *Knights of the Round Table* (1953) or *King Richard and the Crusaders* (1954), contrast with the claustrophobic, studio-shot artificiality and expressionistically lit sets of film *noir*. The archaic idealism of medieval movies may be seen as an attempt to deny the existential angst of film *noir*, especially in its postwar phase. The attempt of medieval movies, as a species of historical films, to recreate a virtual past time and place contrasts with the surrealism and presentness of film *noir*. What I seek to locate in this chapter, however, is an unlikely cross-pollination, one which inflects certain medieval movies with an unsettling modernity, and which raises questions about the relation of the present to the past and about the aesthetic and political uses of an ostensibly faraway time and place.

Because of their settings in faraway lands and past times, medieval movies are often stereotyped as escapist. When they are seriously treated as a form of historical film, as they are in John Aberth's *A Knight at the Movies*, they are judged by a standard of their fidelity to history, or at least to historical documents, though Aberth is attentive to the careers of individual directors and to responses in these films to contemporary political and social developments.[1] But there are other relations and other dimensions to the genre that suggest the interplay of medieval movies to other forms and movements, cinematic, political and intellectual. As Kevin J. Harty observes in *Cinema*

Arthuriana, unlike 'films we classify as films *noir* or westerns or road pictures, films about King Arthur do not easily fit into any one cinematic genre. Rather, cinema Arthuriana is a form of medievalism, the attempt as old as the birth of the early modern or Renaissance period to revisit or reinvent the medieval world for contemporary purposes.'² Harty informs us elsewhere that an uncommon number of early silent films dealt with medieval themes, usually based on nineteenth-century retellings of romances or other medieval stories.³ The medieval past, mediated by revivals and interpretations of the Middle Ages, was therefore a crucial element in the costume drama and historical films that seem to constitute the opposite cinematic pole of film *noir*.

There can be, however, traces of unlikely opposites in film genres. A critical model for investigating such traces was provided nearly thirty years ago, when Daniel R. Rubey published what has become a classic article on the original *Star Wars* (1977) in the journal *Jump Cut*.⁴ Beneath the hypermodernity of a science fiction future, Rubey discerned the patterns of the past. One pattern was the structural dependence of *Star Wars* on medieval romance. Rubey observed that the film highlighted an Oedipal struggle that is also often found in medieval romance. The other was the films' employment of the imagery of the Second World War, particularly its dog-fight battle sequences, which Rubey argued was a way of erasing the reality of America's experience in Vietnam by recalling a successful and clearly heroic struggle of the recent past. Similarly, argued Rubey, the film *Jaws* (1975) also used Second World War references, particularly in its recall of Hiroshima, and of the legendary sinking of the ship that carried the *Enola Gay*, and the loss of its crew to sharks.⁵ Far from being escapist fantasies, films employing medieval subjects and themes in fact revealed what Fredric Jameson called the political unconscious.⁶ But, as Rubey's article implies, the clear demarcation of the Second World War, with its identifiable contrast of good and evil, could hardly survive the complex and compromised experience of the postwar world, in which memories of defeat, collaboration, betrayal and resistance coloured the increasingly paranoid view of even the victors. The McCarthy period turned former friends into informers, and its trials were compared to the Inquisition. The filmic expression of this disillusionment is of course film *noir*, though the origins of *noir* are located in the late 1930s.

Film *noir* can be defined very narrowly, as a particular species of detective or crime drama, or more broadly to refer to a style or a mood or a particular complex of filmic techniques. Raymond Borde and Etienne Chaumeton, who in the 1950s were among the first French critics to define the new, dark series of films – 'oneiric, strange, erotic, ambivalent, and cruel' – emerging from postwar America, could look back from the perspective of the 1970s to find *noir* elements in a wide range of films: 'From the "filmological" point of view, series have their origins in a few old movies, a few scattered titles ... Afterwards, they reach a climax; that's to say, a moment of exceptional purity. Following that, they fade and die, their aftereffects being felt in other genres.'[7] Borde and Chaumeton's somewhat organic metaphor of an afterlife does suggest how *noir* characteristics can be found in medieval movies. They also distinguish film *noir* from other series, in the course of which they mention Jean Delannoy and Jean Cocteau's *L'Eternel Retour* (1943) as an example of an item in a series involving 'mythic evasions'. Modernising Tristan and Isolde in contemporary dress, Cocteau dramatised the public and private conflicts inherent in the plot, emphasising its dark and destructive spirals. Visually, the stark black-and-white photography seemed to glamorise the blonde hero and heroine in such a way that the film was condemned for a pro-Nazi bias during the Occupation. Other film critics have also found *noir* elements in other genres. For instance, Raymond Durgnat offered a map of the way in which *noir* elements could be found across the spectrum of film genres, including Stanley Kubrick's science fiction *2001: A Space Odyssey* (1968).[8]

Some film scholars prefer to limit the definition of *noir* to a very specific set of films. Alain Silver and Elizabeth Ward, in their extensive catalogue of films that satisfy the generic definitions of film *noir*, limit themselves to detective films and thrillers, and also limit themselves by period, emphasising the period from the late 1930s to the early 1960s.[9] Marc Vernet questions whether film *noir* can be defined by intellectual influences – imported European lighting and film techniques, or the other factors normally associated with the rise of film *noir*.[10] He finds what we call *noir* in the American crime film from its earliest beginnings, and attributes the classic definition of Borde and Chaumeton mentioned above to the relative isolation of French film critics and audiences, as well as to a shift towards a certain populism in French culture that allowed the French to view American films in a new, dialectical way. Vernet wonders whether expressionism can be said to influence film *noir* in any fundamental way, a question which complicates some of my assumptions below. In any case my argument depends less on the limits of what constitutes film *noir* than on its status as a dominant genre of postwar American cinema.[11] Moreover, the association of the medieval with *noir* (which in fact might be more accurately described as the Gothic and *noir*) is an association already forged in popular cultural productions of the last decade or so. Fantasy fiction and especially video and computer games combine the maze-like urban setting of film *noir* with a loose symbolic network of medi-evalised images. And *noir* itself is spoken of as a matter of style and fashion, even of mood, in contemporary journalism.

The Middle Ages and *noir* are frequently linked by casual meta-phors in cinema studies, cultural studies and literary scholarship. The collocation of *noir* and medievalism has recently intertwined itself in popular culture. The most famous example of this is Quentin Taran-tino's *Pulp Fiction* (1994), with its reworking of *noir* imagery encap-sulated in the phrase 'get medieval on your ass' to announce a male rape scene. Carolyn Dinshaw comments on the homophobic imagery of the scene in her book *Getting Medieval*, which analyses the ways in which ideas of the medieval past disturb normative sexuality.[12] The phrase 'medieval *noir*' has in fact been widely used, largely outside of academia. In discussing the success of Roberto Benigni's *Life Is Beautiful* (1997), for instance, *Variety* stated that until that film, the most popular movie on Italian television had been *The Name of the Rose*, 'the Jean-Jacques Annaud medieval *noir* pic based on Umberto Eco's bestseller'.[13] The recycling of medieval imagery and motifs in Goth rock and Heavy Metal music is so pervasive as to be almost self-evident. The *L. A. Weekly* referred to a local band, Ego Plum, as partly medieval *noir*.[14] An interesting contrast between the modern world of film *noir* and the vaguely medieval decentring of postmodernism is suggested in one influential study. In *The Sphinx in the City*, Eliza-beth Wilson links 'the medieval "ship of fools", in which the mad were herded on to a ship that endlessly sailed the rivers and seas of Europe' to the place of young women in the doom of Manhattan in the 1980s, especially in the fiction of Catherine Texier: in film *noir*, according to Wilson, 'urban space became a powerful metaphor for the angst and paranoia of the 1940s'.[15] And where the usurping women of film *noir* were controlled and punished ultimately by patriarchal figures, the disorientation of such postmodern fiction is that pleasure and danger are inseparable and even the male figures are now 'petulant, temper-amental and uncertain'.[16] In a thorough study of crime film Thomas Leitch associates the idea of the criminal protagonist in gangster films and *noir* with the passing of the medieval idea of divinely ordered social positions, hence giving rise to 'the suspicion that some people may be occupying places they have no right to – a suspicion that produces the rise of the criminal in literature'.[17] The relationship to courtly love or its absolute breakdown also figures in the metaphorics of *noir*. In *Somewhere in the Night: Film Noir and the American City*, Nicholas Christopher imagines the 'Beatrice' figure who may be distinct from or combined with a 'Circe' figure to constitute the female object of film *noir*, alluding to Dante's association of Beatrice with a protective and beatific light. Christopher's use of this analogy derives from a more or less Jungian panoply of archetypes: 'When she is a Beatrice-type, she is almost too good to be true. Nurturing to a fault, loyal beyond the bounds of common sense, she is like the faithful guide who appears suddenly in a nightmare, or in the "dark wood" in which Dante found himself.'[18]

Because Raymond Chandler, the most typical author of novels whose books were made into classic *noir* films, is explicit about the knight-errantry of his protagonist detective, Philip Marlowe, critics have pointed to the medieval images in Chandler's novels. Marlowe's name not only recalls the narrator of Joseph Conrad's complex narratives, a narrator who does not always fully comprehend the meaning of his own narration, he also recalls Thomas Malory, the author of the great English version of the story of King Arthur and his knights. The discovery of the Winchester manuscript of Malory's work would have meant that mention of the author would have been prominent in newspaper and radio accounts at the same time that Chandler was creating his fictional detective. *The Lady in the Lake* (1947) clearly references Malory's Lady of the Lake. In *Creatures of Darkness: Raymond Chandler, Detective Fiction and Film Noir*, Gene D. Phillips goes as far as to title a section of his book 'Knight and the City'. 'Chandler was at pains', writes Phillips, 'to portray Marlowe in the novel not just as a hard-boiled private eye, but as a knightly hero ... Marlowe views a case as a crusade, whereby he aims to protect the innocent and helpless, and not merely solve a mystery.'[19] Phillips is building here on Chandler's own comments, as well as such critics as David Geherin, who compares Marlowe to a 'knight in shining armor' battling 'dragons', and Robert Merrill, who points to Marlowe's 'knight-errantry'.[20] The connection is made clear in a famous passage in *The Big Sleep*. As Marlowe enters General Sternwood's home, he notices a stained-glass image of a knight 'in dark armor, rescuing a lady who was tied to a tree and didn't have any clothes on'.[21] The medieval image, presumably a medieval revival window, is described in the terms of a pulp magazine cover. Andrew Dickos in *Street With No Name: A History of the Classic American Film Noir* modifies the analogy when he distinguishes the chivalric hero from the American detective, for 'these private eyes maintain a code of personal honour, but it is less proscriptive and judgmental than is usually held to be the case, not like the medieval Christian heroes'.[22] The analogy can go both ways. In his reading of Marie de France in *Fictions of Identity in Medieval France*, Donald Maddox compares the plot of *Equitan* to film *noir*, especially the motivation of the seneschal's wife: 'With the cunning of a heroine of *film noir*, she even foresees the need to dissipate possible suspicions, specifying that the vassals of both the king and the seneschal be convened for a kind of collective "autopsy" to certify that death has occurred by natural causes'.[23]

Disenchanted quests and city settings

Film theory has also drawn some implicit parallels between medieval films and *noir*. Medieval historical movies and crime films share a certain generic status in cinematic taxonomies. Film *noir* historians have always attempted to distinguish between earlier crime films and the unique characteristics of films *noir*. Nino Frank called the former the crime adventure or, even better yet, the crime psychology film. This is one of the most notable of film genres, and it has replaced the western. Interesting conclusions can be drawn from this displacement of a western dynamism dependent on 'pursuits and love stories on the run' by a crime dynamism derived from violent death and mysteries that must be solved, as well as from the displacement of a 'vast, fictionalised natural world' by a realm of social fantasy.[24]

Frank's capsule description of the western, with its 'pursuits and love stories on the run' as well as its 'vast fictionalized natural world' is also a fair description of many medieval films, and, indeed, of medieval romances. Yet it must be admitted that while the description Frank offers of his sample – *The Maltese Falcon* (1941), *Murder, My Sweet* (1944), *Laura* (1944) and *Double Indemnity* (1944) – is certainly captured by his distinction, within a few years the pursuit and the man on the run are reintroduced into the narrative conventions of *noir* crime films. In *noir* revival films of the 1960s and 1970s, as Larry Gross noted, space and setting take on a cinematic life and meaning of their own, independently of the fortunes of the protagonist.[25] As Frank notes: 'The essential question no longer has to do with who committed the crime, but with how the protagonist handles himself. It isn't even necessary that the adventures in which he becomes involved be comprehensible in any detail.'[26] The often obscure plotting and symbolic settings of medieval romance, that is, can be found in film *noir*.

Indeed film *noir* can be said to medievalise its urban and suburban setting. The city, like the castle or the ruin in Romantic and neo-Romantic fiction, was now represented as what Sigmund Freud called the *unheimlich*. In fact Freud's classic essay on 'The uncanny' employs an account of the analyst's own experience, in which he takes a wrong turn in an effort to return home and finds himself again and again in the red-light district of a foreign city, which is nevertheless very close to his own home, where he is subjected to insults and imprecations shouted at him by women from their balconies and windows.[27] Susan Crane has brilliantly observed that Freud's example resembles the relation between setting, subjectivity and gender in medieval romance.[28] As noted above, Chandler famously compared his detective to a knight-errant, pursuing an impossible ideal through these 'mean streets'. In Chandler's novels Los Angeles especially is imbued with a menace often expressed as personal and sexual treachery. As Edward Dimendberg has demonstrated, film *noir* employs an urban, almost documentary setting to an unprecedented degree. Film *noir* in general was set against a particular urban background, captured in the title of the film *The Naked City* (1948). Wracked by the Depression, the great American industrial cities, with their increasingly suburbanised white populations, took on an aura of danger and barbarism. The city, metaphorised organically as 'the inner city', is now a threatening and treacherous landscape.[29] Certainly the anti-urbanism of American literature had resulted in a dystopic view of the city in earlier cultural formations, but what was new about film *noir*'s city was its Gothic quality. The stereotypical visual image of the city of danger – the elevated train tracks, the dark alley, the sinister hidden headquarters of both illicit and official authorities – now acquire a visual force and a local habitation. The city of film *noir*, that is, is gothicised, acquiring the aura of the castle of the eighteenth- and nineteenth-century Gothic novel, with its labyrinthine rooms, its menacing foreign antagonists and its atmosphere of sexual and racial confusion. Where the threat of Gothic romance, however, seems to emanate from a repressed and resurrected past, symbolised by the Middle Ages, the new medievalism of film *noir's* physical world is a vision of the present and the future of the modern city. The city of *noir* has a long and distinguished literary history, going back at least to Baudelaire's images of the demi-monde of Paris. As Mike Davis observes in *City of Quartz: Excavating the Future in Los Angeles*, *noir* is an 'anti-myth' that nevertheless employs Grail motifs.[30] The medieval Grail legends themselves may have been an anti-myth, countering secular Arthurian celebration with a spiritual world that Arthur's knights cannot conquer. An example of film *noir* influencing a medieval film is Robert Bresson's *Lancelot du Lac* (1974) based on one of the Grail continuations, and its medieval as much as its modern roots are responsible for its thorough disenchantment. Raymond Chandler's comparison of his hero to a questing knight has occasioned speculation about the mythic underpinnings of other film *noir* plots. Alain Silver and Elizabeth Ward, who have edited *Raymond Chandler's Los Angeles*, elsewhere pointed to the ironic context of Grail allusions in classic *noir* films. They note especially a line from *World for Ransom*, 'You shouldn't play Galahad. You're way out of character', as an expression of the self-consciously counter-mythic aspect of film *noir*.[31]

Chandler's definition of his detective as a Grail knight is not an idio-syncratic or uncommon connection. Chandler's landscape and city, like the landscape of much early and mid-twentieth-century literature, owes much to T. S. Eliot's *The Waste Land* with its 'unreal cities'. Eliot's footnotes and epigraphs for *The Waste Land* and 'The Hollow Men' play upon a certain association of modern life with the wasted back-grounds of the Grail legends. As Eliot makes clear, that association is one developed in the anthropological and mythic interpretations of literature and culture associated with the so-called 'Cambridge School' and which was widely circulated through Jesse Weston's *From Ritual to Romance*, which associates the Grail with pagan agricultural fertility cults.[32] Weston herself, and Eliot, depended on a work that was as influential for literary scholars as for anthropologists, James George Frazer's *The Golden Bough*, which compiles an impressive set of parallels in religious and cultic practices worldwide.[33] Although it may have done so instinctively rather than intellectually, or perhaps both, since even by mid-century Eliot's poem was still the definitive poem of modernist sensibilities, film *noir* translates *The Waste Land* into film, reflecting a sense of disenchanted ideals, sexual tempta-tions, traps and failures and personal and social alienation. Even the odd characters that people Eliot's poem, Madame Sosostris or Mr Eugenides, would be right at home in *The Maltese Falcon*. The 'Unreal City' of the modern world in Eliot's poem is a modern waste land. As with many such associations of film *noir* and the medieval, the identity of the Waste Land, the Grail quest and fertility and renewal are traceable through an appropriately reversed genealogy. I am referring here to Roman Polanski's *Chinatown* (1974), one of whose secrets is reversed genealogies on a grand Oedipal scale. *Chinatown* takes the Arthurian Grail themes and the Waste Land, and sets it in the southern California of the years of *noir* film-making. The background of a Raymond Chandler novel is combined with the ongoing south-west American mix of greed and water. The water scandal (actually dating from a few decades before the film's imagined period) can potentially bring the land back to life, which, in the *noir* cynicism of the plot, means to profit. The corrupt patriarch of the plot, Noah Cross (John Huston), is a debased version of the Fisher King. He is not only based on real figures from Los Angeles history, notably Colonel Chandler, but he references General Sternwood in *The Big Sleep*. *Chinatown* is as much film *noir* revival or homage as it is film *noir*, and a viewing nowadays will reveal a certain parodic note that was not readily apparent in its original release. Nevertheless, in foregrounding the Grail undercurrent of much hard-boiled detective *noir*, *Chinatown* suggests the depth of the fairly obvious parallel between medieval romance and pulp fiction, at least as regards the interplay of plot sequence and heroic subjectivity. Their pathological combination of violence and a seeking for purification or absolution ties together the *noir* quest and its distant model, the Grail romance.

What Chandler uncovers, perhaps without meaning to, in describing the private detective of his novels and stories as a knight-errant, is the disenchantment, rather than the idealism, of the chivalric quest as it faces the impossibility of its fulfilment. Disenchantment is always already a *noir* attitude, and it is often linked by commentators to the bitterness and alienation of the returning veteran following the Second World War. Chandler, however, began writing stories in the 1930s and served in the First World War. *The Big Sleep* was published in 1939. That is, Dashiell Hammett and Chandler forged a certain sensibility before it was translated into film *noir*, though the reception and cultural moment of *noir* was certainly at its height after the Second World War. The 'Crusade in Europe' was part of Second World War propaganda, but the First World War also employed medieval symbolism, in stark contrast to the reality of the mechanised battlefield. As Allen J. Frantzen demonstrates in his study *Bloody Good: Chivalry, Sacrifice, and the Great War*, such imagery was part of a certain complex notion of masculinity and heroism, as much passive and sacrificial as active, and it formed part of the commemoration of the First World War as well.[34] Film *noir* may have appealed to, and even created, the sensibility of the returning veteran of the Second World War, but it was inseparable from the cynicism about heroism that followed on the First World War. Writers whose careers breached both conflicts, such as Chandler or even Hemingway, demonstrate this lingering disenchantment.

High-art medieval *noir*

German expressionism is one of the most widely cited sources for film *noir*, especially given the exile of so many fugitive film-makers from Nazi Germany in Hollywood. But German expressionist film is also one of the tributaries of high-art medieval movies. The early films of Friedrich Wilhelm Murnau are often described as particularly important for the development of film *noir*. Given the recognition of Murnau's *Faust* (1926) as one of the high points of silent cinema, it is not surprising to discover how much has been written about the film, but especially noteworthy is a monograph on Murnau by Eric Rohmer.[35] Rohmer, after all, views issues of guilt and personal salvation in ways that are substantially different from the views embodied in the Faust legend. It is tempting to regard the sunlit, almost miniaturised *Perceval le Gallois* (1978) as a reversal of *Faust*, purging the themes of temptation and salvation from their Gothic, '*noir*' associations. After all, the Grail quest is one of the organising themes of film *noir*, and it is significant that Rohmer should seek to render its mysteries more precise and even rationalised, at least on a visual level. Yet it is the clarity of Murnau's vision that most impresses Rohmer. If Murnau's daring camera angles, underground themes and shadowed lighting were a possible source of medieval *noir*, especially in the vaguely gothicised sets of *Nosferatu* (1922), another link between the German film production company UFA and *noir* was the films of Fritz Lang. Lang's last great triumph in Germany was the silent *Nibelungen* (1924), reportedly Hitler's favourite film at the time. After his exile to the United States, Lang would go on to make crime thrillers, westerns and other films that transcended genre. His career, that is, spanned both medieval films and film *noir*, and his techniques influenced both.

Indeed, his science fiction film *Metropolis* (1927), one of the most well-known in the history of cinema, imagines the future as an amalgam of Dante's *Inferno* and the Gothic castle, introducing a connection that links dystopic futurity with the Gothic, even through such apparently original films as Ridley Scott's *Alien* (1979) and *Blade Runner* (1982). Lang, and *Metropolis*, are among the acknowledged sources of cyberpunk, which similarly thinks of the future as a return to a Middle Ages as imagined through the Gothic novel. Siegfried Kracauer, in his iconic *From Caligari to Hitler*, predicts the proto-*noir* qualities of even such a ritualised film as the *Nibelungen*: 'This intrinsic action does not coincide with the succession of treacheries and murders, but is to be found in the development of smouldering instincts and imperceptibly growing passions.'[36]

If the high-art examples of medieval *noir* are any evidence, thinking of Akira Kurosawa's *Rashomon* (1950) or Orson Welles's *Macbeth* (1948) or Ingmar Bergman's *Seventh Seal* (1957) to name a few, a case could be made that the medieval movie recognised the aesthetic power of film *noir* and its potential use in other genres and modes before American criticism came to an awareness of the innovative nature of film *noir*; and about the same time as Frank and Bourde and Chaumeton and their contemporaries wrote their revelatory appreciations of American film *noir*, giving it a local habitation and a name. In addition to alerting us to the implicit modernity of medieval *noir* films, the other advantage of the term is that it forces a new look at some acknowledged classics of film history. Films such as *Rashomon*, *The Seventh Seal* and *Lancelot du Lac* have been interpreted largely through an auteur approach, linking the films to the other works of their renowned directors and pointing to the originality and idiosyncrasy of their individual vision. But thinking about the films as medieval *noir* recalls the theoretical usefulness of the original concept of film *noir* in the 1950s and 1960s. The attempts to define film *noir* helped usher in the persuasive arguments about the structural, generic, typological and systematic approaches to film that emerged as film theory, demonstrating how the *langue* of film language was as important as the *parole* of individual great films. Paradoxically, the generic and structural potential of the concept of film *noir* often resulted in the appreciation of the artfulness of certain examples. As Paul Schrader notes, any given example of film *noir* is likely to be a better-made film that any given example of other genre films from a similar period.[37] Schrader in another context had identified Bresson's work as an example of 'transcendental cinema', suggesting that he had developed a film style that carried with it associations of spiritual and philosophical investigation.[38] Like Schrader's own films and scripts, however, *Lancelot du Lac* also reveals the influence of *noir*, in its pessimism, its dark and shadowed landscapes and its representation of the obsessively downward spiral of adultery and passion.

One of the classic associations of *noir* with a medieval setting is *Rashomon*. The setting of the ruined gate recalls the dystopic urban settings of many *noir* films. The fractured narrative reflects the recursive plot lines of the complicated mystery often the subject of film *noir*. In both the bandit's and the husband's point of view, the violated lady assumes the character of a femme fatale, while, in her own retelling, she is a virtuous victim. Except for the optimistic ending, which many critics feel is tacked on rather than developed through any actions or values of the main narrative itself, the unsentimental view of human behaviour and the difficulty at arriving at the truth, with which the film's title has become synonymous, are traits shared by *Rashomon* and by film *noir*. The task of the *noir* detective is not just to solve a crime but to reconsider his own position in relation to a crime which he is supposed to uncover. Kurosawa understands this aspect of *noir* as evidenced in some of his other films. Kurosawa will return to 'medieval' settings (allowing for the different temporalities of Japanese history) later in his career, but *Rashomon* appears not long after Kurosawa's ninth feature, *Stray Dog* (1949), which is one of the first self-consciously artistic homages to film *noir* and which might have influenced *Rashomon*. Indeed Kurosawa is often quoted as saying that *Stray Dog* was inspired by Jules Dassin's *Naked City* (1947). Another well-known Kurosawa film, *Throne of Blood* (1957), sets Shakespeare's *Macbeth* in medieval Japan, also recalling the *noir* world of betrayal, ambition, murder, a recursive plot and a devious and manipulative female character.

If Kurosawa's *Throne of Blood* combines Shakespeare's version of medieval history with certain *noir* characteristics, it is certainly a nod to an earlier filming of *Macbeth*, namely Orson Welles's *Macbeth*. Shakespeare's *Macbeth* is not a *noir* script, but it can be made to seem like one: a femme fatale in Lady Macbeth; an inescapable fatalism; even Macbeth himself, played as Welles plays him, less a Renaissance tragic hero than a somewhat vacillating and self-regarding subject. Welles foregrounds Macbeth's uncertainty and dependence on his wife to the degree that his ability to carry out his own intentions is called into question, partly by Welles's focus on the faces of Macbeth's court and followers. Admittedly the mythic overtones of Welles's staging reflects those aspects of expressionism that decidedly do not find their way into film *noir*, but the often strange surrealism of certain techniques in the film do parallel *noir* cinematography and lighting. Given that Welles himself plays a key, if problematic and idiosyncratic, role in the history of film *noir*, from *The Lady from Shanghai* (1948) to *Touch of Evil* (1958), one can see how Welles's style moved from Shakespeare to *noir*, and, indeed, lent a certain Shakespearian cast to his *noir* output. It might be said that Welles unlocked the *noir* undercurrent in *Macbeth*. A few years later, *Joe Macbeth* (1955) sets the plot in a contemporary American urban gangland, in high *noir* style though, in fact, less coherently *noir* than Welles's film.

The second half of Welles's *Macbeth* is more or less a filmed stage drama, with the exception of its outdoor battle scenes, probably influenced by Sergei Eisenstein's *Alexander Nevsky* (1938) and Laurence Olivier's *Henry V* (1944). In the first half of the film, however, Welles comes close to converting Shakespeare into *noir*. The nighttime exterior shots, usually in front of the hulking mass of Macbeth's castle (this is not the 'green and pleasant seat' of Shakespeare), contrast with the partially lit close-ups of faces, usually Welles's own. Welles is technically limited in this film in terms of his characteristic use of deep focus, but he attempts as much as possible to mimic its effects with the means he has available. The castle itself looms like an archaic expression of Macbeth's interior turmoil, and the mise-en-scène throughout mirrors the mood of the action, though the settings are rarely capable of suggesting ambivalence or nuance. For instance, the triumphant background of Macduff's decision to return clashes with the grief of receiving the news of the murder of his family, but by moving Macduff from the sunlit battlefield to the dark and sinister castle Welles foregrounds a 'problem' in the play, emphasising the tragic, or perhaps ethical, failure of Macduff to earlier secure his family's safety, and thereby drawing Macduff, too, into his Shakespeare *noir*. Perhaps to mitigate the stage-like positions of the characters, angled shots and deep shadows abound, particularly in scenes where Macbeth and/or Lady Macbeth are alone. The fog and perpetual dusk and dawn of the film's lighting and minimal special effects act like the rain-slicked streets and street lamps of film *noir*. Indeed, Welles's characteristic camera angles throughout resemble those of his later great film *noir* productions, though many of them admittedly date back to *Citizen Kane* (1941).

Faith, belief and religion

A number of the films I am categorising as medieval *noir* deal with themes of faith, belief and religion. Indeed medieval cinema has always been a repository for explorations of such religious themes, though sometimes from a secular or sceptical or at best liberal Protestant perspective, viewing medieval religion as a mixture of intolerance and superstition. The structure and politics of the Church and conflicts between Christianity and Islam in films about the crusades often form the background of medieval movies in general. But in many medieval *noir* films, personal faith and doubt and its testing are very much the central themes and also determine the progress of the plot and character, best exemplified by the large number of films treating Joan of Arc, notably Dreyer's *La Passion de Jeanne d'Arc* (1928), with its cinematography of stark black-and-white contrasts and extreme camera angles, as well as obvious attempts to plumb the parameters of faith in films such as *The Seventh Seal*.

The most productive period of film *noir*, from the 1940s to the early 1960s, coincided with developments in theology that at the least raise striking parallels to the ideology of film *noir*, even if film *noir* reflected that ideology in a not exclusively verbal, even non-intellectual medium. The 'Death of God', the attempt to think through theology after Hiroshima and the Holocaust, the attempt by theologians to address the questions raised by existential philosophy and the literature of the absurd, formed a high-cultural intellectual parallel to the instinctive plotting of film *noir* and its obsessions.[39] The hero (or, more rarely, the heroine) of film *noir* must operate in a suddenly (or continually) absurd world, where institutional authorities turn out to be witting or unwitting allies of the forces of corruption and evil; and evil, however mundanely defined, is so pervasive that no one is free from its contamination, not even the protagonist. Moreover the isolation of the protagonist, morally and socially, and the disintegration of a supportive community, as well as the pervasive atmosphere of doom, link film *noir* to the apocalyptic and millennial discourses associated with the Middle Ages, as well as with the theology of the Death of God, existentialism and the absurd. Bergman's *Seventh Seal* and to a lesser extent *Virgin Spring* (1960) are the clearest exemplars of these tendencies. Like Kurosawa and Welles, Bergman was also directly influenced by film *noir* in the 1940s, especially in his *Night Is My Future* (1947) or *It Rains on My Love* (1946); and one can observe the transfer of *noir* style and themes into his medieval movies.

Femmes fatales and knights-errant

Such related resemblances between *noir* and medieval cinema may be coincidental rather than structural, inheriting types and themes that originated with medieval literary traditions but which were transformed in intervening periods and movements. The femme fatale figures of *noir* can be traced back to the alluring and dangerous female figures of Arthurian romance, but they owe as much to Romantic imaginings of female sexuality, as in John Keats's *La Belle Dame Sans Merci*, or to early modern unsentimental versions of hard-boiled sensuality, as, for instance, in Arthur Schnitzler's *Der Reigen* and its many later film adaptations. At the same time the interaction of the male protagonist and the seductive female in *noir* plots replicates the tension between mission and temptation that informs medieval romance, a similarity reinforced by the often quest-like structure of many *noir* narratives. The idealisation of Grail romance as a theme and structure in later literature often obscures the dark and disenchanted view of worldly existence in the original thirteenth-century Grail narratives, them-selves arguably a rejection of the secular values of twelfth-century Arthurian romances. The prominence of fatal heroines in film *noir* and in the hard-boiled detective novels on which they are often based is such that the female antagonists of the genre are as memorable as the male protagonists: Brigid O'Shaughnessy in *The Maltese Falcon* (1941); Cora in *The Postman Always Rings Twice* (1946); Velma in *Farewell, My Lovely* (1944) and others. Because of the star system of Hollywood films, actresses such as Barbara Stanwyck, Joan Crawford and Rita Hayworth become identified with the femme fatale to such a degree that their presence in a *noir* film often takes priority over the specific characteristics of the characters they are playing.

Film *noir* and medieval films both project fantasies of masculinity. The violence enacted around and sometimes by the hard-boiled hero of the detective film is often presented as motivated, however indi-rectly, by the sexual presence or agency of the femme fatale, and some-times appears as a substitute for sexuality itself. In the pulp world that precedes and continues to inform *noir*, sex and violence are in fact inseparable from each other. If the *noir* hero occasionally imagines himself or is imagined a knight-errant, he thereby enacts the sexual fantasy of medievalist fictions and images, especially Victorian medi-evalist plots: a male hero as a salvation figure, the saving of the female in the medieval plot often standing in for sexual congress. This is to say that the sexual fantasy of chivalry in the medieval historical film, at least at its most basic level, is a fantasy of rescue from sexuality rather than an engagement in it.

The almost impossible layering of transgressions committed by Phyllis Dietrichson in *Double Indemnity*, played by Barbara Stanwyck, reflects the misogyny of film *noir*. She attempts to seduce Fred McMurray, the insurance salesman who is the narrator and protagonist of the film. In Lady Macbeth style, she involves him in the murder of her husband, after taking out an insurance policy on his life. She eventually plots to murder McMurray in turn, and we learn that she not only has murdered her first husband but is presently carrying on with the boyfriend of her own daughter. This representation of her behaviour goes beyond misogyny and connects her to a mythic archetype of the destructive female deity. If the male detective in other films *noir* resembles the chivalric knight on a quest, however distantly, Phyllis Dietrichson resembles Morgan le Fay, replete with the murderous, treacherous and incestuous motivations of the latter. It may or may not matter to that distant echo that Raymond Chandler himself worked on the screenplay, but in any event the finished film bears as much the mark of Chandler as of James M. Cain, upon whose novel the film was based. Indeed, *noir* films are unusually script-driven for Hollywood productions, perhaps accounting for the Chandleresque mood.

Neo-*noir*

Neo-*noir*, the self-conscious revival in recent films and other media, is more direct in linking the medieval and *noir*, though in so doing it problematically identifies the medieval with the demonic and sinister associations it acquired through the Gothic novel. A recent widely known collocation of the Gothic, the medieval and the Grail quest, written in a popular thriller mode lightly accented with *noir*, is the film version of Dan Brown's *The Da Vinci Code* (2005). Brown's Opus Dei villains take on the role of the monk or the Jesuit in the Romantic Gothic novel, and the Louvre, as well as the chateau of the hero's apparent protector but actual antagonist, stand in for the castle setting of the Gothic. His hero is the reluctant Grail knight, translated through the imagery of the *noir* detective, at least of literature, as he wakes in the middle of the night and faces his bleary image in the mirror as he sets off to investigate the darkened corridors of the Louvre. Similarly, the film version of Umberto Eco's *The Name of the Rose* (1986) placed the Dominicans in the role of the nefarious prelate of the Gothic novel, making the monastic library into the equivalent of the Gothic castle.

In one of the most disturbing crime films of the 1990s, *Se7en* (1995), in a neo-*noir* atmosphere, a world-weary detective is pitted against a psychopathic murderer who keys his crimes to the seven deadly sins. One victim, presumably greedy, is forced to cut a pound of flesh from his body. Another, presumably gluttonous, is forced into self-cannibalism. The ostensibly medieval origin of the seven deadly sins is discussed by the protagonists. Here again the association of the Gothic and horror automatically assumes the medieval as a motif, with film *noir* as its actant. The detective, Lt Somerset, played by Morgan Freeman, who goes on to play other African American *noir* detectives, makes a copy of a so-called map of Dante's *Inferno*. In a conversation the main characters cite Chaucer's *Parson's Tale* and Dante's *Purgatorio*:

> SOMERSET: The sins were used in medieval sermons. There were seven cardinal virtues, and then seven deadly sins, created as a learning tool, because they distract from true worship.
> MILLS: Like in *The Parson's Tale*, and Dante.
> SOMERSET: Did you read them?
> MILLS: Yeah. Parts of them. Anyway, in *Purgatory*, Dante and his buddy are climbing up that big mountain ... seeing all these other guys who sinned ...

Amusingly, Mills has to turn to *Cliff's Notes* to make sense of the *Divine Comedy*. At a library the camera pans over a shelf of Chaucer-related books and the discussion of medieval texts is meant to recall *The Name of the Rose*, with its effort to link esoteric learning, *noir* and the Middle Ages. The clear implication is that the modern city, in this case New York, is analogous to Dante's hell, and, indeed, a certain existential version of hell, mediated through Sartre's *No Exit*, is coincident with the rise of film *noir* in its classic period.

Identifying the complex dialectic between *noir* and medievalism in film thus changes the way we view and think of film *noir* and of medieval films. The *noir* colouring of a certain subgenre of medieval movies results in a weakening of their allegiance to period film-making. The *noir* characteristics announce that these movies, though nominally set in the past, see themselves as addressing modern concerns. Film *noir* style, almost inextricably linked to the representation of the here and now, especially in the immediate postwar years of the 1940s and 1950s (after which *noir* acquires a self-cancelling nostalgic glow) triggers a response that elicits mid-century concerns such as existential angst, the ambiguation of moral certainty and a general atmosphere of paranoia and suspicion. Conversely, the value of thinking about a term such as medieval *noir* lies partly in the way it complicates our notions of classic film *noir* itself. It demonstrates how underlying even the most immediate and apparently ahistorical of modernisms is a latent medievalism: a dependence on certain narrative structures such as the quest form that achieve their fullest development in medieval romance; a complex of subjectivity, sexuality, surveillance and anxiety that also resembles and stems from certain medieval categories of analysis and thought. The visual denotations of the medieval as transmitted by the enlightenment denigration of the Middle Ages – torture, superstition, treachery – are read as modern and present rather than as phantasms from the past. The two forms are thus joined by a certain version of medievalism, one that perceives the Middle Ages through the enlightenment lens that first defined the medieval period as a negative, an absence or an interruption, summarised in the idea of the Gothic. In both high-art medieval movies and in film *noir*, however, there is no superiority accorded to rational solutions. Far from ameliorating its radical challenge, the medieval undercurrent in *noir*, then, is part and parcel of *noir*'s unanswerable questioning of traditional ethical, moral and cinematic traditions.

Notes

1 John Aberth, *A Knight at the Movies: Medieval History on Film* (New York: Routledge, 2003). See also the widely cited Arthur Lindley, 'The ahistoricism of medieval film', www.latrobe.edu.au/www/screeningthepast/firstrelease/fir598/ALfr3a.htm, accessed 20 October 2007.

2 Kevin J. Harty (ed.), *Cinema Arthuriana: Twenty Essays* (Jefferson, NC: McFarland, 2002), p. 7.

3 Kevin J. Harty, *The Reel Middle Ages: American, Western and Eastern European, Middle Eastern, and Asian Films About Medieval Europe* (Jefferson, NC: McFarland, 1999).

4 Daniel Rubey, 'Not so far away', *Jump Cut*, 18 (1978), 9–14.

5 Daniel Rubey, 'The jaws in the mirror', *Jump Cut*, 10–11 (1976), 20–3.

6 Fredric Jameson, *The Political Unconscious: Narrative as a Socially Symbolic Act* (Ithaca, NY: Cornell University Press, 1981).

7 Raymond Borde and Etienne Chaumeton, *A Panorama of American Film Noir: 1941–1953*, trans. Paul Hammond (San Francisco: City Lights, 2002 [1955]), p. 2. For their update on the afterlife of film *noir* see Borde and Chaumeton, 'Twenty years later: Film noir in the 1970s', in R. Barton Palmer (ed.), *Perspectives on Film Noir* (New York: Hall, 1996), pp. 76–80.

8 Raymond Durgnat, 'Paint it black: the family tree of film noir', in Palmer (ed.), *Perspectives*, pp. 83–98. For a definition of film *noir* as a style see Paul Schrader, 'Notes on film noir', in Alain Silver and James Ursini (eds), *Film Noir Reader* (New York: Limelight, 1996), pp. 53–63. Where possible, I have cited this reader or Palmer (ed.), *Perspectives on Film Noir*, which are more widely accessible than the journals where many of the collected articles were first published.

9 Alain Silver and Elizabeth Ward (eds), *Film Noir: An Encyclopedic Reference to the American Style* (Woodstock, NY: Overlook, 1979).

10 Marc Vernet, '*Film noir* at the edge of doom', in Joan Copjec (ed.), *Shades of Noir: A Reader* (London: Verso, 1993), pp. 1–31.

11 See also James Naremore, *More than Night: Film Noir in Its Contexts* (Berkeley: University of California Press, 1998).

12 Carolyn Dinshaw, *Getting Medieval: Sexualities and Communities, Pre- and Postmodern* (Durham, NC: Duke University Press, 1999).

13 Cecilia Zecchinelli, ' "Life" sets TV rating record', *Variety* (23 October 2001), p. 9.

14 John Payne, 'Third ear', *L. A. Weekly* (17–23 November 2000), p. 61. See also bands such as Corvus Corax, which mix medieval musical style and costumes with both glam and punk rock motifs.

15 Elizabeth Wilson, *The Sphinx in the City: Urban Life, The Control of Disorder, and Women* (Berkeley: University of California Press, 1991), p. 138.

16 *Ibid.*, p. 138.

17 Thomas M. Leitch, *Crime Films* (Cambridge: Cambridge University Press, 2002).

18 Nicholas Christopher, *Somewhere in the Night: Film Noir and the American City* (New York: Free Press, 1997), p. 7.

19 Gene D. Phillips, *Creatures of Darkness: Raymond Chandler, Detective Fiction, and Film Noir* (Lexington: University Press of Kentucky, 2000), p. 22.

20 David Geherin, *The American Private Eye: The Image in Fiction* (New York: Ungar, 1985), p. 75; Robert Merrill, 'Raymond Chandler's plots and the concept of plot', *Narrative*, 7 (1999), 3–21 (6).

21 Raymond Chandler, *The Big Sleep* (New York: Vintage, 1993 [1939]), p. 1.

22 Andrew Dickos, *Street with No Name: A History of the Classic American Film Noir* (Lexington: University Press of Kentucky, 2002), p. 106.

23 Donald Maddox, *Fictions of Identity in Medieval France* (Cambridge: Cambridge University Press, 2000), p. 45.

24 Nino Frank, 'The crime adventure story: a new kind of detective film', in Palmer (ed.), *Perspectives*, pp. 21–4.

25 Larry Gross, 'Film après noir', in Palmer (ed.), *Perspectives*, pp. 110–14.

26 Frank, 'Crime adventure story', p. 22.

27 Sigmund Freud, 'The uncanny', in James Strachey (ed.), *The Standard Edition of the Complete Psychological Works of Sigmund Freud*, 24 vols (London: Hogarth, 1953-1974), vol. 17 (1953), pp. 217–56 (p. 237).

28 Susan Crane, *Gender and Romance in Chaucer's* Canterbury Tales (Princeton, NJ: Princeton University Press, 1994), pp. 160–1.

29 Edward Dimendberg, *Film Noir and the Spaces of Modernity* (Cambridge, MA: Harvard University Press, 2004).

30 Mike Davis, *City of Quartz: Excavating the Future in Los Angeles* (London: Verso, 1990), p. 37.

31 Alain Silver and Elizabeth Ward (eds), *Raymond Chandler's Los Angeles* (Woodstock, NY: Overlook, 1987).

32 Jessie Weston, *From Ritual to Romance* (New York: Smith, 1941).

33 James Frazer, *The Golden Bough: A Study in Comparative Religion* (New York: Macmillan, 1894).

34 Allen J. Frantzen, *Bloody Good: Chivalry, Sacrifice, and the Great War* (Chicago: University of Chicago Press, 2004).

35 Eric Rohmer, *L'Organisation de l'espace dans le* Faust *de Murnau* ([Paris]: Union générale d'éditions, 1977).

36 Siegfried Kracauer, *From Caligari to Hitler: A Psychological History of the German Film* (Princeton, NJ: Princeton University Press, 1947), p. 95.

37 Schrader, 'Notes', p. 61.

38 Paul Schrader, *Transcendental Style in Film: Ozu, Bresson, Dreyer* (Berkeley: University of California Press, 1972).

39 See Robert G. Portfilio, 'No way out: existential motifs in film noir', in Silver and Ursini (eds), *Film Noir Reader*, pp. 77–93.

9

'Medievalism', the period film and the British past in contemporary cinema

Andrew Higson

In recent decades there has been an obsession with the past in Western culture, manifested above all in the growth of the so-called heritage industry. Cinema has participated in this cultural shift in all sorts of ways, particularly in the case of films about the British past. Among such films made since 1980 have been a smaller number that offer some sort of representation of the Middle Ages or medieval literature or which adopt a loosely medievalist sensibility, from *Excalibur*, released in 1981, to *Tristan + Isolde* and *Beowulf*, released in 2006 and 2007 respectively. My concern here is with the extent to which such filmic representations of the Middle Ages are distinctive. What sorts of films are they? Do they engage with the British past in the same way as films set in the more recent past? Do they offer the same sorts of pleasures to the same sorts of audiences? Do they position themselves in the marketplace in the same way?

To answer these questions I will examine the various modes of film practice adopted for representing the Middle Ages, from the epic historical adventure film to low-budget art-house fare. I will suggest on the one hand that film-makers frequently blur the boundaries between different historical periods, but on the other hand that there is something specific about the way the premodern past is represented as dangerous and dirty. This specificity, I would argue, owes as much to generic convention and the audience address of the films as it does to histories of the Middle Ages. I will compare representations of the medieval with representations of the more modern past, arguing that the former tend to adopt a more populist and masculine appeal than the numerous middle-brow costume dramas set in the nineteenth and early twentieth centuries. A key concept in this discussion will be the sensibility of the films in question – the way in which a film is pitched to its audiences, the particular assumptions that are made by film-makers about how a film might address its target consumers, what it can and cannot say, the ingredients that are assumed to be attractive and acceptable in terms of style, theme and subject matter. Another key concern will be the various claims made about the historical authenticity of the films and the increasing extent to which medieval films adopt a dirty realist style. Finally I will consider the ways in which the films engage with questions of national identity and national cinema, in an era in which film production is increasingly transnational. This will in part involve looking at the degree to which films about the Middle Ages are caught up in the kind of heritage tourism associated with, for instance, Jane Austen adaptations.

The approach I adopt assumes that, if we are to make adequate sense of such films and of how they represent the medieval, we need to understand the contemporary film culture and film business out of which the films emerge and the markets to which they are addressed. I therefore situate these 'medieval films' in the context of other contemporary films that work with similar generic conventions, from the British heritage film or quality costume drama to the Hollywood epic. To this extent I am expanding on the arguments I have developed elsewhere about period films with British connections.[1] I work from the perspectives of film studies rather than medieval studies (so, for instance, when I refer to the epic, it is the epic film genre rather than the literary genre that I have in mind). As a film historian I am more interested in historical specificity than grand theory, and seek to examine textuality in the context of production, exhibition and reception. I am therefore more interested in how the films I discuss work for audiences in the cinema than in the extent to which they adhere to scholarly accounts of the Middle Ages. This is not to ignore the problems of authenticity and historical representation, but my chapter is more about historicising the moment of production and reception of the films than of the period they are depicting. Where I consider the claims made about the authenticity of the representations of the past, I do so in terms of the exigencies of film promotion and reception rather than the historical accuracy of the representations.

I will focus on films released since 1980 – a little over fifty of which have offered some version of the British medieval past or sought to represent British medieval heroes.[2] Some seventeen of these films retell or rework an aspect of the Arthurian legend, from John Boorman's *Excalibur* (1981) to the Jerry Bruckheimer production of *King Arthur* (2004), as well as no fewer than four versions of Mark Twain's

A Connecticut Yankee at King Arthur's Court. Another five films deal with the legend of Robin Hood, including the relatively low-budget British version *Robin Hood* (1990); the American blockbuster *Robin Hood: Prince of Thieves* (1991), starring Kevin Costner; and Mel Brooks's spoof *Robin Hood: Men in Tights* (1993). A further eighteen films were adapted from an assortment of other literary sources, from the medieval to the postmodern. Medieval poems and letters and the plays of Shakespeare and Marlowe accounted for *The Wanderer* (1991), *The Anchoress* (1993), *Henry V* (1989) and *Edward II* (1991), for instance. There were also adaptations of novels by writers as diverse as Sir Walter Scott (*Ivanhoe*, 1982), Robert Louis Stevenson (*El Flecha Negra / The Black Arrow*, 1985), Barry Unsworth (*The Reckoning*, 1991) and Michael Crichton (*The 13th Warrior*, 1999).

Modes of film practice: from the blockbuster to the art house

These films embrace a variety of modes of film practice that can be differentiated from each other in terms of production context, production values and budgets; film style, generic convention and star presence; and promotion, exhibition and reception. The majority of the films were American, for instance, with only twenty-one having a British connection in terms of funding or the involvement of a British production company – and several of those made very little impact either with critics or at the box-office. There is thus a huge gulf between a low budget, art-house-inclined British-Belgian film like *Anchoress* and a big-budget, star-driven American film like *Braveheart* (1995).

Representations of the British past have played a vital part in the development of the British film production business and British film culture in the period since 1980.[3] In terms of sheer numbers, however, representations of the medieval have hardly been central to that trend. More than two hundred British productions or co-productions released since 1980 were period dramas in some way about Britain or British culture, or set in the British Isles, and some ninety of them were set in the sixty-year period from the 1880s to the 1930s. Compare that figure to the mere twenty-one British productions or co-productions set in the whole of the medieval period or dealing with medieval heroes or tales.

On the one hand, then, British filmic representations of the medieval period have hardly dominated the representation of the British past in the last twenty-five years. On the other hand, if we take Hollywood

productions into account as well, several of the films about the medieval period have been relatively big-budget films about very familiar
medieval heroes or stories and have clearly captured the popular
imagination and made an impact at the box-office – from *Excalibur*
to *Robin Hood: Prince of Thieves, Braveheart, First Knight* (1995), and
more recently *King Arthur* and *Kingdom of Heaven* (2005). Such epic
historical adventure films are thus quite different from the majority
of the films about the modern British past, which have tended to be
much more modest in scale, more intimate and more middle-brow
costume dramas, the sort of films that reviewers describe as 'intel-
ligent' or 'literate'; or, as one reviewer put it, describing Kenneth
Branagh's adaptation of *Henry V*: 'movie[s] for those who don't like
movies.'[4] To this extent one could argue that the few big-budget films
about medieval heroes have had more of an impact on the popular
imagination than the more numerous but smaller-scale, more intimate
films about the modern past.

As the references to *Anchoress* and *Henry V* indicate, alongside the
Hollywood-funded epics there were also several smaller-scale films
about the medieval past, films which occupy a space on the very edge
of mainstream cinema. Box-office figures can be quite revealing here.
Excalibur, for instance, took $34m on its opening weekend in the US,
while *Henry V* could manage only $12m for the whole of its runs in
the US and UK combined. At the height of its release *Henry V* showed
on just 134 screens in the US and 26 in the UK; *King Arthur* on the
other hand opened on 3,086 screens in the US, taking $22m that first
weekend, and on 400 screens in the UK, taking $6m – and, despite
taking $64m overall in the US and the UK, was regarded as a box-
office flop! *Robin Hood: Prince of Thieves* was the box-office champion among medieval films, taking over $200m in the US and the
UK combined; the relatively low-budget British version of the same
story, *Robin Hood*, on the other hand, could manage only $600,000
in the UK and wasn't even released in the US. There may have been
far more critical and scholarly debate about *Henry V*, a £4m (about
$8m) production, and it may have appealed much more to discerning,
middle-class, audiences – but its hold on the popular imagination was
far less secure than even a relative box-office flop like *King Arthur*,
with its £80m (about $160m) budget and epic canvas.[5]

Clearly, then, there are some important differences between
the blockbusting epic and the more literate art-house movie or the
middle-brow costume drama. One might also note a tension between

the romantic mythology of heroic knights in shining armour, which is there to some extent in *Excalibur* and *First Knight*, and the demythologising brand of dirty realism and historical authenticity, which is where *King Arthur* situates itself (Figure 19). But at any moment both the romantic and the dirty realist can be undercut by tongue-in-cheek comedy or outright parody – whether it is the archly camp villains of the otherwise realist *Robin Hood, King Arthur* or *Kingdom of Heaven*, the postmodern anachronisms of Derek Jarman's *Edward II* or *A Knight's Tale* (2001), or the full Mel Brooks treatment of *Robin Hood: Men in Tights*. Each of these modes of expression, and especially the frequent confusion or tension between them, owes much to the Monty Python brand of medievalism in *Monty Python and the Holy Grail* (1975) and *Jabberwocky* (1977).

Historical myopia: blurring the boundaries between different periods

At the level of popular film culture, however, it is probably the epic more than any other genre or mode of expression that dominates recent filmic representations of the Middle Ages. The epic representation of the past and the conventions of the historical adventure encourage a particular way of engaging with audience expectations, offering a particular set of attractions, with a notably gender-specific appeal, quite different to that of the more intimate romantic costume drama set in the nineteenth or twentieth centuries. The generic types are therefore to some extent historically specific – although filmic history tends to be fuzzy around the edges. There is as a result no clear break

19 Dirty realism in *King Arthur* (2004)

between the Dark Ages, the Middle Ages and the early modern period in film terms, which all to some extent occupy a generic premodern space, while aspects of the medieval can also linger on in the modern period. Thus films like *Plunkett and MacLeane* (1999) and *Rob Roy* (1995), set in much later periods, but still historical adventures, share many of the same characteristics as films about Arthur, Robin Hood and William Wallace.

It is also important to recognise that, for some audiences and for some in the film industry, a period film is a period film: that is to say, it does not really matter in which period the film is set, since the pleasures on offer tend to be the same. In this respect we are bound to find a blurring of the distinction between the medieval and the early modern, for instance, and we are bound to find that film-makers do not get the costumes right. This sort of historical myopia is partly a function of the desire to produce entertaining and commercially successful films, a desire that is embodied in the star system as much as anything else – and clearly the casting of particular stars does indeed blur the boundaries between different periods. Thus Cate Blanchett can present herself as both Queen Elizabeth I in *Elizabeth* (1998), on the edge of medievalism; and in *Charlotte Gray* (2001) as a Second World War spy; Colin Firth can play medieval in *The Hour of the Pig* (1993), Regency in *Pride and Prejudice* (1995, TV) and postmodern in *Bridget Jones's Diary* (2001); and Clive Owen can move effortlessly between the Dark Ages of *King Arthur*, the Tudor period in *Elizabeth: The Golden Age* (2007) and the 1920s of *Gosford Park* (2001). Orlando Bloom on the other hand blurs the boundaries between the 'real' Middle Ages of *Kingdom of Heaven* and the mock medievalism of *The Lord of the Rings* (2001–3).

Films such as *King Arthur* and *Kingdom of Heaven* share as much with other recent historical epics as they do with other representations of the Middle Ages. The producer Jerry Bruckheimer, for instance, made both *Pearl Harbor* (2001), about the Second World War, and *King Arthur*, in the epic mode, while director Ridley Scott made both *Gladiator* (2000), set in ancient Rome, and the Crusader film *Kingdom of Heaven*. Regardless of the period in which they are set, the iconography, the sensibility and the pleasures on offer in these films are similar. The medieval in this sense is simply a vehicle for another version of the historical epic, the historical adventure as blockbuster, pitched somewhere between *Alexander* (2004), *Troy* (2004) and *The Passion of the Christ* (2004) on the one hand, and *Pirates of the Carib-*

bean (2003), *The Gangs of New York* (2002) and *Pearl Harbor* on the other. Filmic representations of the past are always caught between generic convention and historical specificity, and representations of the medieval are no exception.

King Arthur, for instance, was promoted as an historically accurate film, which 'tells the heroic true story behind one of history's greatest legends', and much was made of the discourse of authenticity in advance publicity, in the opening of the film itself, and in the 'making of' documentary on the DVD.[6] The film, then, was in part conceived and presented as historically authentic. On the other hand history is telescoped, and legend reworked in order to produce an engaging story and a familiar filmic experience for the modern multiplex audience. Thus, alongside the discourse of authenticity, the same promotional material heralds 'an immensely thrilling adventure epic', a 'spectacular motion picture', which 'fuses historical grandeur with edge-of-your-seat action'.[7] It is no surprise then that one of the film's main selling points is that *King Arthur* is 'from the producers of *Pearl Harbor*'.[8]

The premodern past as dangerous: medievalism, masculinity and mud

At the same time there clearly is something specific about how not necessarily the medieval but a more general sense of the premodern is expressed in contemporary film culture. The move into a premodern past – but also the move into the epic historical adventure mode – takes us away from the studiedly picturesque landscapes and buildings of so many English costume dramas set in the nineteenth and early twentieth centuries, the genteel drawing rooms of Jane Austen adaptations and the polite bourgeois respectability of E. M. Forster or Henry James adaptations. In its place is a more sublime iconography, with wild, uncultivated and often bleak and epic landscapes (Figure 20). Light is replaced by darkness, and the relative intimacy of the drawing room by vast stone castles and cavernous spaces – or by peasant huts surrounded by mud. In part this is a shift in scale; in part a question of sensibility, the reassuring surface decorum of the films depicting more 'modern' pasts replaced by the terror and astonishment of the premodern epic. What we are faced with here are two quite different regimes of spectacle, for there is no denying that the spectacle of the picturesque is as vital an ingredient of the more modern, domesticated costume drama as the spectacle of the vast battlefield is for the

20 Sublime imagery in *Elizabeth* (1998)

premodern epic. But where one is characterised by surface prettiness and a modest scale, the other is more in the vein of dirty realism and monumentalism.

As the British costume drama meets the historical adventure genre on the one hand and retreats towards medievalism on the other, heritage Britain becomes a far more dangerous space to inhabit, closer to nature, more primitive, less civilised. As Philip Kemp puts it, reviewing *Anazapta* (2001), a film set in 1348, with plenty of blood, gore, violence and eroticism, this is a 'full-throated rejection of the decorous conventions of "heritage cinema".'[9] The bourgeois costume drama offers a much more intimate and conventionally feminine version of history, closer to the woman's film: to some extent, this is history for girls. The premodern historical adventure film, however, offers a much more epic and conventionally masculine version of history for boys, characterised by dramatic narratives full of eventful action, in which strong masculine hero figures are defined precisely by the actions they undertake, and where passions are raw and more overtly threatening. The bourgeois costume drama, by contrast, is characterised by comparatively mundane narratives of politeness, restraint and refinement, in which relatively little happens – but what does happen tends towards romance, affairs of the heart and domestic drama, and characters are less heroic but psychologically more complex.

Film titles are revealing, too. Several of the more tasteful costume dramas depicting the 'modern' past have as their title the name of a woman – *Emma* (1996), *Mrs Brown* (1997), *Mrs Dalloway* (1997) and *Miss Potter* (2007), for instance. Several of the films dealing with medieval heroes, on the other hand, carry masculine names – either men's names or the name of a sword. To this extent, *Excalibur, Henry V, Robin Hood, Macbeth* (1997), *King Arthur* and *Beowulf* identify their core target audience in terms of gender in their titles. The distinction between epic adventure and romantic drama is not simply about gendering the appeal of the different films, however; it is also about class, cultural capital and taste. Thus the epic medieval adventure belongs above all within the realm of popular cinema, while most of the romantic dramas about the more recent past inhabit the upscale niche market for modestly-budgeted, quality films, the point at which the art-house sector crosses over into the mainstream to become the prestige picture.

Generic hybridity: changing visions of the past

As with any such critical construct, this neat binary opposition between two generic modes is far too rigid to represent accurately the range of films to which I am alluding, and there are all sorts of crossovers, exceptions and hybrid developments. Firstly, by no means all of the films set in the Middle Ages are framed in the epic mode or adopt the conventions of the historical adventure. *Anchoress* (1993), for instance, tells the story of a young girl who has visions of the Virgin Mary, and devotes her life to God, enclosed in the walls of her village church, while the potentially epic qualities of a film like *Henry V* are offset by the fact that it was budgeted for the art-house circuit and the margins of mainstream cinema. *Anchoress* is also one of a small number of medieval films that feature a woman as central protagonist, with others including *Guinevere* (1994) and *The Midwife's Tale* (1996). It would be foolish, too, to ignore the romantic elements of some of the historical adventures, such as *King Arthur* and *Kingdom of Heaven*, which also construct their protagonists along modern lines, as psychologically complex, brooding characters. Both *King Arthur* (in its casting of Keira Knightley as a feisty, 'girl power' version of Guinevere) and *Tristan + Isolde* (in its mimicking of the title, not to mention the storyline, of that key romantic teen hit of the mid-1990s, *William Shakespeare's Romeo + Juliet* (1996)) also attempt to extend the audience appeal of the historical adventure by addressing young female viewers. Even so, with its violent battle scenes, its lack of decorum and its often wild and primitive sensibility, *King Arthur* is a quite different experience to most 'modern' costume films. Love and romance are very much side issues, and domesticity is hardly possible. On the contrary the film is powerful, exciting, dramatic.

We might approach the equation from the other end as well, for if the medieval adventures tend to be more obviously epic in scope, sometimes the intimacy of the more refined modern costume dramas is overwhelmed by an epic dimension. Thus the romantic costume drama of the relatively recent past comes up against the conventions of the blockbusting disaster movie in *Titanic* (1997), while Shekhar Kapur's version of *The Four Feathers* (2002), another film about the modern past, situates its romance in the context of an action-adventure film. There are also moments where the dirty realism of the medieval films creeps into and stains the surface prettiness of the more modern costume dramas. If a line can be drawn between the premodern and the modern pasts in recent cinema, it would have to be around 1800, with adaptations of Jane Austen's novels heralding the arrival of a fully fledged modern past. But the boundary is blurred in the 2005 version of *Pride and Prejudice*. The director of the film, Joe Wright, talks of Austen as 'one of the first British realists ... I wanted to treat [*Pride and Prejudice*] as a piece of British realism rather than going with the picturesque tradition, which tends to depict an idealised version of English heritage as some kind of Heaven on Earth. I wanted to make *Pride and Prejudice* real and gritty'. The authors of the screenplay put it slightly differently, explaining that they wanted to make 'the muddy-hem version' of Austen – and it is indeed a very muddy film.[10] Significantly, when Elizabeth arrives at a neighbouring country estate having walked through thick mud, one of the other characters remarks that she looks 'positively medieval'.

This mode of representation is perhaps indicative of a shift in attitudes towards particular versions of the past. In the 'gaslight melodramas' of the 1940s, and in David Lean's adaptations of Dickens's *Great Expectations* (1946) and *Oliver Twist* (1948), it is the Victorian period that is horrendous and threatening, and against which true modernity can be defined. But in many of the refined costume dramas made in the 1980s and 1990s this relatively recent past was more positively valued. Representations of the Middle Ages have moved in the opposite direction, however. In the early 1950s, in films like *Knights of the Round Table* (1953) and *Ivanhoe* (1952), the medieval period is a romantic past, a time of chivalry and pageantry. More recently, it has become a period of terror and uncivilised passions. What we find in films such as the muddy, dirty realist version of *Pride and Prejudice* is an attempt to re-imagine the modern past once again – but it also clearly blurs the boundaries between the medieval and the modern.

Another film that is situated somewhere between the medieval and the modern, and which draws on both sensibilities, is *Elizabeth*, depicting the early years of the Tudor queen. As I have demonstrated elsewhere, *Elizabeth* is an interesting example of the generically hybrid film, which was carefully packaged to draw in both the audience for the more tasteful and genteel costume dramas, and those audiences who sought out the attractions of the historical adventure or the political thriller.[11] The film thus blends the two traditions, both the woman's picture and the historical adventure, both the costume drama and the action film, both the romance and the conspiracy thriller, both the character study and the epic. It is significant, for instance, that the battle scene in *Elizabeth* shows the aftermath of the battle, not the fighting itself, and is presided over by a woman, who *cares* about the effects of the carnage, as she surveys the hundreds of bodies littering the muddy field beneath her towering castle. The sequel, *Elizabeth: The Golden Age*, adopts this same hybrid sensibility, once more under-lining both the feminine pleasures of the romantic costume drama and the masculine pleasures of the action film – and again evoking a gory and grotesque medievalism in its torture scenes.

The appeal of authenticity: romantic mythology, dirty realism and irreverence

I have already noted that claims of authenticity are frequently made about recent films depicting the medieval past, and that such films often adopt a dirty realist style. The truth claims of realist discourse are repeatedly challenged, however, by the status of medieval fictions on the one hand and by the demands of entertainment on the other. Thus the often highly mythologised fictional source material of many of the narratives and heroes of the Middle Ages does not always sit easily with the conventions adopted by the film industry to achieve realist effects. The film industry's consumerist drive towards the production of profitable entertainment too is just as likely to be at odds with what historians in the broadest sense see as historical accuracy.

Excalibur, for instance, produced at the beginning of the period of film production under investigation, remains strongly wedded to the mode of legend, allegory and magic, but, as one reviewer put it, 'there's plenty of bloody realism among the mysticism'.[12] With its explicitly erotic sex scene, this was not obvious family fare either, but serious, adult myth-making, rescuing the Arthurian legend from *Star Wars* (1977) and putting it back in its literary-historical context. A few years later, the carefully deglamorised and frequently muddy, low-budget British version of *Robin Hood* sought to move beyond the heritage industry mythology, and was certainly a dirty and realistic film by contrast with the Kevin Costner version – but even in the British film the glamorous Uma Thurman was cast as Maid Marian. British reviewers identified a dirty realist screen version of Shakespeare in *Henry V*, 'steeped in blood, battle, mud and realism',[13] with Branagh endeavouring to express 'the muddy ingloriousness behind the legend'.[14] Even in this serious and worthy film the Monty Python link was apparent to at least one viewer: 'in keeping with this "realistic" approach, [Branagh] has adopted a visual style which might be best described as early Terry Gilliam. These are the filthy, rain-swept Middle Ages of *Jabberwocky* and *Monty Python and the Holy Grail*'.[15] This sort of medieval miserabilism could also be found in another low-budget film, *Anchoress*, with its bleak landscapes and grey skies, and costumes that, according to Geoffrey Macnab, 'were churned around in a cement mixer until they had just the right, crinkled feel'.[16]

First Knight, however, offers a much glossier, cleaner Hollywood version of the Middle Ages, in which the medieval past is as much about chivalry as violence. It also carefully mixes its modes in order to draw in a range of audiences, crossing the western with the Arthurian legend, and action with romance. Lancelot is a solitary wanderer, a medieval cowboy who lives by the sword rather than the gun, and who seems most at home in the wilderness, roaming through untamed natural landscapes, green hills and woods. Arthur, on the other hand, is a man of the city, his home being the gleaming white citadel of Camelot, even if it is set in a virgin pastoral landscape. Somewhere in between the city and the untamed landscape are the peasant villagers, closer to dirt, and terrorised by Malagant, who is associated with darkness and with a damp and inhospitable ruined fortress. The feuding between Malagant and Arthur means that the premodern past is a highly dangerous place, with plenty of action scenes for the boys. But there is also plenty of romance and finery for the girls, while Guinevere is invested with a certain feminist strength as a leader of her people, who is first glimpsed demonstrating her prowess in an early version of football.

The effort to attract new audiences to the historical adventure film can be seen also in *A Knight's Tale*, a wonderfully anachronistic, historically irreverent blend of rock musical, medieval jousting drama, romantic comedy and Chaucerian pastiche. In effect it tries to do for Chaucer what *Shakespeare in Love* (1998) did for Shakespeare. It is also much more ready than most historical films to acknowledge the extent to which the past is imagined from the point of view of modern sensibilities.

If the period of film-making under investigation opens with Boorman's version of the Arthurian legend, it nears its end with *King Arthur* and *Kingdom of Heaven*, both epics, but both also presented as historically authentic – claims which led to a debate in the British press and elsewhere about the veracity of the films. Ridley Scott, writing about making *Kingdom of Heaven*, proclaimed his love for 'research and the fine details', and described the weaponry used, for instance, as 'completely real ... carefully researched and constructed to fit with the era'.[17] Publicity for the film also bandied about claims such as 'historically accurate' and 'a fascinating history lesson'.[18] Others were less happy to see such claims go unchallenged. *The Times* newspaper, for instance, commissioned a lengthy article from Jonathan Riley-Smith, Professor of Ecclesiastical History at Cambridge University, who dismissed the film as 'invention' and 'nonsense':

> No-one can object to romantic fiction, but the film-makers have boasted that 'authenticity coloured every facet of the production'. If so, they have not had good advice ... Worse, where they could have created fictional characters they have opted for real historical personalities whom they have distorted ruthlessly ... [and] re-manufactured to suit the needs of the script.[19]

Riley-Smith's views were picked up by other newspapers, with several substantial comment pieces weighing up the pros and cons of this sort of historical film-making.[20]

The debate about *King Arthur* was rather different and took a somewhat surprising turn, since the concern was no longer about the failure to adhere to historical fact but about the 'death of a legend', as one newspaper headline had it.[21] Disney, who distributed the film through its Touchstone label, marketed it as 'the definitive version of the Arthur legend', with posters using the tag-line: 'The untold true story that inspired the legend'.[22] Bruckheimer, the producer of the film, went out of his way to stress the amount of research that fed into the production, while John Matthews, the historical consultant employed by Bruckheimer, was widely quoted in publicity material.[23] As one website proclaimed: 'Stripped of the elaborate magic and romance of the medieval stories, *King Arthur* presents a new but authentic image of Arthur, Guinevere, Merlin and the Knights of the Round Table.'[24]

This did not go down well with reviewers in Britain. At one level it was simply a matter of taste: 'This is King Arthur ... as gritty, bloody and dirty rather than mystical and magical, the hallmarks of the best Arthur movie to date, John Boorman's *Excalibur*.'[25] But at another level it was a challenge to Britain's national heritage, with another journalist complaining that an *American* film producer (Bruckheimer) was 'preparing to unleash a film that insists one of Britain's greatest legends, King Arthur, wasn't British at all.'[26] Even the liberal *Guardian* newspaper was moved to express patriotic concern: 'Strip the tale of King Arthur of its chivalry and sorcery and what is left is nothing sort [*sic*] of a national insult.' It was not that history had been misrepresented but that 'Britain's national myth' had suffered a 'catastrophe' and had been 'washed away ... by a river of pseudo-historical garbage.'[27] Disney even had to defend its claims to historical accuracy at the Advertising Standards Authority, to which it had been reported. Following a vigorous defence of the research that had been undertaken, Disney was allowed to continue its promotional campaign.[28]

For many, then, the tale of *King Arthur* was worryingly unfamiliar, but at the same time it was a very familiar film, as an epic historical adventure in the dirty realist mould, which also drew on much more modern heroic and not so heroic tales. In pre-production it was conceived as a sort of squad movie, in the style of *Dirty Dozen* (1967), while, for scriptwriter David Franzoni, the concept of the film was 'King Arthur and his knights as *The Wild Bunch* [1969].'[29] The bloody violence of Sam Peckinpah's western is indeed an apt model for the film and indicates the range of influences at work in a single text, the range of attractions designed to secure different audiences. The debate about realism and historical authenticity underlines one set of attractions, but it also underlines the extent to which claims to authenticity depend on what audiences, reviewers and other commentators are prepared to treat as believable or acceptable. This is in part about familiarity with source material, whether it is historical documentation, folklore or literary texts; but it is also in part about storytelling conventions, and in this particular case about current standards or practices of filmic entertainment.

Beyond authenticity: entertainment and displacement

Filmic representations of the medieval or the premodern serve particular functions, within film culture but also within contemporary
culture more generally. Clearly one function is that such films are
seductive and entertaining dramas capable of providing a great deal
of pleasure to a range of audiences; they thus offer a particular set of
attractions, and are designed to tap into entertainment markets that
appreciate such attractions. Among those attractions are the spectacle
of the past and the discourse of authenticity.

The discourse of authenticity is thus in part a selling point, a means
of attracting certain audiences to a film – but at the same time there
is a tension between the discourse of authenticity and the desire to
produce profitable entertainment, which often dictates that a representation or a narrative is reshaped for the purposes of drama rather
than to achieve a heightened sense of historical accuracy. Historical
authenticity may be one selling point, but it may also then come into
tension with other selling points. Thus the producers and distribu-
tors of *King Arthur* may have proclaimed that the film was historically
accurate, but the costume design was also clearly caught up in a more
modern sensibility, with costume designer Penny Rose explaining that
they wanted Arthur and his knights to come across as 'fifth-century
rock stars'.[30] It is clear, too, from the promotional material for *Kingdom
of Heaven*, that there was a certain commitment to achieving an
authentic representation of the Middle Ages in the film, but Ridley
Scott also admitted that the film was intended as 'a terrific story from
a dramatic age – not … a documentary'.[31] At the same time this is
a story chosen for its ability to address current concerns. The film-
makers thus use a version of medieval history in *Kingdom of Heaven*
to address twenty-first-century tensions between East and West, Islam
and Christianity – yet they managed to invoke the wrath of conserva-
tives in both camps. On the one hand, they received death threats
from Muslim activists who saw any revival of the crusader stories as
dangerous and anti-Islam.[32] On the other hand, right-wing Christians
were incensed by the representation of Salah al-Dīn (Saladin) as a
tolerant Muslim.[33]

The medieval setting can also provide a legitimate and respectable space in which certain modes of behaviour can be played out,
modes of behaviour that are currently considered unrespectable or
vulgar, decadent or debauched, outmoded or primitive. In other words

the 'un-modern' setting of these films is used as a licence to project taboo images and actions – particularly around the body and what might be done to it, or done with it, or how it might be displayed. The un-modern setting thus legitimises what might otherwise be regarded as censorious representations, such as the numerous depictions of post-Peckinpah violence, or the low-budget exploitation aesthetics of *Sacred Flesh* (1999), a pornographic film of sexual fantasies in a medieval convent, or *Anazapta*, a Hammer-style horror about the Black Death, with its 'rich, reeking mix of shit, mire, pus and gore', as Philip Kemp puts it.[34]

National identity and transnational cinema

One might also note the way in which some of the historical films that evoke a medieval sensibility are used to mythologise the emergence of a modern identity and a modern nation in Britain. *Elizabeth* may be set in the early modern period, but it also draws on a popular and very loose understanding of medievalism, as the dark and evil world from which modernity breaks free – a process that is dramatised in the film itself. Thus Elizabeth is represented as an essentially modern woman partly by contrast with other characters who are presented as 'un-modern' – and therefore, in 'historical' terms, medieval (especially in the colloquial use of the term to mean archaic, or old-fashioned). Thus her sister Mary and the scheming nobles around her are presented as still connected to a medieval sensibility, confined to the shadows and to darkness, and bound by ignorance, superstition and intrigue, literally inhabiting their own Dark Age; Elizabeth on the other hand is associated with romance and rationality, light and bright colours. There is a gender politics at play here too: the un-modern is gendered either as barren – in the case of Mary – or as terrifyingly masculine, while the modernity of Elizabeth is coded much more resolutely as feminine. As I have noted elsewhere, the idea of Elizabeth as a modern woman was widely taken up in the critical reception of the film – with the construction of her character repeatedly linked to the discourse of 'girl power', which had great currency in the late 1990s.[35]

Elizabeth and its sequel, *Elizabeth: The Golden Age*, are prime examples of films that construct a premodern space in which to play out dangerously primitive and irrational passions, grotesque torture and gory violence, a space that is filled by murderous priests and untrustworthy nobles, all of whom threaten the emergence of a modern nation. On the one hand, the distinction between the medieval and the modern is dramatised clearly in the films; on the other hand, the lingering medievalism of these two films set in the late fifteenth century demonstrates that there is no clear distinction between the medieval and the (early) modern, at least in popular discourse.

If the *Elizabeth* films are set after the medieval period, yet have medieval qualities, then *King Arthur* takes us back to Roman Britain in an effort to tell us the 'true story' behind a canonical medieval narrative. Camelot, of course, has long been exploited as a symbol of democracy; while the radical revisionism of this film means there is no Camelot as such, and while it purports to go behind the Arthurian mythology, the film still manages to mythologise the emergence of both a British nation and the semblance of a democracy. To this extent this US/UK/Ireland co-production functions as a national epic, about nation-building, about achieving national sovereignty, about the founding of an independent Britain, about fulfilling national destiny, and about a very American concept of 'freedom' (justified here as freedom from the external authority of Rome). There is a fascinating tension in and around this film, then, between the national and the transnational, between 'authentic' history and cultural appropriation.

Like *Elizabeth*, and notwithstanding the concerns of some cultural commentators, *King Arthur* is also about an already highly mythologised 'national' monarch and national hero; but again like *Elizabeth* it is about the making of the legend, the mythologising of the hero: it is about how its eponymous character *becomes* a ruler, how he attains mythic status (which is not to deny that both films at the same time mythologise their characters!).

With its Woads (Picts), its Sarmatians, its Romans and its Saxons, ethnicity is very much to the fore in *King Arthur*, as are the themes of belonging, invasion and resistance – at one point, Guinevere, a Woad, pointedly says to Arthur, a Roman military leader: 'I belong to this land. Where do you belong, Arthur?' It is ironic, then, that the film was made by an American production team, with an African American director, Antoine Fuqua, and shot in Ireland – but then the *Elizabeth* films were made by an Indian director with an Australian star; and the Merchant Ivory team, responsible for some of the best-known depictions of the 'modern' British past, were an American and an Indian. National cinema is rarely what it seems, or what is claimed for it.

Heritage tourism and the filmic Middle Ages

National identity is always to some extent a question of product differentiation among the world of nations, and in the era of globalisation the national has become a tourist attraction. Cinema plays a key role in this process, and a key feature of British film culture in the 1990s and 2000s has been the rise of film-related tourism, with consumers encouraged to visit sites associated with film production. In the case of period films and costume dramas this frequently enables tie-ins with the heritage industry, with films shot at 'authentic' historical locations, and consumers then encouraged to visit those heritage sites by organisations such as the National Trust. Such a process serves further to mythologise the nation. Medieval films partake in this process in various ways. Robin Hood Country, for instance, is well-established as a tourism brand, and tied to numerous film and television productions, as are many medieval castles. *Braveheart* meanwhile fuelled interest in Scottish heritage, with visitors to the Wallace National Monument, for instance, increasing by 156 per cent after the release of the film.[36] More controversially, a statue of William Wallace, modelled on Mel Gibson's features in the film, was erected in the car park to the Monument. In 1999, the British Tourist Authority produced a Movie Map, designed to encourage tourists to visit a range of historical properties: 'Many of Britain's dramatic castles, beautiful stately homes and gardens, and medieval manor houses are featured on this Movie Map. And they are yours to discover with the Great British Heritage Pass – our invitation to the independent traveller to visit almost 600 of Britain's finest historic properties free of charge.'[37]

Among the locations featured on this Movie Map are those associated with *Braveheart*, *First Knight* and *Robin Hood: Prince of Thieves*. Ironically, the attractions associated with the first two films include 'medieval villages' constructed by the film-makers, while the entry for *Robin Hood: Prince of Thieves* notes that the film was shot 'pretty much everywhere except Sherwood Forest'.[38] *Elizabeth* also features on the Movie Map, and provides a good example of how films can be taken up within the discourse of heritage tourism, with the medieval castles on display in the film further showcased as visitor attractions. Thus the Press Book for *Elizabeth* notes of one of the film's key locations: 'With its long imposing battlements, Raby Castle echoes the spirit of medieval England, and is recorded as first belonging to King Canute in the early 11th Century. Its stronghold of soaring towers and impregnable walls stands as a symbol evoking power, wealth and ambition.'[39] Various articles appeared in the travel pages of newspapers when *Elizabeth* was released, encouraging readers to visit Raby Castle and some of the other medieval settings in the film, clearly constructing medieval history as a space for heritage tourism.[40] The film connection remained vital, however, with Alnwick Castle noted in one article as a setting for both *Elizabeth* and *Robin Hood: Prince of Thieves*.[41]

The Tourist Authority, now renamed VisitBritain, produced another Movie Map in conjunction with Disney, to coincide with the release of *King Arthur*: 'King Arthur and his knights have been resurrected and are inspiring tourists to rediscover his land' and 'to help position Britain as the definitive destination for British and international visitors interested in the ancient legend'.[42] Further blurring history, fiction and tourism, the leaflet itself is illustrated with both images from the film and photographs of heritage attractions such as Stonehenge, Hadrian's Wall and Bamburgh Castle.

The sublime architecture of the medieval castle offers a very different visitor attraction to the stately homes of more recent British history – and, as with the epic genre itself, it is a gendered space, more masculine in its appeal than the more refined and domesticated spaces of later centuries. The otherness of such space, and its often geographically spectacular setting, is inevitably played up in the medieval film, inviting the tourist gaze within a filmic context. In certain circumstances, for certain viewers, this look, this display of heritage architecture, can get in the way of the drama of the film. One reviewer of *Kingdom of Heaven*, for instance, dismissed it as 'a delectably pretty twelfth-century castle tour … a mere excuse for exotic spectacle'.[43]

The film-maker with a concern for historical authenticity has other problems too: first, medieval architecture will often be hemmed in by more modern styles, or there are insufficient medieval buildings to provide the space needed for a medieval film setting; secondly, the architecture that does survive has been ruined over many centuries, so often seems too old for the people who must inhabit it in a medieval film.[44] Hence the shiny new version of Camelot in *First Knight*, or the shiny new version of Hadrian's Wall in *King Arthur*. Such spaces cannot exist as 'genuine' heritage visitor attractions, since they have been constructed anew by the film-makers – and will often be dismantled after the shoot, as with the 'medieval villages' from *Braveheart* and *First Knight* referred to on the Movie Map.

This ambivalence about the past can also be seen in the images of landscape that feature in medieval films. Such films provide an opportunity to represent the British past in terms of natural, uncultivated spaces, rolling hills, virgin forests and so on. Such representations mythologise Britain as ancient and primordial, even if it is the Celtic fringes that actually provide the images in the films (*First Knight*, for instance, was shot in Wales; *King Arthur* in Ireland). When we move this far back in the past, however, the green and pleasant land of Heritage Britain will frequently become a dangerous land, less picturesque than sublime. The dirty realist aesthetic thus reworks the natural as wild, primitive and untamed – and sometimes bleak and barren. This is not of course a space that is easily accessible to the modern tourist.

Conclusion

The British Middle Ages in films produced since 1980 have then taken various forms and performed various functions. It would be difficult to argue that the medieval has a distinct representation, or that it is carefully demarcated from the Dark Ages or the early modern period; rather, there is a more generic premodern past. There is a much clearer distinction between the epic historical adventure and the intimate costume drama, but even the smaller-scale medieval films offer pleasures rather different from the much more numerous middle-brow period films set in the Britain of the nineteenth or early twentieth centuries. The chivalry of *First Knight* notwithstanding, the decorum of the modern past tends to be displaced by much wilder and more threatening versions of the past in the dirty realist medieval film. Aspirations to historical accuracy may characterise some of these representations of the past, but the medieval is in the end defined as much by generic convention, and generic distinctions between the premodern and the modern. To some extent medieval films about Britain or British characters work as national cinema, mythologising the national heritage, the nation's heroes and the emergence of the modern nation – except that many of the films in question are *international* productions for which the national has little meaning. As history becomes entertainment, the successful film is one that can market its wares to a range of audiences, and that is at the same time able to meet audience expectations, in terms of genre, star image and the spectacle of the past.

Notes

I would like to thank Jonathan Stubbs and Jane Bryan for assisting me with the research for this chapter.

1 See, for instance, Andrew Higson, *English Heritage, English Cinema: Costume Drama since 1980* (Oxford: Oxford University Press, 2003).

2 Statistical information about numbers of period films released since 1980 is based on a thorough trawl through the film reviews in *Monthly Film Bulletin* (January 1980 to April 1991) and *Sight and Sound* (May 1991 to December 2006), supplemented with searches on the Internet Movie Database (www.imdb.com), and information in Kevin J. Harty, *The Reel Middle Ages: American, Western and Eastern European, Middle Eastern and Asian Films about Medieval Europe* (Jefferson, NC: McFarland, 1999).

3 See Higson, *English Heritage, English Cinema*.

4 Christopher Tookey, 'Once more unto the breach', *Sunday Telegraph* (8 October 1989), p. 44.

5 All box-office figures and budgets from Variety.com; accessed 31 August 2006.

6 *King Arthur: Director's Cut*.

7 *Ibid.*

8 *Ibid.*

9 Philip Kemp, 'Anazapta', *Sight and Sound*, 14:6 (June 2004), 44.

10 Quoted in 'Production Notes', on the Working Title website for *Pride and Prejudice*, at www.workingtitlefilms.com/downloads/PridePrejudice_Production-Notes.pdf; accessed 25 October 2007.

11 See chapter 6 of Higson, *English Heritage*, pp. 194–256.

12 Colin Dangaard, 'King Arthur rules, OK', *Daily Express* (11 May 1981), page number missing on BFI microfiche.

13 Alexander Walker, 'Branagh breaks Olivier's spell', *Evening Standard* (5 October 1989), p. 32.

14 Shaun Usher, [review], *Daily Mail* (4 October 1989), p. 3.

15 Tookey, 'Once more unto the breach', p. 44.

16 Geoffrey Macnab, 'Anchoress', *Sight and Sound*, 3:10 (October 1993), 38.

17 Ridley Scott, 'When worlds collide', *The Guardian* (29 April 2005), Review section, p. 7.

18 These terms were widely used in the press and on the Internet; see, for instance, Cahal Milmo, 'A wound that has lasted 900 years', *The Independent* (3 May 2005), pp. 12–13; and Charlotte Edwardes, 'Ridley Scott's new Crusades film "panders to Osama bin Laden"', www.telegraph.co.uk (17 January 2004), accessed 25 October 2007.

19 Jonathan Riley-Smith, 'Truth is the first victim', *The Times* (5 May 2005), T2 Screen section, p. 13.

20 See for example Milmo, 'A wound that has lasted 900 years'; Jonathan Jones, 'What the Middle Ages did for us', *The Guardian* (10 May 2005), p. 24; Edwardes, 'Ridley Scott's new Crusades film'; and, in an American context, Robert Spencer, 'Crusading against history', www.frontpagemag.com, 3 May 2005, accessed 25 October 2007.

21 Jonathan Jones, 'Death of a legend', *The Guardian* (23 August 2004), p. 14.
22 Adam Sherwin, 'How Disney's once and future king has been dubbed the "true" Arthur', *The Times* (1 December 2004), p. 28.
23 See Luke Leitch, 'King Arthur? Oh, he wasn't English', *Evening Standard* (2 October 2003), p. 29; 'King Arthur', on the VisitBritain website at www.visitbritain.com/VB3-en-GB/experiences/Tour/spotlights/kingarthur.aspx, accessed 31 January 2007; and 'Blood on the Land: Forging King Arthur', 'making of' documentary on *King Arthur: Director's Cut*, DVD.
24 'King Arthur', on the VisitBritain website.
25 Martyn Palmer, 'Blood, sweat and spears', *The Times* (24 July 2004), Magazine section, p. 37; see also Dalya Alberge, 'Did the "real" King Arthur have Georgia on his mind?', *The Times* (21 May 2004), page number missing from BFI microfiche.
26 Leitch, 'King Arthur?', p. 29.
27 Jones, 'Death of a legend', p. 14.
28 Sherwin, 'How Disney's once and future king', p. 28.
29 Quoted in Palmer, 'Blood, sweat and spears', p. 37.
30 Quoted *ibid.*
31 Scott, 'When worlds collide', p. 7.
32 See Milmo, 'A wound that has lasted 900 years'.
33 See Spencer, 'Crusading against history'.
34 Kemp, 'Anazapta', p. 44.
35 See Higson, *English Heritage*, pp. 217–20.
36 www.magicdragon.com/Wallace/Wallace7.html, accessed 25 October 2007.
37 'Movie Map', British Tourist Authority, 1999.
38 *Ibid.*
39 *Elizabeth* Press Book, copy held at BFI National Library.
40 See Hilary Macaskill, 'A castle fit for a celluloid queen', *The Independent on Sunday* (25 October 1998), Travel section, p. 7; and Andrew Wilson, 'All the Queen's castles', *Mail on Sunday Magazine* (10 October 1998), p. 20.
41 Wilson, 'All the Queen's castles', p. 20.
42 'Guide to Film and TV Locations in Britain: King Arthur', VisitBritain, 2004, available online at www.visitbritain.com/VB3-en-GB/experiences/Tour/spotlights/kingarthur.aspx, accessed 31 January 2007.
43 Tim Robey, 'Kingdom of Heaven', *Daily Telegraph* (6 May 2005), p. 21.
44 However, in Chapter 2, Sarah Salih makes a good case for seeing such ruins as integral to the aesthetic of some medieval films.

Further reading

Bettina Bildhauer

In his pioneering article 'The ahistoricism of medieval film' in the online journal *Screening the Past*, 3, Arthur Lindley in 1998 noted 'the absence of books by medievalists as well as of any kind devoted to medieval film'. Since then a field has begun to emerge. Although film studies and medievalism are still very much separate academic disciplines with their own traditions, some medievalists have started to take film seriously; and some film scholars have started to take seriously if not medieval film then at least historical film. The following survey is designed to complement our contributors' references to suggest some twenty-first-century starting points for those interested in the overlaps between medievalism and film.

In 2007 *Exemplaria* published a special issue on Movie Medievalism (19:2), edited by Richard Burt and Nickolas Haydock. It contains six articles on a number of medieval films, predominantly from Hollywood, with reflections on anachronism, simulacra and trauma; and is particularly attentive to the paratexts of these films, like extra features on DVDs, publicity material and director's comments. *Race, Gender and Class in 'Medieval' Cinema*, edited by Lynn Tarte Ramey and Tison Pugh in Palgrave's New Middle Ages Series (2007), also collects interpretations of a number of individual films set in the Middle Ages or considered medieval, focusing on their depiction of race, gender or class. Particularly innovative are the reflections on race and colonialism, and the fact that this volume extends both the films and the plots covered beyond medieval Europe. A somewhat earlier essay collection, *The Medieval Hero on Screen: Representations from Beowulf to Buffy*, edited by Martha W. Driver and Sid Ray (Jefferson, NC: McFarland, 2004), is loosely thematically linked through the topic of heroism, but also deals with wider issues of accuracy and the overlap between medievalism, science fiction and fantasy in films and television. Driver and Ray are now co-editing *Medieval Shakespeare in Performance*, including work on film, forthcoming with the same publisher.

Mittelalter im Film, edited by Christian Kiening and Heinrich Adolf (Berlin: De Gruyter, 2006), combines helpful surveys (on medieval film and epic films in general, Robin Hood, Joan of Arc, and, looking beyond Europe, Samurai films), with seven rather superficial case studies of classic films, and a select filmography. *Antike und Mittelalter im Film*, edited by Mischa Meier and Simona Slanicka (Cologne: Böhlau, 2007), is an unadventurous but useful collection of essays on individual films as well as including general reflections on the characteristics of medieval films as well as films about antiquity.

As regards monographs, Kevin Harty has been a ground-breaker in establishing an impressive corpus of films about the Middle Ages. His encyclopaedic *The Reel Middle Ages: American, Western and Eastern European, Middle Eastern, and Asian Films about Medieval Europe* (Jefferson, NC: McFarland, 1999), listing and briefly describing over six hundred medieval films, was followed by two edited essay collection on Arthurian film with the same publisher, *King Arthur on Film* (1999) and *Cinema Arthuriana* (2002). John Aberth's *A Knight at the Movies: Medieval History on Film* (New York: Routledge, 2003) is an entertaining survey by a historian of films about King Arthur, Robin Hood, Joan of Arc, the Vikings, the crusades and the Black Death. While mostly concerned with accuracy, it contextualises this issue in the often equally fictionalised tales from the Middle Ages about these figures and subjects. Susan Aronstein's *Hollywood Knights* (New York: Palgrave Macmillan, 2006) explores in detail the analogies between the medieval Europe of a wide range of Hollywood Arthurian films and America at the time of their production. Amy François de la Bretèque's most substantial contribution to the study of medieval film to date is *L'Imaginaire médiéval dans le cinéma occidental* (Paris: Champion, 2004). It provides a huge survey of American and European films about the European Middle Ages in a broad sense, listing 290 films. It deals with various forms of creative anachronism and fantasy; and discusses the films by content in terms of the medieval characters, events, areas and stories that they depict. The conference proceedings edited by Xavier Kawa-Topor under the title *Le Moyen Age vu par le cinéma européen* (Conques: Centre européen d'art et de civilisation médiévale, 2001) add further individual studies.

In the large field of the study of the modern reception of the

Middle Ages many general publications mention films, too. The annual *Studies in Medievalism*, for example, has included a number of essays on medieval film, particularly in the issue on *Film and Fiction*, edited by Tom Shippey and Martin Arnold (2002). The irregular series *Mittelalter-Rezeption*, edited predominantly by Ulrich Müller (Göppingen: Kümmerle), is the German-language equivalent. Those interested in adaptations of individual literary works from the Middle Ages, particularly of Arthurian material, can also draw on a substantial tradition of scholarship. Most introductions to medieval characters, stories and events now also include chapters on reception, which often discuss filmic representations. As many medievalists come into contact with film first as a tool for teaching, several publications address the use of film as a teaching tool, too, for example, Martha Driver's survey 'Teaching the Middle Ages on film: Visual narrative and historical record', *History Compass*, 5:1 (2007, 141–61).

There is also a broad range of academic studies about historical film as a genre (also known as heritage film or costume drama, and sometimes still as swashbuckler or adventure film). These works typically defend film against charges of inaccuracy and establish criteria for quality different from those of academic historiography. Pioneering works in this field were published by Pierre Sorlin, Leger Grindon, Vivian Sobchack and Robert Rosenstone, amongst others. Marnie Hughes-Warrington's *History Goes to the Movies* (London: Routledge, 2007) and William Guynn's *Writing History in Film* (New York: Routledge, 2006) are useful introductions to the accuracy debates in academia and beyond. Marcia Landy's star-studded edited collection *The Historical Film: History and Memory in the Media* (London: Athlone, 2001), like her own writing, is noteworthy for encompassing popular memory and fantasy as well as film. Postmodern or theoretical studies of historical films are still predominantly concerned with films about the recent past, especially about the Holocaust.

On the British heritage film Andrew Higson was instrumental in positing historical film as part of a wider heritage industry, which shapes national memory: see in particular his *English Heritage, English Cinema: Costume Drama since 1980* (Oxford: Oxford University Press, 2003). Claire Monk's and Amy Sargeant's edited collection *British Historical Cinema* (London: Routledge, 2002) adds further useful facets. On Hollywood historical films Robert Burgoyne, George Custen and Robert Brent Toplin published groundbreaking work (see now also Toplin's *Reel History: In Defense of Hollywood*, Lawrence:

University of Kansas Press, 2002). David Elridge's *Hollywood's History Films* (London: Tauris, 2006) concentrates on the 1950s and offers useful insights into film production history.

Worth noting for comparisons are the recent studies of antiquity on film, again published mostly by classicists rather than by film scholars. Since Jon Solomon's foundational and Maria Wyke's insightful work, there have been a number of German-language collections (for example, by Ulrich Eigler; Martin Korenjak and Karlheinz Töchterle; Armin Loacher and Ines Steiner), as well as Gideon Nisbet's light-hearted *Ancient Greece in Film and Popular Culture* (Exeter: Bristol Phoenix Press, 2006). On the early modern period, another useful area of comparison, there is a wide range of secondary literature on Shakespeare on film. Michael Klossner's *The Europe of 1500–1815 on Film and Television: A Worldwide Filmography of Over 2550 Works, 1895 through 2000* (Jefferson, NC: McFarland, 2002) delivers what its title promises and can therefore serve as a convenient starting point. (Note: While this manuscript was waiting to go to print, the following two books on medieval film appeared: Nickolas Haydock, *Movie Medievalism* (Jefferson, NC: MacFarland, 2008) and Richard Burt, *Medieval and Early Modern Film and Media* (New York: Palgrave Macmillan, 2008.)

Index

Note: literary works can be found under authors' name; films are listed under their most commonly known title; page numbers in *italic* refer to illustrations

CPSIA information can be obtained at www.ICGtesting.com
Printed in the USA
BVOW04s1545280515

401911BV00005B/6/P